MAX WEBER AND THE CULTUR[...]

Also by Sam Whimster

ALDGATE PAPERS IN SOCIAL AND CULTURAL THEORY (*editor*)

THE ESSENTIAL WEBER

Max Weber and the Culture of Anarchy

Edited by

Sam Whimster
Reader in Sociology
London Guildhall University
London

First published in Great Britain 1999 by
MACMILLAN PRESS LTD
Houndmills, Basingstoke, Hampshire RG21 6XS and London
Companies and representatives throughout the world

A catalogue record for this book is available from the British Library.

ISBN 0–333–68227–0 hardcover
ISBN 0–333–73021–6 paperback

First published in the United States of America 1999 by
ST. MARTIN'S PRESS, INC.,
Scholarly and Reference Division,
175 Fifth Avenue, New York, N.Y. 10010

ISBN 0–312–21302–6

Library of Congress Cataloging-in-Publication Data
Max Weber and the culture of anarchy / edited by Sam Whimster.
p. cm.
Includes letters in German.
Includes bibliographical references and index.
ISBN 0–312–21302–6 (cloth)
1. Weber, Max, 1864–1920—Views on anarchism. 2. Anarchism–
–History. 3. Political culture. I. Whimster, Sam, 1947– .
HX828.M34 1998
320.5'7'095—dc21   97–42334
                                                                  CIP

This book is printed on paper suitable for recycling and made from fully managed and
sustained forest sources.

10   9   8   7   6   5   4   3   2   1
08   07   06   05   04   03   02   01   00   99

Printed and bound in Great Britain by
Antony Rowe Ltd, Chippenham, Wiltshire

Contents

List of Plates

All plates are taken from *Graphic Works of Max Klinger*, by J. K. Varnedoe and E. Streicher (New York: Dover Publications, 1977).

1. *Eve and the Future: Eve*

2. *Eve and the Future: First Future*

3. *Eve and the Future: The Serpent*

4. *Eve and the Future: Second Future*

5. *Eve and the Future: Adam*

6. *Eve and the Future: Third Future*

7. *A Love: Happiness*

8. *On Death, Part I: Death as Saviour*

Preface

This volume of essays was triggered by a visit I made in the summer of 1992 to the Prussian Secret State Archive in Merseburg outside Leipzig where I was a guest lecturer for the semester. I decided to pay the archive a visit as it was known to contain Max Weber's *Nachlass*. With no particular plan in mind I looked at some of the files and came across three marked 'Max Weber an Frieda Gross'. The correspondence and documents seemed mostly legal – wills and court cases – and belonging to long-forgotten private lives. Then another file revealed letters by Max Weber, written in Ascona to his wife Marianne. Frieda Gross was the wife of the infamous Otto. Ascona was, of course, 'The Mountain of Truth' well known from the books by Martin Green and Harald Szeemann. Not only had Max Weber stayed in Ascona for over six weeks, he had sent 35 letters to Marianne, only a fraction of which she had published in her biography.

The letters were circulated at the 1995 Max Weber Study Group conference on 'Max Weber – Politics – Culture', which was supported by the efforts of David Chalcraft and by the British Sociological Association. There were many unexplained threads in the letters; private and public, intellectual and political. This volume grew out of the conference. Not only did the contributions bring an understanding of the issues that were talked about in Ascona, but they also showed how the public and private, and the cultural and the political, intertwined. Equally the world of personal encounters interweaved with the textual Weber. Was Weber bringing his own sociological mindset to Ascona, or did this strange incongruous world impact on his aloof intellectual cosmos? More the latter than the former, is my conclusion.

My thanks are due to John Eidson, Harald Homann, and Johannes Weiss for initital discussions back in Leipzig. Subsequent visits to Germany were supported by the Department of Sociology, London Guildhall University, and by the German Academic Exchange Service to whom I am most grateful. The road to Ascona passes through Munich's Schwabing, where I was looked after by one of its resident spirits, Klaus Friedrich, to whom many thanks are due. Dr Karl-Ludwig Ay provided unfailing support and advice at the Max Weber Arbeitstelle in the Bavarian Academy of Sciences. In Heidelberg the letters editor of the *Max Weber Gesamtausgabe*, Birgit Rudhard was generous with her help and advice, and Professor Rainer Lepsius was, as ever, courteous, humorous and helpful. James Joll, who is greatly missed, read the Ascona letters and gave me much encouragement. The publication of this small selection of letters was only possible through the services of the Geheimes Staatsarchiv, Preussischer Kulturbesitz, in Merseburg, to whom I acknowledge my debt. A debt is also owed to the staff seminar in the Sociology Department at London Guildhall University, who had to experience the amateurish narrative at my first attempts to work out what was happening in Weber's and the anarchists' lives. I am also greatly indebted to Sven Eliaeson, Edith Hanke, Carl Levy, Ulrich Linse, Ralph Schroeder, Mary Shields, Christopher Stanley and Guenther Roth for numerous chats and letters. Martin Green has been an unfailing source of information as well as communicating to me why these people and the values they held matter.

Notes on the Contributors

Karl-Ludwig Ay is the Redakteur of the Max Weber Gesamtausgabe (the editor's editor). He is a historian and member of the Commission for Social and Economic History at the Bavarian Academy of Sciences. He has published on the Bavarian revolutions of 1919 and is now writing on regional variations of the Protestant Ethic thesis.

Christoph Braun is a researcher at the University of Freiburg im Breisgau. He is the author of *Max Webers 'Musiksoziologie'* (1992), which was awarded the Amalfi Prize for most promising young sociologist.

David Chalcraft is Head of Sociology at the University of Derby and is currently preparing a new edition and translation of Weber's essay on the Protestant sects.

Martin Green was Research Professor at the Center for Advanced Study in the Behavioural Sciences, University of Stanford 1996–7 and is professor emeritus of English at Tufts University. His books have covered some of the major figures and movements of the twentieth century: D. H. Lawrence, Max Weber, Frieda and Else Richthofen, Countess Reventlow, Otto Gross, Laban, Gandhi, Tolstoy and, in *Children of the Sun*, the English upper class of aesthetes, dandies and spies. His is currently completing a book on Otto Gross.

Edith Hanke is Redakteurin of the Max Weber Gesamtausgabe. She is author of *Prophet des Unmodernen. Leo N. Tolstoi als Kulturkritiker in der deutschen Diskussion in der Jahrhundertwende*, 1993. She is currently researching Weber's 'Herrschaftssoziologie' for the Max Weber Gesamtausgabe.

Carl Levy is an historian at Goldsmith's College, London. He has published extensively on anarchism and Italian politics and has editied *Socialism and the Intelligentsia 1880–1914*. He is currently writing a major work on the social history of anarchism.

Ulrich Linse is professor of modern history at the Technische Hochschule in Munich. He is Germany's foremost historian of the anarchist movement in Bavaria and is the author of several books on the subject.

Mary Shields is a writer and translator who lives in Oxford. She did her doctorate on German expressionism in the Department of German, University of East Anglia.

Charles Turner lectures in sociology at the University of Warwick. He is the author of *Modernity and Politics in the Work of Max Weber* (1992).

Sam Whimster is Reader in sociology at London Guildhall University. He is currently undertaking research on Marianne Weber, and his previous publications include *Max Weber, Rationality and Modernity* (1987, edited with Scott Lash), and *Global Finance and Urban Living* (1992, edited with Leslie Budd).

Editions and Abbreviations of Weber Texts

ES   *Economy and Society*, ed. G. Roth and C. Wittich (New York: Bedminster Press, 1968)

FMW   *From Max Weber*, ed. H. H. Gerth and C. Wright Mills (London: Routledge & Kegan Paul, 1948)

GStA   Geheimes Staatsarchiv Preussischer Kultur Besitz, Berlin

MSS   *Methodology of the Social Sciences*, ed. E. Shils (New York: Free Press, 1949)

MWG   *Max Weber Gesamtausgabe*, I. *Schriften und Reden*; II. *Briefe* ed. H. Baier, M. R. Lepsius, W. J. Mommsen, W. Schluchter, J. Winckelmann (Tübingen: J. C. B. Mohr (Paul Siebeck), 1984-)

PESC   *The Protestant Ethic and the Spirit of Capitalism*, trans. T. Parsons (London: Unwin University Books, 1930)

PW   *Political Writings*, trans. and ed. P. Lassman and R. Speirs (Cambridge: Cambridge University Press, 1994)

WuG   *Wirtschaft und Gesellschaft*, ed. J. Winckelmann (Tübingen: J.C.B. Mohr (Paul Siebeck), 1972)

1 Introduction to Weber, Ascona and Anarchism

Sam Whimster

It will be recalled that in the final pages of *The Protestant Ethic and the Spirit of Capitalism* Weber speculates on what sort of future awaits humankind now that the spirit of religious asceticism has escaped from the iron cage of capitalism. Religion in the form of the Protestant sects had played its decisive role in the formation of a frame of mind that would reproduce a new form of capitalism. But having made the succession from early to high modernity, what should be done with this mental and cultural 'habitus' – that ingrained disposition that controlled all one's actions in the world? It might haunt us as duty, or it might simply be discarded as in America in favour of the pursuit of wealth as a competitive sport.

Weber's next paragraph deepened and darkened the question. At the end of the tremendous development of modern capitalism would new prophets, new ideas and ideals arise? Or would it end in a mechanised petrification in which the cultural development humankind attained would, as Weber bitterly and sarcastically noted, be that of '"Specialists without spirit, sensualists without heart"; this nullity imagines that it has attained a level of civilization never before achieved'? The quote marks are Weber's own. Nobody has yet found the exact citation, but the reference points to an even more pithy formulation of a section of Nietzsche's *Thus Spoke Zarathustra*. The object of Zarathustra's contempt is the *Last Man*. 'The earth has become small and upon it hops the Last Man, who makes everything small. His race is inexterminable as the flea; the Last Man lives longest. "We have discovered happiness", say the Last Men and blink.' For 'blink' read incomprehension. '"What is love? What is creation? What is longing? What is a star?", thus asks the Last Man and blinks.'[1]

Sociology, having noted these two possibilities – either a future inhabited by nullities, the Last Men, or a future where new prophets and ideals are awakened – passes by on the other side of the road. The discourse on happiness is sometimes technically referred to by its Greek name, eudaemonism. Weber was intensely interested in this subject but to the extent he was a sociologist he placed the issue in the judgemental category and

1

therefore beyond the scope of social science. Weber was, however, forced to confront the future in November 1917 when the Free Students Association requested him to speak on the future of science. His answer was deeply depressing and dispiriting, very much in the specialist without spirit category, and amounted in the eyes of many to a betrayal of the ideals of learning. Then the same student association asked him to address the question of the future of politics, which he did in early 1919. Germany was having to come to terms with not winning the war and was faced by revolutions and the breakdown of the nation-state. In his politics lecture, 'The Profession and Vocation of Politics', Weber counsels resignation but does allow the possibility of new ideals and prophets.

This volume of essays is concerned with charting Weber's thinking between the fully formed genius of *The Protestant Ethic and the Spirit of Capitalism* of 1905 and his two late lectures on politics and science, which however much one disagrees with them – and this volume adds new disagreements – are rightfully regarded among his most mature statements. So was it the disasters of war that forced the hand of the reluctant philosopher? In forcing him to a *public* stance this was largely the case. But the intervening period between the questions left hanging at the end of the Protestant ethic essay and the partial answers given in 1917 and 1919 have been insufficiently probed. Weber was not quiescent but on the contrary vigorously and actively involved in the 'happiness-under-conditions-of-modernity' debate. In its Aristotelian formulation this ranged to the ends and purposes of the human person, the manner in which a life might be conducted, and the ethics of action and how one's own goals are to be reconciled with the actions of others.

The essays in this volume show that these issues were debated both publicly and privately by Weber, that they involved him in major disagreements with friends and colleagues, and it is through these arguments that we can begin to grasp the background field which sourced the development of these debates. Two very large reasons made the debate unavoidable. One was the unstoppable process of rationalisation under way. Weber the sociologist investigated the rationalisation process in factories, churches, bureaucracies, the press, political parties. All these institutions displayed the progressive ascendancy of means–end rationality that Weber termed instrumental. Large scale capitalist units and the rise of white collar bureaucracy in government and industry had created new forms of work discipline and conformity. Max and Alfred Weber criticised this as a 'parcelling up of humanity' in their studies for the Social Policy Association. It was a critique that found a receptive audience, including the young Kafka, who was Alfred's student in Prague. The aspirations which Weber held for conduct became increasingly threatened by these enormous developments. As with Nietzsche, Weber's disdain was most clearly marked by his dislike of utilitarianism, a form of conduct and happiness fundamentally at odds with Weber's own humanism. Yet Weber the sociologist conceded that utilitarianism was the obvious successor to religious asceticism in the field of social ethics under conditions of modern (as opposed to early modern) capitalism.

The other reason was the particular pattern modernisation had locked into in the German Empire of Weber's own day. Structural transformations are indiscriminate in their effects. The Germany of Weber's day was faced with massive problems resulting from rapid industrialisation and urbanisation. Urban planning, zoning of industry, social housing, and public transport were only just being considered even as late as 1900. Dislocation, fragmentation, poverty and widespread prostitution and illegitimacy were endemic to the system.

Taken in their entirety these problems amounted to a very long list on the agenda of reform politics. But to the endless frustration and anger of reform politicians, the Empire was controlled by the Emperor and a Prussian political class who were reluctant to concede any loss of their control to political parties and parliament. The crisis in political governance came to a head in the First World War and was played out to its final catastrophic end. Unsurprisingly the path to catastrophe has been carefully analysed under the heading of politics in Weber studies and the historiography of the Wilhelmine Empire.[2]

Weber's preferred solution was the reform of politics towards parliamentary politics, the granting of rights to trade unions, and the political and domestic emancipation of women. The weakness of Weber's reform position was the inability to muster the political means to force reforms through against the will of the Emperor and the Prussian political class. Friedrich Naumann was the progressive politician upon whom Weber pinned his hopes; yet Naumann spent his whole life, in terms of electoral success, in the political wilderness.

The majority of the upper and middle classes complacently enjoyed the benefits of an unequal society and felt firmly secure in their monarchism, dislike of democracy, and Germany's growing power. The majority of the working class gave their allegiance to the Social Democratic Party in the hope of major change to the system. Beyond these groups, however, were large numbers of people whose profound dissatisfaction with society and politics drove them to look for alternative solutions. They numbered feminists, politicians, trade unionists, health workers, academics, artists, poets, writers, and youth movements, who all tried to force through their vision of an imagined future under conditions of modernity. These groups felt themselves to be outside the political community of the nation and attempted to work out their deeply felt alienation through other routes and through another politics.

Weber was one voice in a much wider chorus of voices looking for a reform of ways of living and conduct that would circumvent an unresponsive politics and the modernising structures of society. Weber research has set out Weber's analysis but in doing so has tended to consign other voices as foils, light-weights, dim-wits, misguided enthusiasts and other epithets of marginalisation. This has created a disservice to Weber himself. His views in no small part developed in dialogue with the voices on the margin. Leaving aside the arrogance that voices 'marginal' to Weber were wrong and the uncritical acceptance that Weber was always right, a major underestimation of the severity of the crisis in Wilhelmine Germany is perpetrated. Weber and his reform solutions imply that through rational social policy a more progressive and whiggist view could have prevailed; there is much evidence to the contrary.

The marginalisation of the excluded, actually the case in Wilhelmine Germany, but also the intellectual marginalisation practised by Weber studies, stems from the conventional political analysis of the three choice scenarios of reaction, or reform, or revolution. This captures the major actors in the political community and those who wanted to be represented through it, including the 'revolutionary' Social Democrats. But it fails to do sociological and historical justice to the many others who felt the pressures of Wilhemine society as intolerable. The labels of rationalisation and modernisation with their imputation of an inevitable progress – all part of becoming modern – diminish the enormity of what was occurring across a broad front of experiences.

The term 'high modernity' signals the explosion occurring not simply in work, bureaucracy and nation-state but in urbanism, religion and culture.[3] Sociologists and social reformers were the progressive and secularised Protestant solution to the multiple transformations in society. But, equally, other types of avant-gardes existed in politics – most notably in anarchism, in experiments in living, and of course in the visual arts and literature. Klaus Lichtblau has recently shown that these modernisms can be taken as revolutions in the basis of thought and the forms through which the world was cognised.[4] Sociology was just one modernism in the human sciences. But within the German speaking world new knowledges and new artistic and cultural movements came into being side by side: Nietzsche in philosophy, Simmel in cultural analysis, the Weber brothers and Toennies in sociology, Menger in economics, Freud and Jung in psychology, Kraepelin and Bleuler in psychiatry, Einstein in science, Kirchner, Kokoschka and Kandinsky in painting, Shoenberg and Berg in music, expressionism in literature and drama closely followed by Dada and surrealism. (See the assessment of the sciences by Karl-Ludwig Ay, in Chapter 5, below.)

Wolfgang Mommsen has complained that the social has been taken in isolation to the cultural and 'basic values and ideals and aesthetic conceptions have been treated separately from the individual cultural sciences.'[5] This volume of essays asserts not only the interaction between politics and culture, but, through an investigation of the avant-gardes of anarchism and culture it also seeks to suggest new possibilities in the relation between the political community and those who stand outside as the unrepresented and the unnamed. This theme has a contemporary relevance as politics and economics is normalised around those who have a stake in the system and its narrowing of a political discourse of inclusion. The unrealised and perhaps unrealisable categories of community and justice are remaindered for the excluded to work as best they may.

To invoke the cultural and aesthetic is, therefore, to challenge the conventional boundaries of the political and to give equal weight to the historical moment of the marginalised. Culture just as much as politics involves the struggle for advantage. David Chaney in his work on contemporary culture has drawn attention to the ways in which cultural resources – forms, styles, and patterns – are deployed for the ascendancy of position. Modern consumption is not a world of aimlessly free choice but the outcome of a politics of culture.[6] The same point can be made for the wider field of politics and culture in Wilhelmine society. Avant-gardes were not simply the reactivity of the excluded (which is largely their portrayal in the historiography). Instead they were pitching for their own redefinition of modernity and to this end were creating and deploying innovative artefacts: new forms in art, literature, life-style and politics, producing entirely new aesthetic and ethical sensibilities. The political has, as always, to be seen as the struggle for the possible. And in this struggle culture as both form and sensibility could attempt to create a new politics of the excluded based on new conceptions of representation, justice and community.

As many of the essays in this volume show, Weber paid the anarchist option great respect. The anarchists, like Weber, read Nietzsche and understood Zarathustra's injunction 'to shoot the arrow of his longing out over mankind'. And the anarchists could react less ambivalently than Weber to Zarathustra's observation, 'I tell you: one must have chaos in one, to give birth to a dancing star. I tell you: you still have chaos in you.'[7] It was culture that provided a common ground between Weber and the anarchists. Culture was the strong force that linked two opposing poles:

Weber's reformism and anarchist renewal. It enabled dialogue across the boundary of those who counted themselves as part of the political community of the nation and those who wanted a wider definition of whom and what the political were to include.

However this over-states the case of culture. Both the anarchists and Weber, and very many others (as Ascheim's book on the Nietzsche reception testifies[8]), could draw a common affiliation back to Nietzsche. Culture was actively being re-defined and open to contention. The encounters of Weber and the anarchists involved both sharp disagreements but also an ability to keep talking to each other despite those differences. Studies on Weber have not got much further than registering Weber's 'fascination' with anarchism. The materials assembled in this collection force a move from interesting explanandum to deeper explanation. Why was Weber cohabiting (literally, in Ascona) with anarchists and how should the dual lines of agreement and disagreement be followed?

In order to pursue these question we need to be a little more sociological in the use of the term culture. Wilhemine Germany experienced what Simmel referred to as the crisis of modern culture: what were the possibilities for a life that was culturally constituted over and beyond the crude determinism of economics and the technology of the modern age? For those brought up and educated within the cultural horizon of Nietzsche, it was an inescapable question that produced a variety of solutions and answers. However the phrase 'those brought up and educated to read Nietzsche' is also a sociological category which, following Bourdieu, I will call cultural habitus. Education, as the contributions by Ay and Levy make clear below, meant the classical humanism of the gymnasium, university education and reserve officer status. This stratum is termed the *Bildungsbürgertum*, or the educated middle class. This was the acquired and taken for granted background of culture. As a habitus it becomes a set of dispositions to understand the world and behave in a particular manner which would be instinctively apparent to any onlooker. An individual's dress, manner, diction, conversation, as well as the far more telling attributes of household, marked a person out as belonging to a particular social stratum. Max Weber's own habitus spelt educated middle class, and the picture of him taken at Lauenstein Castle captures his assumed sense of bearing. Weber's letters from Ascona (published below) continuously demonstrate the cultural assumptions of his social class that are revealed even more tellingly by the anarchists. These are the people who had rejected the bourgeois world of culture and manners, yet their appearance, language and attitudes still signalled the inalienable cultural habitus of upbringing.

However, we need to follow through the theoretical postulates of Bourdieu's sociology.[9] Habitus is an ingrained disposition to see and react to the world in a particular way but this should not be taken for a common determination. It is a practical attitude of acting and performing in the world drawing on the unconscious cues of assumed behaviour. Background cannot determine a world about to happen, especially a world as crisis ridden as Wilhemine Germany, through which Weber like any other person had to find his way. In fact, because of their unrealistic adherence to an honour code, Weber's class failed to reproduce its pre-eminent position in society (see Ay, Chapter 5). Weber and the anarchists developed opposing solutions. These were readable across positions, and either side could unconsciously assume that it would be understood and even accepted by others of the same habitus. Seen in these terms cultural habitus explains commonality. But then actual cultures, politics and life styles should be regarded as open to dispute and conflict. One of the weapons of conflict was to pull your opponent to your point of view through the unspoken assumptions of habitus. Politics, gender, and culture were all open to the deployment of habitus.

The differentiation of culture into a fixed habitus and a set of ideas in flux enables a clearer grasp of Weber's apparent propinquity to the anarchists. It also permits an uncompromised view of how the boundaries of culture and politics were fought over and deployed. The questions that Weber flagged up at the end of the Protestant Ethic essay – nullities, prophets, or utilitarian hedonists – to which he gave his own answers only in 1917 and 1919, belong to the flux of ideas, which at the same time is the encounters of people and their efforts to understand and control the direction of events.

Letters from Ascona

We can track textually what Weber was doing between 1905 and 1917. Schluchter has recently done this with commendable skill, searching the texts for indicators of Weber's late excursion into philosophy. He counts the Freiburg inaugural lecture of 1895, the epistolary rejection of Otto Gross's essay for the *Archiv für Sozialwissenschaft und Sozialpolitik* in 1907, Weber's oral contribution to the debate on technology and culture at the first meeting of the German Sociological Society in 1910, and the 'Intermediate Reflections' essay from 1915 as the important milestones in the development of what might be termed a post-Protestant ethic. However the reader of Schluchter's text quickly discovers a parallel world in his footnotes.[10] The parallel world is the life-world of Weber's reluctant philosophising. The notes bustle with Weber's correspondence to family, friends, colleagues, lovers and enemies. The social and political worlds of Heidelberg, Munich and Berlin are fleetingly glimpsed – a world of houses, tête-à-têtes, walks, Sunday afternoon gatherings, concerts, seminars, conferences, meetings, rallies, and the turbulences of war and revolution. Schluchter with the practised dexterity of the censor keeps Weber's life-world firmly in its place. Occasionally, and most interestingly although not wholly explicably, some of this vitality spills out into Weber's texts. But the above-mentioned references are an inadequate preparation for comprehending, critically, what Weber vouchsafed to paper in 1917 and 1919.

It is an affliction of research that we cannot re-enter this life world and re-capture the tensions, the alarms, the places of stability and the flash-points of contention. But this does not mean it has to be relegated as posterior to the figure and writings of Max Weber. What needs to be re-created, to the extent that this is possible, is the conversation Weber was so actively involved in with the people and the currents around him.

My research method as editor is unusual but nevertheles should be noted. I have taken, and translated, 35 letters that Weber wrote to his wife Marianne, when he stayed in Ascona over the Easters of 1913 and 1914 – a period altogether of at least 6 weeks. Ascona was a little fishing village on the shore of Lake Maggiore on the Swiss side of the border with Italy. Ascona and the wider province of Tessin (or Ticino for its Italian-speaking inhabitants) had a history of attracting anarchists and revolutionaries – Kropotkin, Malatesta, Michael Bakunin and Mazzini being the most internationally famous.[11] Although still primitive, it was touched by modernity in two ways. Refugees from the empires of Germany and Austro-Hungary settled in the gardens and small hills of Ascona seeking a self-sufficient pastoral world. The anarchist historian Ulrich Linse notes, 'From the beginning of the Wilhelmine period to the end of the Weimar Republic 'to settle' was not only an idea but a movement, it expressed a critique of the big city, it incorporated the yearning for the countryside and the striving of 'back to the land'.[12]

In addition Ascona became a rural outpost of Munich's bohemian district of Schwabing and some its leading figures – Erich Mühsam, Franziska zu Reventlow, Otto Gross, Frieda Gross, and Ernst Frick – stayed there.[13] It was not, however, the sort of place, either in comfort or repute, a respectable professor would stay. Weber was entering a 'wild zone'. In 1910 the *Winterthur Tagblatt* bemoaned 'the unwelcome appearance of ambassadors of German metropolitan anarchism, syndicalist wandering preachers, and emancipated females. They have been shown to be

representatives of acute metropolitan sickness, of sexual perversion and of homosexual prostitution.'[14]
     I have used these letters as a sample of the biographical threads in Weber's life at these two points in time. The two points can be taken as a cross-section of Weber's life. Following the 1995 BSA's Max Weber Study Group conference[15] the authors in this volume have contributed to unearthing the overlapping worlds of politics, culture, and quotidian existence of the people whose lives passed though Ascona. Some of these threads can no longer be grasped, others can be followed and then are concealed or disappear without trace, and some have a rewarding longevity. Taken together in this volume (and much more needs to be said and researched) we can approach the world outside the text, that of practical conduct.

Na ja, Franzl, Ascona gehört entschieden zur Biographie

('You see, Franzl, Ascona belongs decisively to biography' – Fanny Reventlow, 1911).

My method in this chapter is biographical. This should not be taken as an aversion to theory and the text. The people who passed through Ascona, and the people they knew, comprise a major segment of those responsible for modernism – in its creative artistic forms and as the new understanding of society and power, pre-eminently in the new discipline of sociology. Within the biographical sketches I will introduce relevant theoretical contributions made by the people of Ascona. What is quite striking about this rich period is just how few people were involved in the project which we now refer to as modernism. Obviously this is a question wider than that of selected individuals, and it is one of the major points of this chapter to show how the pressures and tensions of society and politics forced these individuals into creative solutions either in their own conduct, or sociological analysis, or culture. Also you do not have to be a deconstructionist to realise that at some point the narrative of theory in its infancy becomes part of the narrative of a life. Moreover, as we will see in the case of Gross, Jung and Freud, the ways in which lives intersected, often inharmoniously, have become part of the received narrative of theories (of psychoanalysis). The same point can, and will be made, for Weberian theory. In searching out biographical threads, one excavates the traces of the genealogy of theory.

Max Weber

The first biographical thread is Weber's own. Weber in Ascona is not like any received picture we have of the man. Some, or rather parts, of his letters were published by Marianne as part of the biography of her dead husband. She placed them in a chapter entitled 'Travel Pictures'.[16] This misleads and disguises the deeper issues that were being played out in Ascona. Marianne's biography has been an extraordinarily successful enterprise in ordering and conventionalising her husband's life. But her story covers up much over the particular turbulent period of the decade 1910–20.

Weber's main activity over Easter 1913 was doing nothing. He slept, he rested on the sofa, he sat in the sun outside his lodgings overlooking Lake Maggiore, he went for walks around the edge of the lake, and made excursions into Locarno. His diet was vegetarian 'fodder' of figs, biscuits and fruit, save for lunches at the inn, which provided a proper cuisine, though Weber reports that it was too rich for him. He read novels – the new Thomas Mann (*Königliche Hoheit*) – and some poetry. In a letter to Robert Wilbrandt early on in his stay he declines to enter into academic correspondence – '"ultra posse nemo obligatur"'.[17]

The Easter breaks were an established routine in Weber's life. In April 1907 he travelled to Lake Como in search of spring and recuperation. In 1908 he was away for the two months of March and April travelling on the French Riviera and then on to Italy. He was recovering from the 'enforced labour' of completing the *Agrarverhältnisse im Altertum*. At the end of April 1909 he was at Pallanza on the shore of Lake Maggiore, and he spent the beginning of April 1910 in Lerici near La Spezia. In 1911 he was back in northern Italy and the French Riviera and in 1912 he travelled to Provence.

The picture of the driven scholar tied to his desk has to be amended. Back in Heidelberg he was surrounded by writing, projects and plans. He was deeply involved in writing for and planning the mammoth *Grundriss der Sozialökonomik*, he was working on his other major project 'The Economic Ethics of World Religions', and the essay 'Some interpretive categories of Sociology' appeared in *Logos* later that year (in September, 1913). Yet in Ascona he did nothing, preferring solitude to any other activity. After each winter's work as a private scholar Weber was compelled to go south in search of the sun. It was in these breaks Weber weaned himself from the sedatives of 'Trional and Bromidin etc' which, he tells Rickert, was the price of the *'Agrargeschichte'*.[18] The Ascona visits continued the pattern of rest and recuperation, in which sedative drugs, including those containing opiates,[19] were given up in a regime that necessitated the avoidance of all stimulants. Weber dieted, gave up meat and his cigars, avoided strenuous exercise, kept out of the wind and coped as best he could with insomnia. He humorously refers to his diet as the *Kur*, placing himself in the same bracket as the vegetarians and teetotalers of Ascona.

Breakdowns in mental and physical health are a persistent theme throughout the figures who appear in this volume of essays. There were few robust individuals able to sustain work and a 'normal' pattern of personal life. The theme of the abnormal personality is one of the commonplaces in the literature on Wilhelmine period as well as in the literature of Wilhelmine society. The naming of Weber's psychological affliction, what he referred to as his 'demons', is speculation, just as this period saw the speculation in the naming of personality disorders by Freud, Jung, Bleuler and Kraepelin all of whom connect to the threads of Ascona. The double moment of patient and analyst is a theme repeated in Freud, Jung, Weber, and Gross that has its equivalent in the field of literature with Kafka, and Hesse and D. H. Lawrence (see Green, below) and in philosophy with Lukács. The innovation of naming a condition of modernism only came through living the condition and at the same time analysing it. Cultural habitus produced a character formation but how adaptive this was to the exploration of the modernist psyche by individuals varied from case to case. In Weber's case one suspects that being chosen as a leader of the secular Protestant élite was to take on a character as hard as steel that chafed and tormented his body and mind. In Ascona, cut off from academia and society, he could convalesce his battered and pharmacologically sustained psyche.

Weber's letters of 1913 portray a man at a very low ebb in his personal relationships. His longstanding friendship with the Jaffés appears to have completely deteriorated, Max swearing for some reason to strike Edgar Jaffé dead (see Chapter 2) and refusing to meet Else Jaffé both in 1913 and 1914. The Jaffés were living the outward form of married life, though in fact each had other partners, Edgar, travelling in 1914 with the actress Mendelssohn and Else with Max's brother Alfred. Max and Marianne had helped to save the Jaffés marriage from complete breakdown in 1910 when Else first started a liaison with Alfred. Max himself was romantically besotted by Else and in an atmosphere of sexual jealousy and sibling rivalry it is no surprise that Max was no longer on speaking terms with Alfred and Else.[20] This is some of the background to the farce of Max shutting himself in his room when Else visited her close friend Frieda Gross in Ascona in 1914.

Towards the end of his stay in 1914 Weber's spirits improve noticeably. Firstly he was actively and enjoyably committed in the legal action to defend Frieda Gross from a court action to have her children removed into guardianship. Secondly he was visiting his lady companion Mina Tobler in Zurich;

she was one of the very few people able to humour the sulking bear out of its moods. It was Tobler, as we will note in connection with Christoph Braun's essay, who was the stimulant for Weber's remarkable study of music.

Weber's story and his interconnections with anarchism both pre-date and post-date Ascona and here pride of place will be ceded to the anarchists themselves. I will first mention the women of Ascona who personify an important issue in relation to habitus and new cultural forms. The cultural habitus of the educated middle class was reproduced through the form of the family. The stratum had a strong tendency to endogamy; marriages were made predominantly between the sons and daughters of the same stratum and marriage between cousins was not uncommon. Boys were brought up for careers founded on the humanistic curriculum of the gymnasium and the university patent. Girls were brought up with a schooling more in line with the liberal arts and languages and their careers were to be that of the husbands, if and when they found one. Dress, decorum and manners had to be observed by ladies and mothers and their ambitions were turned inwards to family and household.[21] Men were groomed for the public world of work and despite the humanistic reputation of the German university, duelling, and drinking were the expected accomplishments of a young man.

Franziska zu Reventlow

One of the first topics of conversation and correspondence when Weber arrived in Ascona in 1913 was the Countess Franziska zu Reventlow, who had achieved legendary status in the academic and bohemian circles of Munich and Heidelberg. Reventlow had been very strictly groomed for an aristocratic marriage. But she rebelled against her parents and schooling. She married a lawyer at an early age and he supported her studies at an art college in Munich. She soon ended this marriage, objecting to the demands of respectability and household made by her husband's career. It was as a seventeen year old girl in her hometown of Lübeck that she had joined the Ibsen club and discovered the contemporary literature of Ibsen, Tolstoy and Theodore Storm. She absorbed an alternative code of authenticity and personal freedom.

> For us 'modern' human beings, to which we of the younger generation belong, many of us – most of us, have to fight a difficult struggle before we can free ourselves from the so-called influence of good upbringing and its archaic moral principles and outlook in order to attain the basis for a freer conception of life.[22]

Her legendary status derived from her status as queen of the long running carnival of Munich's Schwabing where she not only pursued her own sensual and aesthetic needs in defiance of patriarchal convention but through that pursuit created and contributed to a new cultural habitus. It was the expectation that members of her circle should be extreme, outspoken, outrageous, colourful and creative. In breaking convention she became a role model for educated bourgeois daughters who did not want to embrace marriage, at least not immediately. Otto Gross is usually singled out for spreading the gospel of the erotic movement, as Martin Green terms it,[23] first in Munich and then in Heidelberg, but Reventlow's rebellion predates Gross and was a palpable demonstration of independent womanly conduct, which Gross's theory and practice failed in crucial respects to achieve. She was a role model of independence for Else Jaffé, and her sister Frieda, for Frieda Gross, and probably Mina Tobler. And latterly she was the inspiration for the book that became the film '*Jules et Jim*'.[24]

But Reventlow was hardly a role model to be lightly copied. Having broken with patriarchal norms, there was no way back and her parents disinherited her. Her quest for independence owed much to her qualities of courage. Avant-garde bohemias tend to be short-lived. By 1908 she regarded Schwabing as no longer so vital and she was considering moving with her son to Ascona, which she did in the autumn of 1910. She realised that in the absence of a career for women, she had to make a career of herself. She needed to maintain the momentum of her life, always being ahead of her biography, as she put it. When Max Weber met her in 1913 and again in 1914, when she acts as his temporary secretary, the downside of bohemianism was apparent. Age had slowed the pace of her liaisons (she was born in 1871) and some of her more adventurous occupations such as circus performer were no longer an option. Weber witnessed the closing stages of the farce of her arranged marriage to a Baltic baron, Rechenberg-Linten, who lived in the village of Ronco close to Ascona.

Rechenberg-Linten's parents had refused to pass on any of the family inheritance unless he married and reformed himself – he was a notorious drunkard. Rechenberg-Linten and Reventlow agreed a contract with local lawyer (Weber's landlord in 1913), prior to their marriage, to split the inheritance that would come with marriage. Unwisely Rechenberg never paid for the contract and the lawyer Signor Abbondio turned to his father to pay the debt, so revealing the sham of the arranged marriage.[25] Some 15 000 Swiss Francs did come to Reventlow in 1914, which Weber sourly notes was being spent on dresses, but the majority of this was lost in the Tessin bank crash of that year. As Reventlow wrote to a Munich friend,

'Otherwise things are brilliant. The short-lived luxury was beautiful, the crash was great fun and the decision to travel abroad was liberating. In short the Lord has given, the Lord has taken away, praised be the name of the Lord!'[26]

Despite the insouciance this was a humiliating return of patriarchy. Her story dramatically illustrates the price of liberation from patriarchalism. Her case also raises some of the limitations of the proponents of open marriage as advocated by her friend the anarchist Erich Mühsam, which are noted by Linse in this volume (Chapter 6) and lead into a wider debate on the essentialist conception of women held by the advocates of free love in Germany.[27] For Weber Reventlow would have raised the issue of living according to convictions and living with the consequences of those convictions. But Weber is less than gallant in his estimation of Reventlow, as can be read. (Although he may well have not wanted to appear as too complimentary about the countess to Marianne; and it is Mina Tobler who actively complains about his association with the countess).

Else von Richthofen

Else von Richthofen, who married Edgar Jaffé in 1902, showed a more studied but by no means successful attempt to achieve independence. Her parents belonged to the minor aristocracy and were impoverished. As the eldest child of three daughters it was Else who was sent by her mother to the officers' mess to sort out her father's gambling debts. She attended school at the Institute Blas in Freiburg. It was here that her friendship with Frieda Gross (née Schloffer) started, and it was Frieda who introduced Else to the academic world of Freiburg. Frieda was looked after for long periods by her aunt and uncle, Sophie and Alois Riehl. Riehl was professor of philosophy at Freiburg and among his publications was the first serious study of Nietzsche's philosophy. Max Weber, the new professor in political economy, was a visitor at the Riehls and it was during this period that Else commenced her friendship with the Webers. This was clearly a biographical moment of some import. As Hennis notes, this was the point at which Weber's language became inflected with the vocabulary of Nietzsche.[28] For Else it must have been a clash of two habituses: her own rather rackety background of aristocratic privation and military officialdom, and that of the young Freiburg professors, their smart flats and advanced talk of scholarship and social reform. David Chalcraft records below (Chapter 10) Else's shock on entering the Webers' flat and confronting the provocative Klinger etchings that were hung on the walls of the flat. (See Plates 1–8) This was a world whose tastes and values were radically different from those she was used to. She decided to enter this world, very much a pioneer, as one of the first women in German higher education. In a sense her choice meant re-equipping herself with a new habitus. As if to emphasise the dangers of her parents' world, Marianne Weber wrote to Else in 1899 advising that she could study in Berlin only so long as she had nothing to do with society.[29] That other choice was taken up by her youngest sister, Joanna, who married a regimental commander and aristocrat and lived the society queen to the full.

After the completion of her degree in 1901 she became Baden's first female factory inspector. This indicates the extent to which she had been drawn into the reform circle of Marianne and Max and the wider movement of Protestant led reform in Baden.[30] Her baronial parents must have been less than proud; factories and women workers were not words in their vocabulary. It was probably a move too far outside her habitus and after a short period she resigned the post, opting for marriage with a rich merchant and Heidelberg academic, Edgar Jaffé. At this point the trajectory of their marriage and lives becomes a personal and complicated biography. But for this volume it needs to be noted that Edgar joined Kurt Eisner's Bavarian Republic as Finance Minister in 1918–19; and that Else had an affair with Otto Gross in 1907, so marking the arrival of the erotic movement in Heidelberg.

Frieda Gross

Emanuel Hurwitz wrote in his study of Otto Gross of the difficulty of being the son of a famous father.[31] Frieda's difficulties stemmed from being married to a notorious husband who had a famous father. More so than Else, she was at home in the world of the university. After the death of her mother, she used to stay in the household of Alois Riehl. Then, in her own home town of Graz in the Austrian Steiermark she met, and later in 1903, married Otto Gross who was studying at the psychiatric and neurological clinic of Graz University. Her father-in-law was Professor Hans Gross who laid the foundations of forensic crime detection and ran his own university department. A repeating theme in the many accounts of her was the striking and favourable impression she imparted. Her friend Frieda Lawrence (Else's younger sister) portrayed her in a short story as 'a strange, blond "Nixe" [water sprite] kind of woman, living in a world of her own, abstract like a visionary, brooding in her own way.... She was very musical, her voice had a slow, gentle quality.... She was Austrian with all the soft cultured quality of an old race.'[32] Frieda Gross drew on a cultural resource and fashioned it into a habitus all of her own. Despite the alarms and devastations of her life her appearance conveyed an inner coherence and stability. She favourably impressed Freud who commented, 'I have great sympathy for his [Otto's] wife, one of the few German women I really like.'[33] Carl Jung was obviously taken by her courage and integrity. And Weber really does seem to have been transfixed by her, to judge by his descriptions in his Ascona letters (see below Chapter 2). Despite going beyond the boundaries of 'society' she was able to deploy habitus to remind would be critics that she was a more stylish example of their own cultural formation.

When Weber met her in Ascona at the start of his visit in 1913 the curious triangular relationship between her, Otto and Hans Gross had come apart. Frieda had believed in marrying Otto she was attaching herself to a rising star in academia. The father likewise had hoped his gifted son would follow in his footsteps in psychological research into criminality. Otto's research followed other lines, however. One side of his research related to Freudian psychiatry and therapy, and the other to neurology and the behaviour of the brain. Around 1905 these two sides were combined into a radical theorisation of abreaction, repression and neurological development. Repression blocked nerve development; instead the patient should try and lift repression by acting out his or her desires. What in Freudian theory had been a process of the analyst aiding the catharsis of the repressed unconscious became for Otto the need to defy convention and patriarchy. Men's desires were blocked by the looming authority of the father, women's sexuality was denied. Otto did not distinguish the boundaries of theory, practice and life. In his understanding of abreaction (or catharsis) the analyst should form a personal relationship with the patient in order to help what was for him a fellow human being, out of the prison of repression. Otto was convinced by the goodness and honesty of his theory and actions which he held to be free from hypocrisy. If a desire was sexual then it was perverse to deny it. The healthy development of nerves demanded the hygiene of sex and to this end Otto entered into a number of sexual relationships with women patients. Otto's own candour was frequently intensified by consumption of cocaine, a habit he made fashionable in the literary cafés of Schwabing.

In towns like Munich and Heidelberg which had large academic, artistic and bohemian stratums with an already overdeveloped affectual sensibility, Gross found a ready audience. His activities were not unleashed upon a naïve and prudish public. To sit in Café Stephanie with an analyst was to invite outcomes which would not have been wholly unexpected. His wife Frieda and Franziska Reventlow prudently refused his analytic charms,

Reventlow being especially caustic. Mühsam and Leonard Frank allowed themselves into sessions with Otto and they both regretted it,[34] as Ulrich Linse reveals below (Chapter 6).

As these examples show, Otto Gross was emotionally dangerous, exactly in respect to the consequences of his praxis for which he had no response. One of his patients, Charlotte Hattemer, committed suicide, seemingly with Otto's approval. Another patient Sophie Benz, who was badly depressed and lived with Otto in Ascona in 1910–11, committed suicide with opiates supposedly forgotten by Otto after he had left for Berlin. In defence Otto said they were incurably depressed and that ultimately he could not deny their wish to end their lives. His close associates, such as Ernst Frick and Erich Mühsam, condemned him unreservedly over the Benz case.[35] In addition Otto was a danger to himself, fuelling his writing and work with cocaine and opiates.

By 1911 Hans Gross had decided that Otto Gross was so seriously imbalanced he should be confined. This followed Carl Jung's analysis of Otto in 1908 when he entered the Burghölzli for a cure for drug dependency. Jung came to the conclusion that Otto suffered from dementia praecox, a very vague label of madness. By late 1907 Frieda was 'in a profound state of resignation over her marriage'.[36] Despite the freedom each had granted to the other within their marriage, Otto was very much dependent upon Frieda as well as his father. Hans paid for his drug detoxification cures, which occurred about every two years from 1902 onwards, while Frieda persuaded him to voluntarily enter the clinics. In addition Frieda had to cope with Otto's phobias which included not washing, not clearing up anything, and refusing to relinquish his scientific manuscripts which Frieda helped to transcribe and make sense of. Also Hans Gross, who as a result of his scientific reputation and books had become a rich man, paid money to Frieda to look after Otto and their son Peter (born in 1907). Otto was something of a St Francis figure – he gave his money away, and according to his father had an immoderate love of animals that made him a convinced vegetarian.

Hans had managed to get his son into a clinic in Mendrisio in Italy during the furore over the Sophie Benz affair and had by then given up hope that Otto would ever be fit for work. In a will drawn up in 1912 Hans stipulated that after his death his son should be placed permanently in an asylum 'lest he be exploited and misled by his "friends" (people of the worst Bohème and anarchists'.[37] Hans was not amused by anarchists. His life had been devoted to law and order and he was a proponent of the deportation of vagabonds, homosexuals and persistent criminals.[38] He received secret intelligence from police authorities in Prussia, Austria and Switzerland on the movement of his son and daughter-in-law within anarchist circles. From 1908 onwards both Otto and Frieda had moved into the anarchist bohemia of Schwabing as well as Zurich. In 1913, publishing in the Berlin anarchist magazine *Aktion* he had proposed sexual libertarianism as a form of anarchism.

But it was Frieda's association with anarchism that ended the alliance between Hans and his daughter-in-law. In 1910 Frieda had started a relationship with a Zurich anarchist, Ernst Frick, with Otto's approval. Indeed they all went on holiday together to Ragusa in 1910. That same summer they stayed in Graz and introduced Frick to Hans Gross who was not told about Frick's anarchist background. Hans was most impressed by Frick's fineness and cultivation and considered him a stabilising force over his son. This pretence fell apart when Frick was arrested for a terrorist offence in June 1912 and Hans was informed by his police spies of the relationship of Frick and Frieda Gross. Frick was sentenced to a year's imprisonment and Frieda visited him in Regensdorf jail. Hans's informer, a Zurich state prosecutor named Kronauer, noted that she spoke 'softly to him and brought him money, flowers and fruit'.[39]

So when Weber arrived in Ascona in 1913 Frieda had been cut off from her main supply of income, Hans. Her husband had not returned to Ascona since the Benz affair of 1911. She had two children: a six year old boy Peter and a two year old girl Eva whose father was Frick. Otto had declared Eva to be a legitimate child of their marriage, though this statement was given no credence by Hans. In 1914 matters had been made much worse by a series of court cases brought by Hans Gross. He had had his son forcibly removed from Berlin, driven to the Austrian border and taken in protective custody to an asylum in Troppau. In an action brought in Graz he applied to have his son certified as insane and himself made his son's legal guardian. He started another legal action to have his grandson removed from Frieda and be brought up by a guardian, and he changed his will so that Otto, Frieda and Eva were cut out of any inheritance.

These, I think, are the main strands of an intrinsically complex situation. It is a subject of articles, monographs and books[40] and even now is not fully researched. Edith Hanke adds new details on Frick's terrorist offences (see below, Chapter 7). As might be expected, Weber's participation in the case, as revealed in his Ascona letters, adds further important knowledge.

Over and beyond the intrinsic interest and complexity of the case, the Gross affair throws into relief many of the fault lines and intersections of German-speaking society. The case became a significant *cause célèbre* in Zurich, Vienna, Prague and Berlin. Petitions were organised, protest articles appeared in the anarchist press, a letter of pathetic intensity by Otto was smuggled out of his asylum and published in a leading Viennese paper, to which Hans replied, completely rubbishing the character of his son. As Weber commented of Frieda, 'she has been dragged through the press in the most vulgar way' (see below, Chapter 2).

The deepest fault line was that of patriarchalism. The private and public became one through Hans's actions. Hans had acted in an authoritarian manner against the rights of his son whom he had reduced to the legal status of a child. And in pursuing his case in the courts the Prussian state had acted arbitrarily and without legal process in seizing Otto from the home of Franz Jung in Berlin. There could not be a starker illustration of the arbitrary power of the father and state and the obvious implication that patriarchalism was an undifferentiated fusion of the public and the private.

Since Otto had started writing for the Berlin anarchist journal *Die Aktion* and had been seized from the home of the anarchist writer Franz Jung, the anarchist campaign claimed him as their own. But both within and outside anarchism the intersections were complex. On the basis of my enemy's enemy is my friend, Otto could command a wide support, which in part explains the involvement of the Webers and the support of the progressive intelligentsia. But the issue also showed up differences within the radical movement between bohemians, anarchists and sexual liberationists.

Max Weber while supporting Frieda and her children was violently opposed to the anarchist campaign for Otto and Frieda, in particular venting his spleen on Erich Mühsam. But as Ulrich Linse shows below (Chapter 6), Mühsam was himself against publicising the case as a form of propaganda against the state. Mühsam could act as responsibly as Weber and could equally count himself a good friend of Frieda. Weber's intemperate attack against Mühsam indicates his determination that the case be fought within the camp of bourgeois reformers and not *entgleiste* (derailed) bourgeoisie. Weber's considerable support[41] was based on the assumption that despite Frieda's libertarianism, which had placed her irretrievably outside even the advanced mores of Heidelberg (Chapter 2), she was still 'one of us'. Reasons of chivalry (*Ritterlichkeit*) and not those of political principle demanded that she be defended. Frieda was obviously well aware of this and played upon it. The acceptance of anarchists as persons of a certain class and habitus, rather than what they actually said and did, becomes a discernible pattern in Weber's encounters with the anarchists.

Despite Weber's disagreement with Mühsam that the matter remain a private legal matter, politics did come to be mobilised under the banner of the reform wing of the women's movement. Weber comments to Marianne 'You see the whole of the women's movement before the car of Aphrodite' (see below, p. 66). Weber's slightly sarcastic note indicates that Marianne's public role in the women's movement was a far more powerful card than any reputation Max himself might possess.

Marianne Weber

Marianne Weber did actually accompany Max at the start of the 1914 visit to Ascona, but then she journeyed back to Freiburg staying with Sophie and Heinrich Rickert before returning to Heidelberg. Max instructs her not to talk back to Heinrich Rickert or she will become exhausted. Likewise he admonishes Marianne to conserve her strength and 'don't let yourself be plagued by superfluous women'. Marianne was an important link in Heidelberg in the defence of Frieda Gross. She was a confidante of Professor Emil Lask whose money was footing the legal bills for Frieda. In 1908 and 1909 Frieda Gross and Emil Lask had a close personal relationship and Frieda was looking for a way out of her draining relationship with Otto. Eva Karádi has written most interestingly about Lask, who was held in high esteem by Weber, Lukács and Rickert. It was hoped that he would advance neo-Kantian philosophy by providing a new foundation for the validity of values. But these hopes were dashed with his death in May 1915 in a battle on the Eastern Front. Much still needs to be said about Lask. His meeting with the bohemia of Schwabing through Frieda (though Otto he greatly disliked) may have been responsible for a late move toward vitalism in the same way that Simmel turned.[42]

The communication between Frieda Gross and Lask appears to have been through the Webers. Marianne's main role was to provide a character reference for Frieda and perhaps Ernst Frick as well. Frieda's legal tactic against Hans Gross was to deny her relationship with Frick. She would claim legally that her right to remain mother of her children was inalienable. Hans's patriarchalism said otherwise and the shadow of his estate and who would inherit it hung over the legal proceedings. (In his will of 1908 Hans estimated his wealth at 270 000–280 000 crowns.[43]) Everybody realised that Frieda's claim to be a proper mother to her children was compromised by living with another man, who was a convicted terrorist and who was living off Frieda – Max's reference to '*homme soutenu*'. Max pleaded with Frieda that she give up Frick at least until the case was over. Frieda refused. Meanwhile Hans was approaching the case with the thoroughness of a well run police investigation, collecting and paying for witness statements over the last two years. Frieda's lawyers sought to counter this by collection of character references.

Marianne was the authority on marriage and legal rights.[44] Max tells her in rather humiliating detail exactly what to write in her character reference to the court (pp. 52–3). Looking beyond the details, again, it was what Marianne represented and what she would be seen as representing that is important. Marianne's branch of the women's movement saw marriage as ennobling where both partners recognised each other as equal. She did not think that women should gain autonomy through work, nor did she think that an attack on legitimate marriage was the way to deal with single mothers. The League for Mothercare and Sexual Reform argued for both of these policies, and it was Marianne Weber who along with her friend Dr Gertrud Bäumer campaigned successfully against the role of the League and its leader Dr Helene Stöcker in the umbrella organisation of the German Women's Federation. Moreover, as Guenther Roth has written, Marianne argued against the move for a more naturalistic ethos in sexual relationships and in favour of marriage as the attainment of high cultural values through the practice of ethical integrity.[45]

In writing a character reference for Frieda, she was countermanding her own public position, though whether she did this for Max, or Frieda or for Lask we don't know. Frieda's own sexual activities, which she refused to curb, lay in the category of libertarianism, an extreme version of Helene Stöcker's position. As Linse shows below, Erich Mühsam developed a sexual libertarianism in his play 'The Open Marriage' – written in 1911 – that drew on Frieda Gross's and Reventlow's experiences. Its central character, Alma, asserted an autonomy to take and dismiss lovers as she wished, to keep her eroticism separate from love, and to bring up *her* child (not the man's) as she wanted, which meant outside marriage.

Mühsam's anarchist bohemianism was consistent in taking libertarianism to the core of personal behaviour. The anarchist revolution would arrive through a revolution in private behaviour. In part this philosophy worked for Frieda and Reventlow to the extent that they made a project out of their own lives, but equally the history of Ascona showed how precarious those projects were. Mühsam's fellow Munich anarchist Gustav Landauer sharply criticised his libertarianism and Otto Gross's sexual ideology. Like Marianne, Landauer believed that marriage was the best protection for women, although unlike Marianne he saw women as essentially different to men. He blamed the brutalisation of Wilhelmine society and the war years as a failure of the feminine principle to be carried into society. But in marriage, like other institutions, the different qualities of man and woman should work together for the building of a better society.[46]

Mina Tobler

Tobler, like Miss Brüstlein, benefited from the advanced education open to women in the progressive Swiss canton of Zurich. The Swiss advocate Miss Brüstlein, who comes up to Ascona in 1914, is described with some wonder in Weber's letters – educated, a career and personally autonomous. Tobler herself was a professional musician and concert pianist. Tobler obviously had feminine qualities that Weber despite his tormented masculinity could trust.[47] The women of Ascona, whom at the end of his second stay he can relaxedly call the enchantresses, obviously found him, to judge from Weber's reporting of their comments, stiff, unbending and unable to say what he felt. They saw him as attracted to women but unapproachable through a wall of intellectualist posturing (see for example, pp. 64–5).

Weber's landscape descriptions are the key to his moods. When together with Tobler on Lake Zurich and during their excursion to Rapperswyl, the waves, wind and colours boil up into a little ecstasy. No reliable documentary evidence about Tobler's relationship has been published and the publication of Weber's letters to Tobler is still awaited. However Christoph Braun on the basis of some of the Max Weber and Mina Tobler correspondence shows not only that Tobler inaugurated him into a new appreciation of the expressive and sensual, but deepened his understanding of the technical rules of music through the discussion and playing of musical scores.

Weber's study 'The Social and Rational Foundations of Music' re-assesses the whole interpretation of the rise of western rationalism. Instead of this being a history of ascendancy and superiority over other civilisations, rationalism becomes a matter particular to each civilisation. Christoph Braun explains that Weber pursued the 'logic' of harmonic rationality in western music which is evident in its notation, its chromaticism, the development of functionally optimal musical instruments, and the orchestra and the concert, but then Weber turned the analysis around by showing the limitations of harmonic rationality. Firstly, it was only an approximation to the 'true' acoustic sub-divisions of the scale. The modern diatonic scale and temperance fudges the actual acoustic gaps between notes. Music, in the West, is then emblematic of the whole of western rationalism: it is only rational up to a point, and this rationality is only valid according to the direction in which a technique or set of rules – whether musical, legal, economic, or literary are 'evolved'. The second point is vital to the matter of cultural significance. The drive to harmony is a degradation of the acoustic ear of the listener.

All other musical tonalities, other than modern western harmonic music, operate melodies according to tuning scales that exploit music's harmonic and melodic richness. Chromatic harmony offers only the semitone, the tone, and the predominance of certain 'harmonic' intervals such as the third and the fifth. This allows a complex musical evolution but at the cost of an inferior acoustic sensibility and other musical freedoms of expression. Modernism in music, such as atonality (which Weber was informed about by the composer Paul von Klenau), in one sense is a submission to the limits of rationality.

Christoph Braun concludes his chapter by noting Weber's admiration for the studies of Karl Vossler into medieval Provençal poetry. The literary convention of this poetry is the heightening element of eroticism in courtly love, yet the sociological and historical evidence reveals a Christian asceticism practised by the courtiers. This opposition between a substantive morality and a literary form is replicated in Weber's musical studies in which the rule-bound nature of western music contains a substantive highly emotional affect. It is a theme taken up in David Chalcraft's essay where the overt eroticism of the Webers' Klinger etchings which were hung on the walls of their Freiburg flat contrasts with the Webers' contract to a chaste marriage, as opposed to nuptial sex on the sofa under the gaze of the naked 'Eve'.

The rationality of forms can never capture the substantive nature of the aspects – musical, legal, religious, and so on, – of life. The quandary, when reading Weber, is whether to give assent to the tension which he generates from this opposition; or whether to query the basis on which he formulates the tension. The reader generally follows the first path because of the ever-present insistence that there is at the end some resolution of the tension, which of course never is resolved. But in doing this the reader tends to become caught up in the tensions, which Weber manufactures and of which we need to be wary. Chalcraft shows (Chapter 10) that the Webers interpreted Wagner's *Tristan and Isolde* as a combination of the utmost eroticism with the strongest injunction against sex, namely death. For Wagner himself, by contrast, it was a consummation of form and substance, and for the aggrieved Mrs Wagner obscenely so (see Chalcraft). The example is extreme and, as ever, open to the judgement of taste.

This criticism needs to be held in mind when considering some of Weber's own resolutions of the tension of form and substance.[48] In the space of two months (October and November 1917) Weber had attempted to impose his dry conception of form on the substantive demands made by German youth movements and student associations. At Lauenstein Castle (see Toller section below) in October Weber disabused German youth from the idea that a national politics could be built on a new cultural awareness. In his lecture 'Science as a Vocation' in November he reduced science to the method of the pursuit of truth, and demanded the university become the preserve of specialists in place of the classical idea of Bildung of the educated generalist. The complexity of Weber's analysis of science has ensured its place in the canon of social science methodology. But this should not obscure Weber's superimposition of a method of truth-finding against a much wider tradition of learning. And the rhetoric he employs is disabusal and denial against the dangerous enthusiasm of students, who were staring into the intellectual and moral bankruptcy of the universities and the annihilation of war. Weber also refuses the terms of Zarathustra's question he had so confidently thrown out in 1905 at the end of the Protestant Ethic essay. Weber's minimalism on science, while seeking to curb the more unrealistic aspirations of students – not least their 'New Age' enthusiasm for experience, was hardly a constructive contribution in the face of the crisis the university system was undergoing.[49]

On politics in 1919 amidst circumstances where resolution of the crisis could not be denied personality is asserted as a substantive force against the rules of ordinary politics. And on culture and religion, the area of Weber's sociological genius, the limits of rationality, to use Brubaker's formulation,[50] are discovered to point up the particularities of civilisational difference. This requires further elaboration which I will return to in connection with Mary Shields's chapter on expressionism and Ernst Toller.

Raphael Friedeberg

Friedeberg receives a mention in Weber's Ascona letters. 'Already the wife of the anarcho-syndicalist – ! – Raphael Friedeberg – from Berlin won't let her children play with the Gross kids'. The exclamation mark denotes the difference between respectable anarchism and that of Frieda and Ernst Frick. Unfortunately nothing is recorded in the Ascona letters about anarcho-syndicalism. Friedeberg had retired to Ascona for health reasons but mainly as a result of his expulsion from Germany. Friedeberg represented a failed attempt to improve the political and economic condition of workers through a direct attack on the boundaries of the political community that excluded the urban proletariat. Friedeberg was a medical doctor who had set up a clinic specialising in tuberculosis which was rife in the unhygienic slums of Berlin. In his work he may unknowingly have walked the same pavements as Weber's mother Helene, who was an active charity worker in Berlin. From similar middle class consciences they took very different routes. Helene's conscience was driven by religious conviction and she founded and funded aid organisations for women. She was active in the Germany's Evangelical Social Congress movement and funded Pastor Friedrich Naumann's political activities.[51]

Friedeberg reached the diagnosis that tuberculosis was a social not a medical problem. He joined the Social Democratic Party, seeing this as the most effective way of improving wages and living conditions which were the root cause of so much urban malaise. This was a radical move for a middle class doctor, yet he became quickly disillusioned by the Party, whose radical political rhetoric covered an inability to alter the unequal terms of power and wealth. A capable and practical man with an ability to lead and innovate he set up a mutual health insurance scheme for workers.[52] He campaigned for the politics of the general strike, a form of collective action that could force a decisive change in the economic conditions and political rights of workers. At the height of his syndicalist fame in 'red' Berlin he was addressing rallies of 20 000 workers in 1905. His agitation was successful enough for him to be exiled by the Prussian authorities and his position vilified as 'anti-parliamentarian cretinism' by the Social Democratic Party leader Bebel.[53]

Friedeberg's route to expanding the political community was not Weber's whose views on syndicalism are known from his discussions with Robert Michels. Weber's basic criticism of syndicalism attacked what he took to be its fundamentalism – its conviction that the syndicalist movement, as a form of political process, was morally superior to the instrumentalism of party politics.[54] Weber made the same accusation against his mother's protégé Friedrich Naumann's belief that an ethically correct position of Social Gospel (see Green, below, Chapter 3) could triumph over the realities of the power of the state and interest politics. This debate recurs throughout Weber's encounters with anarchists. Weber defines the political community in terms of an inclusive nation, to include the proletariat, its parties and trade unions, but only on the terms of what Weber sees as the national interest and national culture.[55] From this assumption Weber attacks everybody else's politics for its lack of realism. However, as we will see, this is very much open to debate. Friedeberg was driven by his sense of realism, to the tactic and the strategy of the general strike, not out of purity of process and because the movement was all, but because it offered a chance, albeit risky, of breaking open the closed system of Wilhelmine politics. Weber excluded all ethical concerns in the name of the political community of the nation. (See Levy, below, Chapter 4.) The arguments on ethics surface in relation to Frick, and the arguments about who defines the political community are taken up in relation to Ernst Toller.

In his chapter Martin Green considers pacifism and violence in the characters of Gross, Weber and D. H. Lawrence. Lawrence and Weber had been made aware of the challenge of Gross through the Richthofen sisters, Else (Jaffé) and Frieda (Weekley, soon to become Lawrence). Otto's place was Ascona, a refuge of non-violence beyond the authoritarianism of the nation-state. Neither Lawrence nor Weber could assent to Gross's message of non-violence, each being drawn into the insecurities of nation-states at war. But each man acknowledged the charm of Ascona and the sincerity of Gross: Lawrence in *Twilight in Italy* – a magical description of travelling through the Italian Lakes during his elopement with Frieda Weekley. For Max it was a special place – 'an oasis of purity'. Max is as yet unclaimed by the roller-coaster of war, and nor is he, wholly, the Heidelberg intellect – this is perhaps the real charm of the Ascona letters.

Ernst Frick

Frieda's anarchist lover Ernst Frick was not only an '*homme soutenu*' but something of an '*homme inconnu*'. Frick was not at Ascona during Weber's first visit in 1913, he was in Regensdorf jail serving a one year prison sentence. Nobody has yet unearthed the document listing the charges against Frick but there appear to have been more than one charge made against him. Edith Hanke outlines below what is known about the case (Chapter 7). In 1907 three or four anarchists burst into a police station in Zürich waving and discharging pistols and freed a Russian anarchist and assassin who was to be deported to Russia and execution. A bomb was set off as a diversion. Frick went to trial in November 1912 for complicity in the bomb attack, having been denounced by a police informer. Weber comments that he thinks Frick has been treated unjustly. Frick certainly had an active anarchist past which embraced the 'propaganda of the deed' (see Linse, below, Chapter 6), although whether this extended to terrorist attacks on police stations is debatable. Martin Green notes Frieda Richthofen's comment that he could not hurt a fly (see below, Chapter 3). Green also notes that Frick was drawn toward psychoanalysis under the influence of Otto Gross who was almost saintly in his rejection of violence (leaving aside the violence of emotions). Existing police files on Frick needless to say cannot be taken as truth, given police forces' proclivity for *agents provocateurs* and unreliable informers. As Kubitschek notes, police files did not distinguish between violent anarchism and what Green terms non-violent, or the village anarchism of pacifism, vegetarianism and teetotalism (see Green, Chapter 3). Even Reventlow was subject to police observation, and perhaps the Swiss censors were the first to decipher Weber's letters.[56]

A further complication in the Frick case, which is the trigger for one of Weber's own disquisitions on ethics, is a charge of perjury. Margarete Faas-Hardegger, an anarchist from Zurich and supporter of Gustav Landauer's Socialist League, was arrested on charges of perjury, in part as a result of something Frick had said to the authorities.[57] She was soon released but the issue of honesty and goodness, and the injustice of his own prison sentence, greatly perturbed Frick, with whom Weber converses in 1914.

Weber's reference point for Frick, as indeed all anarchist thought, is Tolstoy. Edith Hanke details below the enormous influence Tolstoy commanded across the political spectrum. Tolstoy was more than a 'great writer'. People avidly read his novels whose issues and characters became the currency of literary, moral and sexual discourse. Weber's reference point is the late Tolstoy, who had turned his back on the city and material civilisation and lived the life of the simple peasant alongside his muzhiks on his country estate. He became the advocate of anti-capitalism, and a return to the simplicities of nature and working on the land. He preached pacifism and non-violence. He attempted to practise the abstinence from pleasures: smoking, meat eating, alcoholic drink, and sexual intercourse. He condemned the sensualism and the worldliness of his earlier novels, such as *Anna Karenina*, and instead penned the desperately bleak fate of characters like Ivan Ilich in *Death of Ivan Ilich* and Podznyshev in the *Kreutzer Sonata*. It was the *Kreutzer Sonata* and its realism of carnality and ordeals of motherhood that so shocked Weber's mother and her sister; yet also explained some home truths about men and their husbands that the elevation of sensibility had made inadmissible (see Chalcraft, Chapter 10).

Martin Green points out below (Chapter 3) that the Tolstoyan outlook is what today would be referred to as New Age. The original Ascona settlers (Gräser, Oedenkoven) were Tolstoyans. Reventlow's new brother-in-law Rechenberg lived in the neighbourhood as a Tolstoyan hermit. Weber dismisses the politics of the anarchists on the basis of his ascription to them of 'New Age' characteristics – an alleged lack of realism in relation to power, violence and capitalism.

Since it was an attribution Weber applied to all anarchists, it is worth examining the Weber/Frick conversations. Frick, says Weber, is a believer in the absolute goodness of mankind. This is akin to Tolstoy's gospel of the realisation of the Kingdom of God in the here and now, an earthly paradise of goodness (and asceticism). Weber brought to this conversation his theoretical concept of 'acosmicism' which he had aired at the Frankfurt Sociology conference in 1910.[58] This becomes a much more important theoretical concept in the 'Intermediate Reflections' essay that Weber wrote soon after his Ascona interlude of 1914.[59] Acosmic brotherhood represents a contemporary rejection of the world and a secularised version of New Testament brotherhood. For Weber, Frick is discovering the consequences of living acosmic brotherhood. 'That the outcome of virtuous action is so often quite irrational and results in evil when one has behaved "virtuously"' (p. 57). It is the naïveté of Frick to tell the truth to the police authorities, assuming the goodness of the world, without considering the consequences to other people. Any successful politics has to take into consideration the effects of actions and decisions. Frick, just like all anarchists, has broken the cardinal rule of politics.

But Weber does not leave the philosophical and ethical emphasis on consequentialism.[60] Weber is *worried* lest Frick become cynical and calculate all actions in terms of their consequential outcomes. Frick's dilemma is whether 'one should do the good thing at all – an evaluation of moral action in terms of its *consequences* [Weber's emphasis] and not its intrinsic worth!' This formulation is repeated in the 'Intermediate Reflections'.[61] These are the Scylla and Charybdis of Weber's moral universe. Unworldly Tolstoyan conscience, a fundamentalist ethic of conviction, on the one side; the calculation of outcomes on the other, which as the tradition of Kant and Nietzsche has noted, has no moral force. (The ethics of conviction and responsibility and the influence of Tolstoy are analysed below by Edith Hanke, Chapter 7)

Weber recommends some reading: Dostoyevsky (discussed by Charles Turner below, Chapter 8) and Lukács (discussed by Edith Hanke). There is no way out of this dilemma. Being in the modern world enjoins both conscience and knowledge of outcomes. However, what Frick needs to understand is the ethical irrationality of the world. The good intention, a *sine qua non* of ethical action, is often de-railed by circumstance. Weber the sociologist is the great commentator on de-railing and displacement, what as Martin Green notes might now be called 'institutional violence', to use a sharper formulation. But Weber the ethical person insists on the necessity of conscience.

The Frick/Weber dialogue should be taken as an important stepping stone in Weber's formulation of ethics and as they are deployed in the lectures of 1917 and 1919. But what needs to be brought into these (Weberian) debates is the ascription of community: Weber's notion of political community, and the impossible, but no less ascribed, community of anarchism. Weber defines the political community as the community of the nation whose ultimate bonding is the comradeship of war and death.[62] The Tolstoyans ascribed community on the basis of an all-including brotherhood irrespective of nation and culture; the one prone to pathos, the other bathos.

Charles Turner provides an answer to these questions through a reading of the novel Weber recommended to Frick: Dostoyevsky's *The Brothers Karamazov*. This and especially its chapter 'Poem of the Grand Inquisitor' is one of the great texts of what Weber termed the 'ethical irrationality of the world'.[63] Dostoyevsky has a number of Tolstoyan characters in his novels, who through their ultimate faith in the goodness of love, good intentions, and the ethical totality of the world cause chaos in a world not so constituted. For Weber this was a feature of Russian Christianity, and the Russian people's adherence to the injunction 'resist not evil'.[64] As Turner notes (Chapter 8) this is a religiosity that disdains social forms and a refusal to accept the inescapability of domination and violence, which is such a central feature of Weber's political thinking. While Russia elicits Weber's compassion, the same phenomena among the German anarchists triggers Weber's opposition and contempt. But behind Weber's angry and vigorous responses, Turner suggests that Weber was less than confident about Germany's development of suitable political forms. Just as in Russia, the anarchists were forced to fill the void with a personalist and ethical conception of a political beyond politics.

Turner notes the Durkheimian or Tocquevillean way of filling the void: with intervening associations and institutions occupying the gap between citizen and individual. Such a political sociology was not Weber's way, which adhered to the more direct model of the leaders of the nation and the led. But drawing on recent work of Hennis,[65] the issue becomes one of the political education not only of leaders but of citizens. Weber slowly came round to the idea, as Karl-Ludwig Ay as a historian also notes, that the returning soldiers had not only earned their right to suffrage but were, through the experience of war and the defence of the nation, morally qualified to be citizens. Turner observes, in concluding, that the requirement of moral capacities on the part of the individual citizen, for Weber, was not assisted by the culture of character types. The Prussian ruling class was not only inimical but inimitable as a democratic model, in a way that wasn't the case for the English gentleman and the Latin cavalier; a case of the 'wrong' cultural resources.

Otto Gross

It is through Frick that Weber makes a partial engagement with the absent figure of Otto. Weber's great sin of omission was not have published Otto's 1907 paper, the most famous paper never published by the *Archiv für Sozialwissenschaft und Sozialpolitik*. (The paper has never been found.) In his rejection letter, sent via Else Jaffé who was pregnant with

Otto's child, Weber asserted the superiority of a cultural Nietzscheanism of distinction (*Vornehmheit*) over biological Nietzscheanism.[66] Otto's use of Nietzsche was consistent with his biologism of nerve development, and today's Nietzsche studies would be more sympathetic to Otto's rather than Weber's interpretation. Besides, this is yet another example of Weber's deployment of his own cultural habitus in the argument over, in this case, life style and conduct.

Weber's antagonism had abated somewhat by 1914. Weber reveals the important information that Otto's parents knew he was mentally ill before his marriage to Frieda in 1903 (and had already undergone one cure for drug addiction in 1902). Weber also confirms Franz Jung's accusation against the father that Hans wanted his son locked up in an asylum because Otto was about to publish a study that drew on the Gross family history and Hans's brutality to his wife. 'Starker Tabak', as Weber notes, also amazed that Otto had the naïveté to send the manuscript to his father.

Otto Gross belonged not only to the back-to-nature world of Tolstoy but was a figure of the metropolis and the margins of the city. Otto is also marginal to the modernist discourse of psychoanalysis. Holding forth in Schwabing's Café Stephanie he pronounced Freud to be 'nonsense, complete nonsense' ('Freud – alles Unsinn, glatter Unsinn').[67] He had once belonged to Freud. He was incensed by the doyen of German psychiatry Emil Kraepelin's dismissal of Freudianism, and in 1907 at the International Congress of Psychiatry he had praised Freud, comparing him to Nietzsche. A year later Gross underwent a drug cure in Bleuler's Burghölzli clinic where Carl Jung undertook his psychoanalysis. Jung was most impressed by the psychoanalytic theories of his patient and when Jung lost the initiative in marathon twenty hour sessions over a period of three weeks Otto became Jung's analyst. This is one of the episodes in the infancy of narratives. Was Otto to be consigned as outcast within the annals of psychoanlysis, which was certainly Freud's wish? Or did Jung obtain valuable insights into his subsequent theory of introversion and extroversion?[68] Jung was shaken by his inability to carry the therapy through to a successful conclusion – Otto absconded over the wall. Freud wrote Gross off as a liability to the psychoanlytic movement and Jung reluctantly agreed with Freud's diagnosis of Gross as suffering from dementia praecox and cocaine paranoia. Gross had put himself beyond psychoanalysis, although he claimed it was his insights into the divided mind, his theory of sejunctiva, that later became the basis of Bleuler's classification of schizophrenia; just as he claimed his theory on the deep emotional mind in contrast to the superficial rational mind became the basis of Jung's later classification of extroversion and introversion.[69] We have seen how Otto placed himself beyond the women of Ascona. Else Jaffé had extricated herself with what must have been remarkable strength of character from the charismatic Gross. She wrote to her sister Frieda Weekley, warning her off Otto, 'You have to see the tremendous shadows around the light – can't you see he has almost destroyed Frieda's life?'[70] And in the fight against the patriarchal Hans he formed an alliance with the expressionist anarchism of Pfemfert and Franz Jung in Berlin; yet he was never a socialist anarchist.

Gross remains an unclassifiable figure, disruptive to ordered conduct and to ordered utopias. He is a trace in the history of modernism that resists personal and intellectual biography. He belonged to fiction and to a discourse of transgression, and he could be allotted no part in the history of scientistic Freudianism. Although Ascona was the scene of his play-acting of orgy, his own mythical presence was taken up in the artistic and political cabaret of Dada of the cities of Zurich and Berlin. Dada's break-ing of artistic forms tended to formlessness. It was, as Martin Green has noted, the expressionism beyond expressionism.[71]

Ernst Toller

Toller was not a pre-war anarchist and he did not stay at Ascona. Nevertheless he is the successor to Weber's unfolding relationship with anar-chism after Ascona. And it is not hard to find a linking thread from the many lives of Ascona. Eugen Diederichs the publisher had links with Ascona and it was he who organised the conference where Toller and Weber met.[72]

It was an unlikely relationship. Toller, who had volunteered at the out-break of the war, had been in the trenches on the Western Front and had been invalided out. As a result of his experiences he turned to pacifism. He pursued his literary interests in Munich and was recognised by Thomas Mann as a significant new talent. Weber's patriotism and cultural national-ism were aroused by the war, complaining that he was too old for active service. But he threw himself into war work, administering at one point over forty hospitals in the Heidelberg area. (See Ay, Chapter 5.)

They met at Lauenstein Castle in October 1917 at a conference to discuss the future of Germany after the war, entitled 'The Problem of Leadership in State and Culture'. It was an unlikely friendship. As Mommsen has written, 'Weber justified the First World War above all with cultural arguments. He saw the historical mission of the German Empire as that of hegemonial power defending the smaller European countries and upholding German culture in central Europe against "Anglo-Saxon convention" and "Russian bureaucracy"'.[73] This was Germany's responsibility before history. Lassman and Speirs point out that Weber followed the cultural historian Burckhardt's views that such an exercise of responsibility inevitably involved 'the diabolical character of power'.[74] Toller accepted no such cultural territorialisation of the world. 'A Jewish mother bore me, Germany nursed me, Europe educated me, the earth is my homeland, the world my fatherland.'

The meeting at Lauenstein Castle was more than just a chance encounter of the idealist Toller and the power realist Weber. The late Professor Tenbruck used to say that Lauenstein was the last occasion that the German cultural nation met in conclave; a similar thesis underlies Nipperdey's view of this period, except he focuses on the aspiration of a 'metapolitics' by the free cadres of youth groups that congregated on the Hohen Meissner in 1913.[75] Behind Tenbruck's *obiter dictum* lies the counter-factual hypothesis that a historic opportunity was missed.[76] Carl Levy shows below that the publisher Eugen Diederichs, despite his own brand of right wing romanticism, cannot be faulted for not inviting a wide spectrum of Germany's cultural, artistic, academic, feminist, reform, and business life to Lauenstein Castle. These opinions encompassed left and right, authoritarian and anarchist, *völkisch* and democratic, romantic and expressionist, feminist and patriarchal. Diederichs felt that something new could be created for the future. One criticism of Weber is that he went too far in deriding some of the more extreme romanticist and organicist conceptions being aired. The only thing that mattered for Weber was a successful outcome to the war, and then, afterwards, the cultural questions could be addressed.

The counter-factual to this is that had a broad based cultural alliance been in place before the end of the war, then the post-war situation might not have polarised as badly as it did. Levy makes the pointed observation that the people who had conversed within the congenial setting of Lauenstein Castle became daggers drawn in the events of revolution and counterrevolution in 1919 in Munich and Bavaria. Assassination, reprisal shootings, hostage-taking, hostage execution, and counter-revolutionary terror were the downward spiral of violence, which as Levy observes involved both the intensification of anti-semitic racism and the establishment of movements like the Thule Society that became a forerunner to Hitler's political party. Weber justified his realism in terms of Germany's 'responsibility before history'. But as Karl-Ludwig Ay shows, even when Germany had lost the war, Weber remained completely out of touch with the realities of what Germany was then capable of after November 1918, and the true condition of the mass of the people and returning soldiers. In a letter to Marianne's aunt in October 1918, Weber opined that the situation was not as hopeless as Ludendorff had by then come to accept. Whereas, as we know, it was Ludendorff's reckless intransigence of the final push that cost countless lives, as Weber knew from his contacts in Berlin, and took Germany beyond the point of exhaustion.[77] In the face of President Woodrow Wilson's peace proposals Weber was calling for armed citizens' resistance and the setting up of German irredenta in Central Europe (Levy, Chapter 4). And when the revolutions started under Eisner in Bavaria, Weber was scathing in his condemnation, again because this would compromise the power position of the German nation.

Toller had joined a peace movement in Heidelberg in 1917 and had asked Weber to be a signatory (Levy, below). Toller was the man who mistook Weber for a pacifist. This takes some explaining. Karl-Ludwig Ay (Chapter 5) brings us back to cultural habitus again. As a leading member of the educated middle class Weber interpreted Germany's interests and conditions as if his class were the moral leaders of the cultural nation. His class adhered to an honour code based on devotion to Empire and the mores of the reserve officers' corps. The educated middle class were above the people, never ever of the people. Weber remained completely intolerant of any aspersion of German war guilt, because to accept a peace treaty under the sign of guilt, was to accept dishonour. Kurt Eisner as prime minister of Bavaria had published diplomatic documents that revealed the German government's expansionist war aims prior to 1914. He hoped to show that the new democratic regime was ready to atone for the past misdeeds of the old regime, and so hoped to ameliorate the terms of the peace treaty. Who then was the realistic realist, Eisner or Weber? Levy raises the question to what extent Weber exploited the inclusivity of cultural habitus to co-opt the anarchists and potential revolutionaries to stay within the fold of Weber's definition of an internal political community, itself governed by the pragma of geo-politics.

Weber of course refused to sign Toller's peace document. 'I wrote to their leader, Herr Toller, and declined to take responsibility for that sort of thing. Either resist evil with force nowhere and then live like a St Francis.... Anything else is a fraud or a self-deception.'(see Levy below, Chapter 4) But Toller's idealism underwent the ordeal of fire as the commander of a red army defending Munich against an attacking white army in April 1919. Toller's conduct proved not to be fraudulent. Weber rhetorically overstated the idealism of the anarchists (as latter day St Francises), in order to force them off the political stage as he saw it. Toller's own idealistic pacifism was tested against what Weber always demanded, the lessons of life. In prison after the collapse of the second Bavarian republic, saved from execution not least because of Weber's own magnamimous testament before the court, Toller reflected on these lessons. His conclusions were informed by Weber's lecture 'The Profession and Vocation of Politics' which he had attended in January 1919. But his reflections differ significantly from Weber's.

Weber had lectured on the necessity of separating culture (literary, romanticist, *völkisch*) from politics. Politics was a hard profession that demanded an endless amount of application, the political judgement of what was possible, and convictions that came from the depths of personality.[78] Convictions were an indispensable part of the ethic of intention. Fundamentalist convictions belonged, however, to Tolstoy and St Francis. And the politician without convictions was a light-weight or opportunist. These statements have qualities of sense that has made the lecture justly famous. And of course when directed against the Bavarian republic of soviets, which was triggered into a brief existence by the outgoing prime minister Kurt Eisner's assassination, made even more sense. Mühsam belonged to Café Stephanie not government office. Bavaria would never be ready for Landauer's thoughtful and intriguing form of anarchist state. And, as Weber commented, what kind of joke of the gods was it to make Toller the pacifist, poet and writer commander of the red army?

Carl Levy shows below, however, that Toller acquitted himself with both realism and conscience. He refused the orders of the Communist Party to shoot hostages, and he saw that the unstable coalition of the soviet republic did not warrant extreme measures. This raises the question, debated in this volume, as to what was the school of politics and political education, and what defines the political community. Weber's universal desiderata for the politician have to be particularised as to how such people are to be produced (and we have aleady noted Turner's answer to the question).

In Landsberg jail Toller had time to reflect on the turbulent months of the two Bavarian republics and it sounds as if he took to heart Weber's admonition on the need to think through the consequences of political actions and decisions (Levy, Chapter 4). However in thinking through the contradictory demands placed on the politician by the lessons of life, Toller came up with solutions that drew on his literary creativity as an expressionist. Mary Shields (in Chapter 11) makes clear that the term expressionism contains some very diverse artistic output. But this was the one artistic movement in Wilhelmine society that confronted the impasse of politics and the bureaucratic iron cage. In *Masse Mensch* (*Masses and the Man*) Toller drew on expressionist devices that were used to penetrate the absurdity and repression of society. One of these was to use characters in a generic way. The one character 'Woman' speaks for individual conscience and the human individual. The other is called 'Nameless' who speaks for the logic of collective action and the necessity of any means to achieve the end of socialism. Woman seeks to stop bloodshed, Nameless stands for its unavoidability:

The Woman: No you do not love the people!
The Nameless: Our cause comes first.
I love the people that shall be,
I love the future.
The Woman: People come first.
You sacrifice to dogmas,
The people that are now.[79]

Toller's commentary on this in his autobiography was to pose the question,

Has the acting person to become guilty again and again? Or if he does not wish to become guilty, does he perish? Is not man individual and mass at the same time? Isn't the struggle between individual man played out in the interior of man as well as society? To me this contradiction seems insoluble, because I experienced it in my own actions. Thus originates my play *Masse Mensch*.[80]

In her discussion of expressionism Mary Shields argues that it articulated an awareness of the disruptive force of irrational elements within the personality and within society. She shows that the images of threatened landscapes, as in Meidner's canvas *Apocalyptic Landscape*, and the metaphors of imminent destruction in poetry and drama, were also shared in the metaphors of Weber's own thought. At its blackest the Wilhelmine subconscious was troubled with impending catastrophe and disaster. Weber and Toller should be considered as different responses to a crisis of anxiety that has also been termed at the level of identity, one of ego dissociation. Personal identity could no longer be held together by the force of acquired habitus. It had started to break up in the last decade of the German Empire. At that point creative and innovative impulses were required by the far seeing, and these were both political and cultural. Weber dug down into his deepest roots for what he understood by political community and what forces should animate the political leader in Germany's crisis. These roots went beyond the conventions of habitus to a culture of romanticism: the romanticism of the nation united as community before the sacrifice of death where the sign of eros is transfigured, as in *Tristan and Isolde*, into death. For Toller the brotherhood of humanity in the exigencies of hunger and necessity cannot depend on Tolstoyan brotherliness. Neither can the logic of collectivism override the rights of the living person. Instead the generic anonymous person with no special qualities of Nietzschean distinction has to rise to the sacrifice of her individuality in the name of a common humanity. Which one, we may ask, learned most from the other?

It is not a question that can be answered in terms of idealism and realism. Realism is too excluding and idealism all including. This suggests instead that the issue is what is taken to be the unit of living together, within which the commonality of lives is recognised by individuals. Ethics and conduct refer not only to the conduct of self but to an acceptance of an otherness beyond self. For Weber and for Toller the reasons why one would accept an otherness beyond self cannot be explained by rational calculation or ordered through a politics, whether liberal or socialist, alone. The expressionist experience indicated not only the irrational in man but also the absurdity of the assumption of a rational ordering of politics and society. Not without reason did Toller place his actors in jail and in cages. The sense of a possible humanity in Toller was a very minimalist assumption. Toller was drawn to Weber not for his charismatic conception of politics but for the confirmation of the deeper motivational roots as to why individuals may possess a sense of otherness beyond self.

As Mary Shields notes, these roots are cultural. When Weber stepped down as a hospital administrator he turned to the completion of his studies of the world religions in which the fundamental relations of man to man and man to the world were formulated according to the cultural interpretation of religion. In modernity religions can no longer provide such a cultural manifold. Undoubtedly many modern societies are sustained by the manners of civilisation. But in crisis, when the civilisational forms prove dysfunctional, the questions of self and other, and self and conduct reduce to an uncomfortable set of antinomies, and these same antinomies are themselves held within the fragile constructions of humanity and community. The *Kaissereich* provides a lesson – rich and complex – in the sociological and cultural analysis of modernity, but it was a regime that ended a long time ago. The optimist would say we are at last beginning to learn these fundamentals.

NOTES

1. F. Nietzsche, *Thus Spoke Zarathustra* (London: Penguin, 1969), pp. 45–7. My thanks to Nicholas Gane for drawing this passage to my attention. Hollingdale translates Nietzsche's 'der letzte Mensch' as 'Ultimate Man'. This rather obscures the point that the last men are nullities, not to be confused with Superman.

2. W. J. Mommsen, *Max Weber and German Politics* (Chicago: Chicago University Press, 1987). The current historiography of the Wilhelmine period is dominated by terrifying Dreadnoughts locked in perpetual 'Streit'. On the historians and their current books, see the first three reviews of the *Bulletin* of the German Historical Institute, London, Vol. XVIII, 2, May 1996.

3. On the sociology of modernity see A. Giddens, *The Consequences of Modernity* (Cambridge: Polity 1990). Martin Albrow characterises modernity and modernism and bids them farewell in *The Global Age* (Cambridge: Polity, 1996).

4. K. Lichtblau, *Kulturkrise und Soziologie um die Jahrhundertwende* (Frankfurt: Suhrkamp, 1996). On protestant leadership see Gangolf Hübinger, *Kulturprotestantismus und Politik* (Tübingen: Mohr, 1994)

5. W. J. Mommsen with E. Müller-Luckner, eds, *Kultur und Krieg: Die Rolle der Intellektuellen, Künstler und Schriftsteller im Ersten Weltkrieg* (Munich: Oldenbourg, 1996), p. iii.

6. D. Chaney, 'Lifestyle sites and strategies', paper given at Theory, Culture and Society Conference, 'Berlin '95'.

7. F. Nietzsche, op. cit., p. 46.

8. S. Aschheim, *The Nietzsche Legacy in Germany 1890–1990*, (Berkeley, California: University of California Press, 1992).

9. P. Bourdieu, *The Logic of Practice* (Cambridge: Polity, 1990), pp. 52–65. Bourdieu has in part developed his own theory from Weber's analysis of material and ideal interests and how these are used by priests and rulers to manoeuvre into positions of advantage over the populace. See his 'Legitimation and Structured Interests in Weber's Sociology of Religion', in S. Whimster and S. Lash eds, *Max Weber, Rationality and Modernity* (London: Allen & Unwin, 1987), pp. 119–136. My use of Weber in this chapter, therefore, is a case of using Weber against himself.

10. W. Schluchter, *Paradoxes of Modernity. Culture and Conduct in the Theory of Max Weber*, trans. by N. Solomon (Stanford: Stanford University Press, 1996), pp. 7–101; footnotes pp. 255–303.

11. See M. Green, *Mountain of Truth, The Counterculture Begins. Ascona, 1900–1920* (Hanover and London: University of New England Press, 1986) and H. Szeemann, *Monte Verita. Berg der Wahrheit. Lokale Anthropologie als Beitrag zur Wiederentdeckung einer neuzeitlichen sakralen Topographie* (Milan: Electa Editrice, 1980).

12. U. Linse, *Zurück, o Mensch, zur Mutter Erde. Landkommunen in Deutschland. 1890–1933* (Munich: Deutscher Taschenbuch Verlag, 1983) p. 7. See also his *Organisierter Anarchismus im Deutschen Kaiserreich von 1871* (Berlin: Duncker & Humblot, 1969).

13. Green, op. cit. and Szeemann, op. cit.

14. Quoted in Hurwitz, *Otto Gross. Paradies-Sucher zwischen Freud und Jung* (Frankfurt: Suhrkamp, 1988), p. 203.

15. 'Max Weber, Politics, Culture', Max Weber Study Group Conference, London, May 1995.

16. Marianne Weber, *Max Weber. A Biography* (New Brunswick: Transactions, 1988), pp. 486–94.

17. *GStA*, Max Weber to Robert Wilbrandt, 2 April 1913.

18. *MWG II/5*, p. 478.
19. *MWG II/6*, pp. 6–7. On Weber's psychological health see the recent work by J. Frommer and S. Frommer, 'Max Webers Krankheit – soziologische Aspekte der depressiven Struktur', *Fortschritte der Neurologie-Psychiatrie*, 61, 5 (1993), pp. 161–71.
20. See the editors' comments *MWG II/6*, p. 367.
21. R. J. Evans, *The Feminist Movement in Germany' 1894–1933* (London: Sage, 1976).
22. F. zu Reventlow, *Autobiographisches. Novellen, Schriften, Selbstzeugnisse* (Frankfurt and Berlin: Ullstein, 1986), p. 482.
23. M. Green, *The von Richthofen Sisters* (Albuquerque: University of New Mexico, 1988), pp. 10–11.
24. Ibid. pp. 92–7.
25. B. Kubitschek, *Franziska Gräfin zu Reventlow, 1871–1918. Ein Frauenleben im Umbruch – Studien zu einer Biographie* (Chiemsee: Kubitschek, 1994), p. 424.
26. F. zu Reventlow, *Briefe, 1890–1917*, ed. Else Reventlow (Munich: Albert Langen, 1975), p. 573.
27. See U. Linse in this volume, Chapter 6; also H. van den Berg, '"Free Love" in Imperial Germany; Anarchism and Patriarchy 1870–1918', *Anarchist Studies*, 4, 1, (1996), pp. 3–26.
28. W. Hennis, *Max Weber. Essays in Reconstruction*, trans. K. Tribe (London: Allen & Unwin, 1988), p. 148.
29. Letter Marianne Weber to Else von Richthofen, 1899, Archive, Tufts University Library.
30. G. Hübinger, *Kulturprotestantismus und Politik. Zur Verhältnis von Liberalismus und Protestantismus im wilhelminischen Deutschland* (Tübingen: Mohr, 1994) pp. 95–113.
31. E. Hurwitz, op. cit., p. 35.
32. Quoted in Martin Green, *Mountain of Truth. The Counterculture Begins. Ascona, 1900–1920* (Hanover and London: University of New England Press, 1986), p. 25. This book is an indispensable guide to Ascona as one of the most important proving grounds of cultural modernism.
33. Quoted in Hurwitz, op. cit., p. 132.
34. Kubitschek, op. cit., pp. 432–3.
35. Frieda Gross to Else Jaffé (12 March 1911, Tufts University Library) reports the Benz incident and how Frick has a bad conscience because he did not kill Otto. Frieda is also staggered by Otto's behaviour. She also knew Benz well, however, and thought Benz and Otto had a madness in common. She thought Sophie Benz, who knew how hopeless her case was, had died with honour. Otto's talent for releasing abreactions caused uncontrollable emotional shockwaves within his close milieu.
36. Quoted in J. Byrne, *A Genius for Living. A Biography of Frieda Lawrence* (London: Bloomsbury, 1995), p. 81.
37. E. Hurwitz, op. cit., p. 217–9.
38. See W. Müller-Seidel, *Die Deportation des Menschen: Kafkas Erzählung "In der Strafkolonie" im europ. Kontext* (Stuttgart: Metzler, 1986), pp. 50–58.
39. Hurwitz, op. cit., p. 228.

40. In addition to the cited works by Green, Hurwitz and Szeeman, see Jennifer Michaels, *Anarchy and Eros* (New York: Peter Lang, 1983).

41. Weber maintained his correspondence with Frieda in Ascona up until 1920.

42. E. Karádi, 'Emil Lask in Heidelberg oder Philosophie als Beruf', in H. Treiber and K. Sauerland, eds, *Heidelberg im Schnittpunkt Intellektueller Kreise* (Opladen: Westdeutscher Verlag, 1995).

43. Landesarchiv Graz.

44. *Ehefrau und Mutter in der Rechtsentwicklung. Eine Einführung* (Tübingen: Mohr, 1907).

45. G. Roth in Marianne Weber, op. cit., p. xxix.

46. C. B. Maurer, *Call to Revolution. The Mystical Anarchism of Gustav Landauer* (Detroit: Wayne State University Press, 1971), pp. 124–5.

47. Edith Flitner has recently given a pungent assessment of Weber's machismo, 'Geschlechterbeziehungen im Leben und Werk Max Webers', unpublished paper, University of Potsdam.

48. On the antinomies of form and substance see the informative discussion in Edith Weiller, *Max Weber und die literarische Moderne. Ambivalente Begegnungen zweier Kulturen* (Stuttgart and Weimar: Metzler, 1994).

49. See also the discussion by Lassman and Velody in their edition of Weber's *Science as a Vocation* (London: Allen & Unwin, 1989), pp. 159–204. Their volume reveals just how wide were the terms of the debate on science and not mere 'methodology'.

50. R. Brubaker, *The Limits of Rationality* (London: Allen & Unwin, 1984).

51. See Flitner, op. cit.

52. P. Weindling, *Health, Race and German Politics, Between National Unification and Nazism, 1870–1945* (Cambridge: Cambridge University Press, 1989) pp. 79–80.

53. H. M. Bock and F. Tennstedt, 'Raphael Friedeberg: Arzt und Anarchist in Ascona', in Szeemann, ed., op. cit., pp. 38–53.

54. See Carl Levy (Chapter 4); also the discussion in D. Beetham, *Max Weber and the Theory of Modern Politics* (London: Allen & Unwin, 1974), p. 175, and L. Scaff, *Fleeing the Iron Cage. Culture, Politics and Modernity* (Berkeley, California: University of California Press, 1981), p. 101.

55. Wolfgang J, Mommsen, 'Max Weber und die deutsche Revolution von 1918/19', *Kleine Schriften/Stiftung Reichspräsident-Friedrich-Ebert-Gedenkstätte* (Heidelberg: Stiftung Reichspräsident-Friedrich-Ebert-Gedenkstätte, 1994), pp. 5–6.

56. Frieda Gross complained to Else Jaffé that her post was being opened, 17 June 1912. See also Kubitschek, op. cit., p. 447.

57. H. Szeemann, op. cit., p. 34.

58. W. Schluchter, op. cit., pp. 57 ff.

59. The 'Intermediate Reflections' appeared at the end of December, 1915. See Schluchter, op. cit., p. 59.

60. For a statment on the status of consequentialist ethics see Roger Scruton, *Modern Philosophy* (London: Sinclair-Stevenson, 1994), pp. 284–6.

61. 'On what basis in an individual case should the ethical value of an action be determined: whether from the *success* of this undertaking or from its *intrinsic* value, however this may be ethically defined? Thus, whether and to what extent the responsibility of the actor for the consequences justifies the means,

or, on the other hand, the value of the conviction [*Gesinnung*] at the basis of the action should give the actor the right to deny responsibility for the consequences...' *FMW*, p. 339. (The emphases belong to the 1921 German edition.) I have used the translation by Neil Solomon in Schluchter, op. cit., pp. 283–4. The 'Intermediate Reflections' essay is saturated with the Ascona experience. It was written after the outbreak of war and the opposition of the pathos of death to the eros of the here and now is manifest.

62. 'As the consummated threat of violence among modern politics, war creates a pathos and a sentiment of community.', *FMW*, p. 335; 'Hence, the concept [nation] seems to refer to a specific kind of pathos which is linked to the idea of a powerful political community...' *ES*, p. 398.

63. *FMW*, p. 122.

64. Johannes Weiss has pointed out that this is a feature of current Russian sociology, which interprets Max Weber's views as a positive endorsement of the Tolstoyan injunction that all violence is evil (Unpublished paper, 'Max Weber in Russia, Russia in Weber' 1996, Fb5, Gesamthochschule Kassel).

65. Hennis, op. cit. and his *Max Webers Wissenschaft vom Menschen*, (Tübingen: Mohr, 1996).

66. *Max Weber. Selections in Translation*, ed. G. Runciman and trans. E. Matthews (Cambridge: Cambridge University Press, 1978), pp. 383–8.

67. Reported by Leonard Frank, cited in Kubitschek, op. cit., p. 431.

68. See Green op. cit. 1988, p. 60, and J. Kerr, *A Most Dangerous Method. The Story of Jung, Freud, and Sabine Spielrein* (London: Sinclair-Stevenson, 1994), pp. 186–9.

69. See J. Michaels, op. cit., pp. 36–7.

70. Quoted in Green, (1974) op. cit., p. 53.

71. A. Mitzmann, 'Anarchism, Expressionism and Psychoanalysis', *Drunken Boat*, ed. M. Blechman (New York: Autonomedia and Left Bank Books, 1994), pp. 83–116.

72. Gangolf Hübinger, ed. *Versammlungsort moderner Geister. Der Eugen Diederichs Verlag – Aufbruch ins Jahrhundert der Extreme* (Munich: Diederichs, 1996).

73. Mommsen, 1994, op. cit., p. 6.

74. *PW*, p. xv.

75. T. Nipperdey, *Deutsche Geschichte. Vol 1. Arbeitswelt und Bürgergeist* (Munich: Beck, 1993), pp. 120–2.

76. Although Tenbruck would not have blamed Weber for this missed opportunity.

77. *GStA*, Max Weber to Alwine Müller, 10 October 1918.

78. *FMW*, p. 128.

79. R. Benson, *German Expressionist Drama* (London: Macmillan, 1984) p. 45.

80. E. Toller, *Eine Jugend in Deutschland* (Hamburg: Rowohlt, 1963), pp. 158–9. See also the chapter by Dittmar Dahlmann in W. J. Mommsen and J. Osterhammel eds *Max Weber and his Contemporaries* (London: Allen & Unwin, 1987), pp. 367–81.

2 Letters from Ascona[1]

Max Weber

Ascona, Casa Abbondio, 26.3.1913.

Liebes Schnäuzele,[2]

Today it is cold, but there is some sun after yesterday's endless rain. Having got up late after a middling night, I am sitting in my spacious digs, three or four flights up, with a view of the steeply rising little garden next to the house and of the lake. The room has two beds, a small closet, a chest, an old, broken-down cabinet, a large sofa for sleeping, a large table, a tin washstand, a night table, a few pre-historic easy chairs, an electric lamp, no bell (four flights up), an ancient oleograph, a mirror, a clothes tree, and the walls done in a yellow wash. With room go a small kitchen, a lavatory next to the bedroom, and everything can be locked during the day. So it is ideal for 'a happy loving pair' of Ascona back-to-nature [*Naturmenschen*] people who cook nothing more than some porridge. In front of the house there is a chaussée, then one steps down into a small, luxuriant garden by the lake with an intoxicating smell of violets. A chicken run, a little landing for boats. The husband, *avvocato e notaio*,[3] is at his office in Locarno every day. His wife, once obviously beautiful and even now very good looking, is the large farmer's wife type. She scrubs the floors together with the maid, trots off to the post office – in short, in rank she is the same as Signora Quattrini in the local tavern. It is a really filthy Italian hole [*Italienernestchen*], although the tavern has some class because of the people staying there. The cooking is really too good for me. In the mornings I eat biscuits and dried figs, it's easy to get these things with the trade for the back-to-nature people. There's nothing in the house.

Today I'll go quickly into Locarno before Bernays[4] gets there, and read the paper – one doesn't know a thing about the world. It would be a great favour, though, if every couple of days you sent the evening pages of the Frankfurter. Otherwise one is as cut off as Wolfgang Gothein.[5]

Now for another bad night and then the 'cure' starts for sure. What has Mädele[6] been doing? Twenty years ago today she went to Oerlinghausen[7] and I to Strassburg-Heidelberg.

41

s just come to make the bed, poor thing she has a tooth
\cate the room for a bit. Hope all goes well with you, dear,
issing you a thousand times. Yours Max.

Ascona, 29.3.1913.

Lieber Schnäuzel,

When I returned from the post office yesterday after sending your
postcard, a blonde woman met me at the entrance of my house here with
one blonde and one dark child – Frieda of course.[8] We greeted each other,
she told me about the countess – financially she's quite well off, her father
in-law has died[9] – and about the children. God knows, she lives in my
house, the children with the maid diagonally opposite by the harbour.
However as you will be able to gather, we do not see each other. She was
somewhat constrained, her appearance is somewhat proletarianised, otherwise as always. A very good night after a bath. The weather is mild now
and completely overcast, one can sit outside. It could be hotter, but we
hope it stays as it is.

Now you don't have to worry about B.,[10] you can 'live it up' can't you?
But send me per Kreuzband [Swiss post] the 'Sieben Stationen des
Leidens' by this Phillips.[11] I'm curious about what it really is. The head
isn't all that clever but sends you a thousand kisses. Your numbskull Max.

Ascona, 30.3.1913, Sunday.

Lieber Schnäuzel,

Early yesterday when I sat on the garden bench at the roadside,
Bernays appeared recognisable even at a distance – with her head stuck in
the illustrated 'Guida' rather than looking at the scenery. First going one
way, then coming back. I hope she now sees this way is not rewarding. I
sent her down the road and she found that it led nowhere – although I was
very friendly. Thank goodness she didn't see Frieda sitting by me – she
turned up soon after. But now she is going to Zurich even this time at
midday won't be available any longer – in the morning and for the whole
afternoon she is occupied with the children (Peter is presently being
'taught' by her). She was very affectionate, she is still the old Frieda, she
is basically in good humour, somewhat dishevelled, her flimsy scarves etc.

peppered with cigarette burns, very unsophisticated in appearance and within herself very simplified in style. The younger child Eva [is] highly sensitive, shy, and totally dependent on her mother (cries at any stern word from her), protected as the apple of her eye, – the lad [*Bengel*] is like the father,[12] brutal, unlovable, she makes promises (which are difficult to keep) to make him behave 'nicely', he remains surly, defiant and unjust, [and] because he must surely be unbearable for the 'step-father'[13] he will be hard work. One cannot be of any use to Frick, for there is no need for him to be sewing mail-bags and he wants to be doing something of his own choice, but under the illiberal Swiss law he would have to pay fifty thousand francs for his court case.[14] Thank goodness the sum is so high and one cannot even think about helping. She sees him through a screen, as in Tolstoy's 'Resurrection'. Since the state prosecutor had demanded fifteen years, one year in jail is lenient for the stupidity and healthwise it's manageable.

Jaffé has lent three hundred marks to the countess at her request against the security of her next translation royalty from the publisher.[15] That is where she earns her money from (besides she is at the moment supported by her 'boyfriend'[16]). She couldn't have travelled to Majorca without that money. She has a crazy fear of growing old – more so than of dying – the doctors hide behind a wall of silence because of the operation (evidently she can no longer endure this and they recommend wholesome nourishment). The old father-in-law, Rechenberg, knows about the marriage of convenience with his drunken son who lives in the district (Frieda is very proud of having arranged this[17]). Until now he has only received pocket money and his father has made sure in his will that nothing will go to the countess. Anyway in emergencies she can still tap the 'husband' for money – they address each other as *Sie*, as they always have, (and *Gnädige Frau*) – things surely must improve.[18] He hasn't adopted the son,[19] because for emotional reasons the countess didn't wish it.

I think if one makes such an arrangement – then the whole thing! – So, that was the important bit. I now live here in Frick's old room. The appartment diagonally across from the harbour, where the children live with the fat good natured Lisi[20] and Frieda has her meals and where she 'lives' in the afternoons. In the mornings it's well heated, otherwise one has to say it's a small Italian pigsty.

The Frankfurter has just arrived, yesterday your dear letter, many thanks, and many most beautiful spring greetings, it is tolerably warm, sleep is moderate, but the strong disturbance of the previous year is gone. Obviously the unfavourable times are yet to come. I embrace you, yours Max.

Ascona, 31.3.1913, Monday.

Lieber Schnäuzel

I sleep with long disturbed intervals but get enough rest if I lie long enough. Everything is dead still as if created for me. Lunches at Quattrinis, mornings and evenings vegetarian fodder: oatmeal biscuits and figs, which one can get from the shops. Should it become colder, Frieda's Lisi would bring me warm water for a lemon-punch. Contact with Frieda is very limited. I sit a lot on the garden bench at the roadside looking over the garden to the lake. Then she talks to me – about God and the world, also about the Jaffés – I answer: I am morally quite prepared to strike Edgar Jaffé dead, that is not morally reprehensible but the only decent thing. Unfortunately our crazy laws forbid it, but as a favour to Else [Jaffé] I could not do anything better. It is better and would be better to carry on these things with less publicity, that would be more generous. But enough of that. She speaks a lot about herself, divorce from Otto Gross (he has Dementia Praecox)[21] is legally impossible since they had a Catholic marriage in Austria. The oldest boy makes a lot of trouble and will make more, he is presently being taught by her but that has now stopped. She is absolutely alone here and badly wants to get away. Only it is so cheap here and for her: no constraints. Also the countess talks with her incessantly. The son looks as if he's going to turn out badly. That is no wonder since everything is talked about in front of him very coarsely and everything is gone into in a cynical manner, above all the mother mocks everything and everyone even the closest friends not excluded. For the boy then every belief in anything is naturally dead, no signs of love or chivalry, only his brutal nature. Yes it is indeed as one would have thought: please be careful when telling Gruhle[22] about this, for he will hold it against her [Frieda]. Although she is very impressed by the countess, she agrees with everything I said, she conforms but in some things she stands up for herself. The countess knows that in this respect her life is nothing and defends herself against it. Now she sits in Majorca, waiting to see if the Spaniard will arrive or not, – suddenly that's all she can think about, the actual 'experience' ['*Erlebnis*'] – so she's not the cool, unattached technician of love ('Technikerin' des amourosen), as she presents herself in her book,[23] – which is her saving grace.

I read various things and make notes, since it's raining heavily today with clouds over the lake, while the last days have been overcast and mild, a wonderful soft air, a proper sanatorium and one lives completely outside.

What is this about your sudden bad sleep? Don't you think you should go away? It must be the effect of the unaccustomed work on your nerves [*Nervensystem*]? I don't find this intermezzo very heartening, my love.

A bouquet of camellias from Bernays has just arrived! oh wow! I must visit her in Locarno this afternoon, in order to settle that. That desperate woman! [*Das Desparate Frauenzimmer!*] Thousand kisses and greetings, your Max.

Ascona, 1.4.1913.

…It rains an unimaginable amount day and night, the lake has disappeared but the air is still mainly soft and beautiful and not too cold; that will probably come since up on the mountain the rain naturally turns to snow. One can't go outside for five minutes without getting soaking wet, so I lie on the large sofa and read and dream; then sleep comes broken by long intervals, so I have to stay in bed a lot to get enough sleep. Even after a week without medication, no collapse yet. I only go out for meals. My head is relaxed and does not feel quite so dull, it even 'thinks' in bed in the morning and joins in taking notes. Obviously it isn't quite right. I will write to the Tobelkind who has sent me Thomas Mann's 'Königliche Hoheit',[24] she had wanted to give it to me rather than send it. It will be just the right thing to read now. Keep in touch, my dear. With kisses, Your Max.

Ascona, 2.4.1913, Wednesday.

…The night was as usual, I lie thirteen hours in bed, sleep seven with breaks, I'm curious to see how it will go. It has poured down for the last two days. One was confined totally to one's room. Today there is no rain, overcast sky, wind, cool. It could be warmer without the wind. Nothing to report. Obviously I have not seen Frieda, although her room is half a flight of stairs below mine. But she knows that I must exist alone. I hope you will soon get over your spring cold, my dear, you now have time to rest.…

Ascona, 11.4.1913.

Liebes Schnäuzel!
Nothing from you today. Yesterday I went to Brissago-am-See by boat and came back by omnibus. A very merry party, which only marginally

disturbed my night. Otherwise nothing spectacular, things 'middling' – except that in spite of meagre eating there's no sign of being leaner.

Yesterday evening it seemed as if it would clear, the moon appeared as a small sickle in the sky. But today the blasted cold wind has returned, which is unpleasant, and it doesn't lessen. Oh for a burning hot summer! This great isolation is beautiful. Still haven't heard anything of Frieda, she is obviously still away. I read some Goethe, otherwise nothing. It seems as if it will remain peaceful! Keep happy little one and accept my kisses, Your Max.

Ascona, 13.4.1913.

…Yes it is a terrible shame you are having such an awful spring; it is also very cold here, but today is clear and sunny and I think it will stay. I lie in bed till 11 o'clock, and at 8 in the evening back in bed. That's already happened. Frieda is here again. I saw her yesterday briefly in her digs – an incredible tangle of toys, ladies hats, crockery, books, cigarettes, she herself in a nightdress of faded grey material – Good Lord! But her bloom is going, though her mouth is still fine and her face the same though more pointed. The hair badly done etc. And all 'problems' grossly simplified. More on this tomorrow. I read Marie Donadieu,[25] much escapes me, but it is really very fine and it's very much Paris with the Moulin de la Galette![26] Isn't it? Otherwise I don't do anything. I don't take anything but to be sure my nights are accordingly very disturbed and with very little sleep. But that's no wonder!

My fingers are numb from the cold, you will be scarcely able to read this. I wrote to mother yesterday. A thousand kisses and greetings, your cold Max.

Ascona, 14.4.1913.

Liebes Mädele!

Send me the Lukacssche book,[27] I can read it here. I've read the Marie Donadieu book and given it to Frieda who in return gave me the latest book of the countess: a Schwabinger Schlüsselbuch [*roman à clef*] with George, Wolfskehl, Count Adrian etc and herself.[28] Well written but only for those interested in Schwabing and very indiscreet. The Marie D.

is beautifully written, with depth and delicacy, a very high level critique of the erotic – but the ending is somewhat contrived: travelling in the Persian Gulf and the like is surely not a sufficient expression of the richness and the greatness of the extraordinary-erotic [*aussererotischen*] life. But I will read the book again. Many details escape me, since my French vocabulary is weak, very weak. In the freezing cold here – I write with numb fingers – I sat with Frieda yesterday by her fireplace for a few hours. She has a great need to talk things out. Her life is completely wrecked. *How so* can be quickly told. Dementia praecox was already diagnosed before her marriage to Otto Gross. The parents had concealed this from her. Then it went as Jaspers predicted of Bloch:[29] she became dreadfully over-taxed, completely and wretchedly eaten up and on top of this – which she confesses – the terrible drain of emotions owing to her polygamy. It's of no consequence who started this: mentally she *couldn't* meet the demands of her husband, she has become a complete nervous wreck, and *must* have 'the other' (so for the opposite reasons as Else!).[30] And with Frick? He also has a 'religious belief' in a future society free of jealousy, of really 'free' love, that is free from within. She herself also theorised about this, but when I said: 1. noble action in respect to jealousy is a fine thing but how could one find it chivalrous to *allow* oneself to accept everything from a person, to whom one has become so indebted? 2. Isn't the pursuit of this odd idea [*Schrulle*] a mad waste of emotional [*seelische*] energy? Then [she] burst out with it: *Yes*, it is terrible and completely hopeless and her strength was gone, she was capable of hardly anything else. And that's how it is. She is *very* neurasthenic. And then the children: both fathers are called 'Otto' and 'Ernst' in front of them, the boy pays close attention and is quite unrestrained, hates his father and step-father, appears very pathological. It was lamentable to see this faded yet still delicate being just sitting there in the chaos of her coquettishly disordered room. For *both* of the last monthly visits – only one monthly visit is permitted – she had let the countess visit Frick! He himself is a complicated person, who hasn't the remotest idea what to do. 'If only he knew what to do with his life when he is out again.' Obviously the prison sentence is equally a holiday for both of them.

She always speaks of moving to Munich. But that is difficult: he is Swiss, and as an anarchist would surely be quickly expelled from Germany. And she is apathetic and incapable of making decisions. *And* it's cheap here.

Enough for today, I'm off to Locarno to sit in a café – the air is really clean, Bernays is away. It's too bleak and cold here. The papers came, many thanks. Stay loving, your frozen Max.

Ascona, 16.4.1913, Wednesday early.

Liebes Mädele,
...Yesterday I sat with Frieda. I had brought marbles for the children and chocolate, also for the children, from Locarno, but she took this as a personal present – it's so unusual for anyone to give her anything. Her main yearning is for another child. But Gross Sr, her father-in-law, has made threatening noises should this occur. He very much wants to have Otto certified and is attempting to have him arrested.[31]

Also it transpires that Else and Jaffé are expected here on their way back from Rome. I said, then I'll go off for the time to Orta. 'Was I angry with Else then?' It turns out that Else has told her everything in minute detail. I said that that was not the issue but, in the first place, it was not proper on account of Alfred for me to see Else – it had nothing to do with my approval. Secondly, a meeting would be embarrassing for Else. For she would say to me: that she had started something very wrong and I would see no point because I have become so completely estranged from her and that my relations with her have been of such a kind that they would be inadequate and little conducive to what she counts as a friend, so that almost nothing of value would result. Then there was a theoretical discussion about Freud, non-erotic relationships and so on, and this point was dealt with. Should Else come, I'll stay two nights at Orta on Lake Orta, where we experienced that terrible downpour coming from the Simplon and we couldn't see. A thousand kisses for you, your Max. It is clear and cold.

Ascona, 17.4.1913, Thursday.

It is warm again here but dull as a result, after yesterday which was a very beautiful day. Perhaps I'll go into Locarno again to listen to a concert. Frieda summoned me to her bedside. She is plagued with neurasthenic problems, in my opinion because she smokes too much – from the moment she wakes up. I should remove the drunk – the Countess R's legal husband, when he comes, since he falls about and wants advice about his inheritance, which is still completely unresolved.[32] I didn't see a copy of it, since he arrived when I was eating.

Yes, there isn't very much one can do with her life, she does not see this completely, only at certain times. She hates Zurich. She is uncertain whether she could remain in Munich with her husband and everywhere else is more expensive than here. This seems to be very important. She remembers Freiburg with happiness[33] and becomes very sentimental. Above all she's still got her humour, which is highly amusing and charming and often most naïve and grotesquely uninhibited. So, for example, her relationship to Lang[34] and its end! More on this by word of mouth. However if difficulties occur with the children, then it's different. One cannot help her, since the relationship with Frick determines everything. As long as this continues she cannot fit into a bourgeois environment, not because of matters themselves but because of all the toing and froing and because it is *only* the chaos and changing scandals that keep her going.... A thousand loving greetings and kisses, your Max.

Ascona, den Qi,[35] 18.4.1913.

Liebes Mädele!

Thank you so much for the Lukács and your letter. Else apparently is not coming (although in her letter she gives other reasons, since she knows through you that I am here). Frieda says that it was a firm date. It is most agreeable not to have to leave now.

Yesterday Frieda and the little girl went to Locarno with me, where she had to take care of something. We sat in the café when shockingly all of a sudden this refined and elegant being began to play the complete coquette – only [to show up] the 'middle class' ladies who were there. I don't know what it was – whether in the hasty and dishevelled appearance (within ten minutes of having got up, she had suddenly made a decision and had dashed on to the boat), the cigarettes, the loud voice or the way of holding her head and gestures: however the neighbouring tables stared and turned up their noses, and how she unconsciously reacted to that! Defiance against 'society'. The feeding of self-esteem through 'the pathos of distance' against society and all such feelings were at once there. I can imagine her in Munich's Schwabing but not in Heidelberg, she doesn't fit into the ensemble; Gruhle thinks she could be integrated again, but I do not. She should move to Zurich. There was even a law proposed to permit concubinage for foreigners who are not able to divorce – or only with difficulty – , but it was rejected after a referendum. That the law-making corporations had decided on this shows, however, there is a tolerance and she would not be an 'outlaw' there.[36]

Otherwise nothing new. It is dull and mild but still too cool. The grey and steelblue colours are very beautiful, sleep futile. I read a little, think a little, and the odd small thought occurs to me now and then....

Tobelchens[37] sister sent the Zuricher Lekerli[38] – terrible stuff! On the first delivery I was insincere enough to praise the child. This saves me two evening meals and one breakfast because it is so filling.

It seems that things are only middling with you? Stop working so continuously, dear. A thousand kisses and greetings, your Max.

Ascona, 19.4.1913.

Frieda was laid up in bed again yesterday – there at any rate her beautifully striking head seems distinguished, quite in contrast to her appearance when promenading [*für 'die Promenade'*]. She always has a headache, almost certainly from her constant cigarette smoking, in bed in the morning and her nocturnal existence, aside from the continual psychic excitement. We talked yesterday most friendly and openly about various things. Frankness naturally has its limits, as one can notice. Also she obviously says only what she wants to about her relationship with L.[39]... Now everything will be well with you, I will see you again in a week and that is fine. Hopefully it is good weather with you. A thousand kisses from your Max.

Ascona, 20.4.1913.

The weather is cloudy and mild, it's beautiful to see the lilies and the sides of the mountains through the silver grey and even more beautiful to watch the gradual fading of the colours with their steel-grey undertones in the long twilight. Perhaps I'll travel to Locarno today or leave it till tomorrow as a birthday celebration, when, my God! I reach my 50th year! – I can hardly believe it. One is strangely still so youthful! Or is it your youth, my dear, which so deceives me? For a birthday present we will have the cement posts on the bridge to the garden crowned with wooden tubs and plant some beautiful flowers in them. That's suddenly occurred to me now, I don't know why.... Sending you a thousand kisses from your Max.

Ascona, 21.4.1913.

Mein liebes Mädele,

Your dear beautiful letter has just arrived[40] and 'Tristan' as symbol – it is something that you can 'still' think of him after 20 years, or perhaps only think properly and perhaps more deeply of him than 20 years *ago*. Whatever else changes inside, there can't be anything more. My dear, all that you have said to me is indeed a beautiful 'poem' of your great love – I cannot look at myself with such great and beautiful eyes as you do and so all that is 'given up' rather than 'given'.[41] However equally, now is not the time to inquire what is true and what is not but to enjoy the beauty that makes it possible that such 'poems' happen. It is always possible for me not to disavow them at least and to be able to protect your soul for ever new 'poetry' – since the poems are indeed 'true' as people [*Menschen*], on which ground the truth is summoned. Keep your love for me, most trusting 'Mädele' – since you are still so young that one cannot call you otherwise – then in the coming year and the years that are allotted to us we will be happy and always going forward together.

Nothing new here. I am ludicrously frozen, now that the weather is becoming warmer. Spring is very late here. I go to Locarno again this afternoon. Frieda takes advantage of this to go with me and to go on from there for two days – where to? who knows? 'To someone' for a single afternoon, which will take a whole day to get there and back; yesterday we sat in a small bar by the lake on the road to Brissago. As always she spoke a lot about herself and the countess, then of Gruhle in whom she finds absolutely nothing, he is totally without significance. The countess also thinks the same and said further: she never knew how she, the countess, actually stands with him, and also has never known: 'Perhaps she lies about this.' I strongly agreed. This lack of perception, only because the man is not an 'erotomorf'![42] And the countess is completely unfaithful and cynical! Then she talked about 'Aunt Sophie'[43] and Schulze-Gävernitz (the aunt had once written to his mother and she found the reply in a cupboard when she herself had dropped in on Schulze-Gävernitz and so on[44]); – Yes, 'she's only coquettish in her outward gestures: the voice, the smoking, her movements, the smudged and disordered toilette. Beyond this nothing. Otherwise her conversation is charming and refined. She is completely bound up with the legal case, which has obviously excited her to the point of exhaustion. She herself has been dragged through the press in the most vulgar way.

And now let me love you and gratefully embrace you, my love. I'm already thinking of seeing you again in five days. Your 'old' Max.

Ascona, 24.4.1913 Thursday.

Liebes Schnäuzel,
    Still a final greeting from you before leaving. It pours with rain almost non-stop, but it is warm. I eat later with [the] Braus, then a talk with Frieda – she still wants to tell me what I shouldn't say and think of her – then it's concluded. This came out in conversation yesterday: (to Peter) 'Yes, yes, you'll notice when the women won't let their children play with you on account of....'(already the wife of the anarcho-socialist – ! – Raphael Fried[e]berg[45] – from Berlin won't let her children play with the Gross kids.) It is *always* the children who have to pay the price. She pleased me again yesterday with her sense of honesty. One never stops learning, even if they are things which explain themselves.
    I very much hope that my beautiful wife isn't in bed when I return and in spite of your cold (or whatever it is) kiss you a thousand times. Your Max.
    Please get the manuscripts from the bank.

Ascona, 29.3.1914.

Liebes Schnäuzel,
    I hope you are now safe and happy at the Rickerts and you're not overdoing it with too much talking. Leave that to Rickert and listen instead of arguing.[46]
    I have been fasting since Friday evening, that is I only drink water and eat nothing. So far I notice nothing whatsoever, my stomach rumbles but is losing rather than gaining [weight], I have not yet become more handsome, but also not weaker or more 'agitated' ['*nervoes*'] so far. I am curious to see how it will go. I'll continue it until this evening. Then a pause till tomorrow evening, then another 48 hour fast. We'll see what happens! I'm feeling somewhat dull, but that doesn't really matter. I sleep sufficiently.
    Frieda meets Alfred today in Bellinzona, at his telephoned wish. It's not clear what he wants. Perhaps only news.
    Now dear Schnauzel, consider your reference [*Bescheinigung*] for Frieda.
    So: 1. the impression of Peter and your relationship to him, his being properly looked after by her. You can say that briefly and then you can offer to go into it in detail.
    2. On Frick's character [*Persönlichkeit*] (refinement, education, passivity, passive and unpolitical opinions, thoughtful and kind manner and so on).
    Best if both on special sheets of paper.

At the start of no.1 that you have *entirely* different ideals and views than Frieda's! (important!) And then send what you've written to the court and trial lawyer (Hof und-Gerichtsadvokat) Dr Otto Pellech, Wien, Rathaustr. 5. Your book is ordered for him from Siebeck.[47] Refer Herrn Pellech from your side to the last chapter for your views and make reference to Rosin's *Deutsches Recht*, Riehl, Endemann, Gothein[48] as witnesses to the absolute ethical correctness of your views. If possible, try and do this in Freiburg. Since in Heidelberg a thousand little things await you! A thousand best wishes, kissing you, your 'Bub',

Ascona, 30.3.1914, Monday.

Liebes Mädele,

Today is the third day of a complete fast and moderate sleep, after a brisk walk and car journey and incessant reading. I'm not really suffering any side-effects except for a rumbling stomach, but scarcely as bad as in Heidelberg at one o'clock when Marie Bernays is around visiting you. No trace of any effect on the *Embonpoint* and looks, I am quite unchanged as God intended me to be (*Schöpfungsplan*). Writing is a little less physically hard than before. This evening I'm calling a halt and going over again to a fruit and vegetable diet.

Now I hope you are reasonably restored – or the reverse? Severely strained by Rickert? I'm glad to think you will be back at home tomorrow, and I hope people will leave you in peace. This bunch thinks to be sure that you've gathered new strengths in order to listen to their nattering....Stay well, dearest girl, hugging you a thousand times, your Max.

Ascona, 31.3.1914, Tuesday.

Liebes Mädele – so now you are at home again and I hope you won't find too much to do. Yesterday evening and this morning I ate a couple of oranges, otherwise 'niente' since Friday evening. I'm feeling reasonably well, sufficient sleep without any medication. Apart from these world shattering events there is nothing to report. We are anxiously awaiting news of Pellech's discussions in Graz, which ought to arrive on Friday.[49] And consider the possibility that the judge will say to him:

If she gives up the relationship with Frick, then she keeps 'the child', she will at best only pretend the former and possibly would prefer to give up Peter. She is, however, remarkably clear that Frick will not and cannot remain here, and of course she has absolutely no idea what will become of him. Apparently he awaits for the moment of great inner illumination when he will perform a great prophetic act. The poor devil, he is totally preoccupied with his sentence and this is rather alarming; if one is convinced, as he is, of the absolute wickedness of the whole basis of 'society' – Frieda finds it quite inexplicable how these ideas come to be so 'overvalued' ['*überwertig*'[50]] by him. Anyway he would like to realise 'goodness' and 'brotherly love' [Nächstenliebe] through the acosmicism of the *erotic* [*durch Akosmistik der* Erotik]. I had already told Frieda why that is not possible, and she admits that the only possible path was that of Tolstoyan asceticism, towards which he constantly tends. This is where he will end up, if he still has the strength for it. But something has snapped in him, one can feel that strongly. But enough for now, I still have things to dictate. – More tomorrow! Your always loving Max.

Ascona, 1.4.1914, Wednesday.

Liebes Schnäuzele,

Thank God, as your dear little letter shows, you are still alive in spite of everything and the beautiful spring days will hopefully take away the strain of the trip ['*Tour*'] and restore you, since it was also stressful here to see the strain in you.

Here everything is in full swing. Yesterday I dictated the commentary for the legal case etc. Today I'm drafting my report on Frick which tomorrow will be dictated to the countess to be typed. In return and with a bad conscience I have fabricated at her request a report for the possible release of her lout [*Lümmel*] from nationality [military service]. Hopefully it will come to nothing and the guy will have to serve![51]

On Friday we expect Pellech's report and in the meantime Frieda is happy it is not here and she isn't faced with making a decision....

I will ask Tobelchen, who surely is back in Zurich now, whether she has a half-day free for the Ufenau and can direct me, if it goes ahead. Other than Lang[52] I have to speak to the lawyer Fräulein Brüstlein. Perhaps I'll search out Sieveking[53] and if there's a little time left, the museum and the trade-hall–

From Friday night until this Wednesday I have had only five orange quarters but my fat belly [*Mostbürgertum*] doesn't budge an inch. I'm destined to be this way. Apart from that I look very well. Yesterday's sleep was again reasonable, and I am not 'agitated'. I walk and read or dictate the whole day. Only a certain dullness and my head feels a little neuraesthenic. Weather is *heavenly*. Not a single day from the year before was like this. If only the spring stays until I come home. With a thousand kisses, my dearest girl, your Max.

Ascona, 2.4.1914, Thursday

Liebes Schnäuzele,

No letter from you. I only wanted to say a happy 'good morning' to you and to tell you that there is nothing to tell – before I go and dictate my portrayal of Frick [*Steckbrief*[54]] to the countess. Wonderful weather… still eating only oranges. The paunch *remains* temporarily! – I walk, read, work, and chatter with Frieda and (yesterday very interestingly) with Frick. And Friedeberg is of the view that Frick will go anywhere since he *suffers* in the present situation. He thinks he could fix him up as a salesman in a business and the like. Huh! I don't think he's any longer capable of it and and won't become so in the future. And when he (Frick) talks of the affirmation of death, many things spring to my mind.

What are you doing? Or rather I know that you'd prefer quiet and be spared from Bernays and all the horrors of everyday things and people. Has your written piece for Pellech gone? Kissing you my dear heart, your Max.

Ascona, 3.4.1914, Friday afternoon.

Liebstes Mädele,

Very many thanks for your little card. You poor tormented little thing [*Peterle*[55]]. It's raining here today on a day when there's nothing to do. The report from Pellech still isn't here, why? Nobody knows. *Hopefully!* not because of another break-down, that would be too dreadful. One's had enough of these incidents. Today's the seventh day of fasting. During the past week in the evening I've had only four and a half kilos of oranges, two lemonades without sugar, and three cups of tea. I feel just as

I did on the first day, that is, my stomach often rumbles, and one is not completely healthy; but also not essentially different to normal. No change in the embonpoint, no raised nervosity. I walk and read as I always have, only writing is a bit of a strain. Tomorrow morning I shall start my nourishment again with a raw fennel. Keep well today, dearest girl, kissing you, your Max.

I talked to Frieda about Lask.[56] But she's very hard to motivate.

Ascona, 4.4.1914, Saturday.

Liebes Mädele,

Still no report from 'our' Pellech (except for a letter to Peter and the news that the court has extended to 1 May responsibility for the little Gross). Hopefully, nothing has happened to him. Here there's nothing new. I have begun to eat raw fennel as well as oranges. The stomach rumbles as before, writing a little easier, head feels normal, brown suit is still too big. I don't think I've changed at all. So you could look after me quite cheaply. Per day my meals cost 3 finocchi = 30 cent. Else Jaffé comes today and remains till tomorrow. Since I cannot go away it is decided that I should stay unseen in my room and Else is told I'm away.

Now that Frick no longer sees me as the 'reference writer' he's more forthcoming. However by any permutation he is still very withdrawn, poor fellow. His Shakespeare translation (sonnets) on the other hand is very good, quite outstanding. Hopefully dear girl you have got over the strain! I think with fury of the females (Bernays, Blank etc) who tear you to pieces! It rained yesterday and was cool. Today marvellous weather. A thousand kisses, your Max.

Ascona, 5.4.1914, Sunday.

Liebes Mädele,

I am blockaded in my room today, because yesterday Frieda installed Else in the room directly opposite. On my instructions she has explained that I am away and there is no way she can see me. So I am not allowed to be here. Also I do not wish to see her. Also from what Alfred said to Frieda in Bellinzona the nasty and cowardly absence of chivalrous behaviour of both of these people to me has become only too apparent –

there can be nothing more for me than a chance meeting. Had I been aware of this situation somewhat earlier I would have gone to Zurich yesterday and today. News is awaited here from Vienna – a telegram arrived in response to my question – negotiations about the abandonment of Eva hang in the balance without any end in sight and an understanding is possible only with difficulty.[57] So now I must see what happens, but when? Yesterday it rained cats and dogs and I did nothing, and I now find the women's blockade rather tedious and this whole business with these people simply 'stupid'.

Frieda meanwhile has told me much about the relationship between Otto Gross and his father which is strange enough. I understand now why the old man wishes to have him isolated. Some years back Otto Gross had among other things the naïveté to send his father a manuscript with the aim that he, the father, should find a publisher and bear the costs of publication: yet the manuscript was a conspicuous example of something despicable, the marital sexual life of the same father in detail including naming of names! That is strong stuff [*starker Tabak*] and I haven't concealed from Frieda that if I was the judge I would lock up a lout who did that without any psychiatric reports.[58] There are things emerging in this way about Otto Gross's life which leave me in no doubt that Frieda is only too happy that he is detained, and she fights only out of 'principle'.

The countess neither improves, nor loses anything on closer inspection. In between my dictating we have only trivial conversations, but she does sometimes come into Frick's room. But then her lad comes in and when he's there one can't talk about anything reasonable. Then I tell mostly anecdotes, only so that the young rascal doesn't continuously interrupt. Frick has depth. But he lacks powers of expression even for simple things. Prison has had such an effect on him that he cannot leave off brooding on the significance of goodness. He has been driven to distraction by the insight that the *outcome* of virtuous action is so often quite irrational and results in evil when one behaves 'virtuously', so much so that he questions whether one *ought* to act virtuously: an evaluation of moral action in terms of its *consequences* and not its intrinsic worth! For the time being he cannot see that there is a mistake in this, so I will see to it that he gets a copy of *The Brothers Karamazov*, and then later Lukács's dialogue,[59] in which this problem is dealt with.

Many thanks dearest for your letter. I can't remember whether I thanked you in my note yesterday. I hope you will be able to get much peace and quiet in Berlin before the preparations for Mama's birthday begins.[60] 1000 kisses my dear heart, yours Max.

I eat raw fennel and apple. I am not any slimmer or better looking.

Ascona, 6.4.1914, Monday

Liebstes Mädele,

You are indeed completely silent! Yesterday nothing, today nothing. And tomorrow I'm in Zurich and return the day after tomorrow. It was fifty fifty whether I went, since I could visit on the way back home at the end of April, but a thick letter from Pellech arrived today that now forces me to go. It all rests on tracking down people who can testify to Frick's qualities – his political harmlessness. Since we have only until the end of April before the outcome [of the case], it is now high time to do everything possible in order to set things in motion. I will see if I can drive to the Ufenau with Tobelchen despite the changeable weather, or whether I shall remain in Zurich and stay with her at her nice sister's. She wrote highly indignantly about the 'seduction arts of the countess' – I wrote to her about what I did for the countess about her lad.[61] Anyway I have not seen the countess for 3 or 4 days.

Else blockaded me in my room here till half past three, then she finally went. Apparently she was very tired after their visit to Naples with her husband and his actress friend Mendelssohn.

I must go and advise Frieda in detail today, so look after yourself dearest child, there is nothing to report anyway. The letter from Pellech contains too many details of the outcome to go into, but the result was: concessions for Eva against concessions in respect to Peter. But the old man is being very reserved.

Unless your letter arrives just before I leave tomorrow I won't hear anything from you till Zurich. I will write from there. Yesterday I met Troeltsch[62] who is in Locarno. A thousand greetings, dearest girl.

Zurich, 7.4.1914, Tuesday

Liebes Schnäuzele,

So I'm here. If it continues to rain like this then I'll leave the outing to Rapperswyl until tomorrow and will recompense Tobelchen with a visit to the museum. I also hope to see the pleasant Otts[63] for a couple of hours. But there's a lot to do. I might have to go to Bleulers.[64] Also the mission to Lang I can now say is a 'diplomatic' one and therefore was urgent. So I won't entrust it to paper now.

Meanwhile in Graz Pellech and the person representing Professor Gross circle around each other aiming to extract the maximum in concessions from each other. Pellech has baldly asserted that Eva is Otto Gross's child. That has only induced the opposition to say finally: abandon Eva as a condition for all concessions in respect of Peter. But Pellech doesn't believe the moment has come to make concessions. Because otherwise one can extract too few counter-concessions. One sees that it's going to be tough and not without some blatant lying [*starkes Lügen*].

Concerning Frick he suffers above all in my view because of his behaviour in this trial – he has been unfairly sentenced but was somehow involved – the others, his alibi witnesses, have been put in prison for falsely testifying and that has wrecked his tactics. But as he has explained to me, honesty would have led others to be accused, who would then have come under suspicion.[65] Thus there remains only insincerity. So these theories: that one should not do good, since it leads to evil consequences. In prison he has obviously brooded over this with an anxious monomania. 'Monogamous' *he* isn't, since Frieda wasn't monogamous either during their relationship (nor was she when he was in jail, nor does she intend to be). So what can he do? However enough. Naturally it is painful for him to answer the question put by the judge through Pellech: how have you lived all these years? He comes across as a kept person [*homme soutenu*] and it's good this pressure is applied!

I don't know whether you are in Heidelberg or whether you are already travelling to Charlottenburg. Probably the latter – the post won't reach me anymore, since I left earlier than I originally intended. If I still visit Bleuler and Sieveking, then I would not be home till early Thursday. A thousand greetings, dear, from your Max.

(Pellech's letters are most graceful. I'll send one in the next post.]

Rapperswyl, 8.4.1914, Wednesday.

Liebes Schnäuzele,

I found the letter I wrote yesterday night in my pocket.[66] I had forgotten to post it since the Tobelchen had in the meantime arrived. At Herr Langs I was very taken with the beautiful house on the Zurichberg with the most beautiful views, his nice and quiet wife – though a little boring but nevertheless obviously capable, and a daughter studying music who is nice but not very grown up. Lang is a strange chap, judging from long conversations. I'll write more about him from Ascona. It was a gamble coming here in this bad weather. It still remains windy and dull. The rain always comes back. To wait for a favourable half an hour, then it would be wonderful; in this cloudy weather who knows what can be done. But the Tobelchen who is very cheerful, lively and, apart from some coughing, quite well is still hopeful. But if the weather doesn't improve it will be time to return, since I would like to talk to the lawyer, Fräulein Brüstlein before I go. Rapperswyl's location is quite wonderful. It is a pleasant idea to think we could sit here together, three quarters of an hour from Zurich, before or after a mountain trip. Since the trip to Zurich I've been eating regularly again. I'll go back to fasting in Ascona. I hope to find good news from you there. Kissing you, your Max.

9.4.1914, Thursday, very early morning, Zurich.

Liebes Mädele,
　　Many beautiful thanks for your letter yesterday, which Frau Ott sent me. Yesterday I completely failed to meet up with these good people because the communications are so bad, and I only saw Tobler's mother, old and somewhat conventional. Now time to return 'home',[67] if one can so call this world full of enchantresses, grace, danger and desire for happiness; as long as there are still things left to do which now must be done, so that all my troubles haven't been in vain. I must say: in and amongst this beautiful and in a certain sense 'human' world based on sensations *lacking any depth*, that it was a sort of *oasis* of purity – one cannot really describe it differently. Yesterday a trip to the Ufenau with the far less loud but in her reserved and gentle effusive way, a 'noble' child.[68] Fate smiled on us in respect to the weather. It was pouring with rain when we came to Rapperswyl (did you get my letter from there which I had put in my pocket from the evening before yesterday?), so that I thought we would only sit by a warm stove and look at the beautiful expanse of the lake with the veiled mountains behind. But look! After lunch the sun broke through the spring storm and it was a quick trip in the little motor boat over the still choppy lake. All the mountains surrounded by clouds were clear, it was almost as warm as summer and the tiny island – a green plate with some small hills on which stood two ancient chapels otherwise only an old inn, fruit trees and bushes round the shore – was dead still and completely empty and was really delightful. (Rapperswyl would be quite the place to unwind in late summer!) So now the beautiful northern contrasts against the unending southerly splendour of sunny days is over – Ascona was incredibly summery last time.

Frieda was expecting me at the station to hear how Herr Lang had behaved – since she has 'not had the heart yet to tell him that everything that was once between them was now finished'. I admit I was quite astounded when this came out (obviously I have made a *faux pas* by not taking into account his jealousy toward the person for whom he was acting as a character witness). And then her childish face – 'You don't hold me in too much contempt do you?' So I just laughed. During Frick's court case Frieda's interest very conveniently waned and then was quickly over. For him it was obviously a late romantic stirring [*Johannistrieb*] which he remembers and clearly reproaches himself about (and naturally nothing was said of this between him and me!) And now he will do his duty.[69]

I had a meal with him on Tuesday. He and his wife send their best greetings. The daughter is awkward and adolescent, studies music. A long evening and I stayed up until one o' clock with him brooding and talking all the time about Frick whom he mightily distrusts. But I did not meet the lawyer [Fräulein Brüstlein]. She was and remains out of town, which had the sole advantage that I went to bed early yesterday, but it cost me three long letters. So when I arrive at Ascona, Frieda has to be clear, what concessions she might make. Obviously I'll be deeply involved in advising on the settlement. Pellech handles things superbly. Obviously, as he admits, with an unbelievable amount of 'under-handedness', but then the other side has a very strong suit.

Greetings to mother – what would she say!! Dear child, as a castaway in a fairytale world your lad embraces you.

Ascona, 10.4.1914, Friday

Lieber Schnäuzel,
Many thanks for both your letters which were waiting here. The weather is superb, perfect spring, everything in blossom and green. I had a bad night again. I think the fasting, which I'll undergo again, will perhaps make things better. Frieda picked me up at the station yesterday; nothing new has happened, everyone waits to see if Gross Sr. will have recommendations submitted which could be grounds for giving up Eva.[70]

The main thing now is establishing Frick's unassailability. Naturally the (unspoken) claim is that he is a kept man [*homme soutenu*], close to anarchism and that is very difficult to counter conclusively, since for years he's lived on Frieda's money.

About seeing Else – I couldn't really do that. (She was only making sure whether I had gone – it's not proper. For years now basic decency [*Ritterlichkeit*] has demanded that she come to me and say, 'Is it so, or was that so?' Since she won't do this for the sake of the comfort of her soul, she will have to take what comfort she can. I won't tax her with this, but I will not respect her anymore....[71]

Please don't let yourself be plagued by superflous women in Berlin, of which there are indeed too many. More tomorrow, for today let yourself be kissed by your Max.

They had the Easter procession here yesterday with Chinese lanterns and pictures of Christ carried and so on. Everything illuminated with lights and lanterns, vivid pictures of the 'annunciation' [*'Verkündigung'*]. On the street in front of the café with a full moon! It was magical.

Ascona, 11.4.1914, Saturday.

Liebstes Mädele,

Many thanks for your letter. I hope mother remains strong over these days and leaves in good spirits for Hanover....That Alfred stays away is most unjust. Had he told me, I would at least have considered whether to come. One would have then said to Arthur, leave everything as it is. To have both of those two together with me – that would have been asking too much.[72]

Here the weather is *magnificent*, so completely different to the 'Culture' of Lake Zurich. The little houses on the green meadows right up to the mountains, creeping into all the smallest crevices, carrying everywhere human hearts with their sorrows and joys, and then in the background the giant mountains. Up there the villages are glued on like a piece of nature, and the people are like them yet also closed, not revealing anything of themselves. This is *also* nice though less human [*'menschlich'*] and without intimacy like a study of a nude, just like Frieda's life – without background, yet not without pride and form.

She asked me yesterday not to say anything about Lang to you. Obviously for his benefit. In any case it would be right if you did keep Lask in the dark, since he repeats everything to her.

The recommendation of the settlement [*Vergleichsvorschlag*] was sent off today to Pellech. 1. The brother from Prague as guardian, and guarantee that Peter enjoys bourgeois schooling, otherwise complete freedom for

Frieda, 2. Money: 200 crowns now, later more according to need. 3. If possible: common petition to annul the marriage on account of madness. 4. Promised: Otto Gross to be freed from internment after cure [*Entwöhnung*].[73] A non-partisan expert agrees to this.

Can it be achieved? Pellech is amazingly industrious and very clever. I must still quickly dictate something, fasting again. Let me kiss you a 1000 times, many greetings to mother, from your Max.

Ascona, 12. & 13.4.1914

Easter Sunday!

Liebes Schnäuzel,

No little letter from you today so far and there probably won't be one now. You really don't need to write daily. I also will only send this short letter, – nothing happens, beautiful weather, rather overcast, *fasting* (in moderation), I eat about a pound of apples a day. Both children are down in the garden searching for eggs. The only event was the visit yesterday of Fräulein Brüstlein the barrister, whom I missed three times in Zurich. A very splendid woman, probably over thirty. Surely was once wonderfully pretty, and still is with brown eyes, beautiful brown hair, and radiating health, businesslike, industrious, humorous – and according to Frieda's estimate far from being a virgin, but not an 'erotomorf'[74] like the crowd [*Volk*] here.

A box arrived yesterday from Lang, also from Lask (Easter delivery) which was taken by Frieda as proof of Lang's petit bourgeois taste: boiled sweets [*Malzbonbons*] and the like and it was happily 'acknowledged' by Frieda with a disrespectful humour, while 'Abel's sacrifice pleased the Lord'. Lask had bought the most wonderful things – a little furry hare, a stuffed duckling, and all sorts of other things. 'Children you have good reason to be thankful to your mother' was the remark which provoked general amusement (Fräulein Brüstlein, Frick and I). Little Peter incidentally is a child with a graphic mind. His definitions of people are wonderful: 'Who was that Peter?' 'That was Gina' (the daughter of Mrs Abbondio) – 'Who is Gina?' – 'The one whose nose runs when she fetches her milk in a jug.' Does one need to know more about a girl?

Yes I certainly have sympathy for Frieda because she has remained the way she is, but I could not breathe for long in this atmosphere. The countess is utterly uninteresting to me. Anyway she has already frittered away ca 8–10,000 francs before the bankruptcy occurred[75] (that's where the clothes come from). Now the need for money is predominant, but Frieda knows from me: there's not one penny.

Early Easter Monday. Your letter just arrived from Charlottenburg. No, it wasn't an act of conquest with Lang but simply the adventure, though he was obviously very pressing. He then immediately disappointed her greatly. I'll take this letter to the post before it closes. Adieu etc. I wrote to mother yesterday,[76]

Ascona, Tuesday, 14.4.1914.

Liebes Schnäuzel,

Although nothing has happened, I am writing today so that you have a letter before you leave Charlottenburg, as far as I know maybe as early as Thursday. Weather is warm, the delta in all its splendour. I sleep with some fasting and rather too much chatter, but bearable. The answer to the action concerning Eva is sent off, again a lengthy piece of writing. Hopefully the last in the correspondence. The old man has called Else as a witness, to say that Frieda had the child extramaritally...

Yesterday, after this was dictated, Frieda had a long conversation with me about lying. She didn't want to see why Else couldn't simply lie as a witness. The 'state' is no 'friend', Prof. Gross an 'enemy'. Therefore both couldn't ask for truthfulness from her and her friends, on which only friends have a claim, no-one else.

I observed to her that I was one of those, who taking this position, would never be sure whether he was the 'friend' he claimed to be. Then she demanded to know whether this was the reason why I remained so aloof from her. I said the reason lay in the experiences with Else. Under certain circumstances I could indeed be fond of erotic women both now and in the future – as she herself must know – but for myself this would never be an inner attachment on which a friendship could develop. Since I'm not an appropriate friend of such women, as I have shown, for whom in truth only the erotic man would have value. I could never rely upon the permanence and certainty of such a strongly subjective perceived sense of camaraderie of such women, since even with the best will every word and feeling would be invalidated at the first test. Now that didn't suit her at all, but that is how it was left.

Her passivity in her own affairs is tiring. She does *nothing* for herself, even simple things (enrolling Peter in school, producing her own witness statements in order to be able to establish a separate domicile here, writing to the brother in Prague) – so that I created a scene and said openly to her: you must do *something* for yourself. Frick always takes my side on this. I've had several individual conversations with him, which are difficult to summarise, and I'll relate them by word of mouth. He is genuinely fine and clever and one can see it more and more. But what is to be gotten out of him –?

Yes obviously, one can only swallow some of this with difficulty in this kind of life (*Lebenswandel*) and Peter isn't being looked after ideally. But I have only just and gradually some picture of the 'principles' of the elder Gross and – to the devil! – and must one say it; also the relationship between Frieda and Otto I now begin to understand slightly. Enough for today – I'll write to Heidelberg unless I receive another address. No letter came today, otherwise I've received everything. 1000 greetings to mother and you, your Max.

Wednesday evening, 15.4.1914,[77] Ascona.

Lieber Schnäuzel,

Nothing new here. I already think of the journey home. Today very early I went on to the delta the sky was overcast with the dark mountains in clouds and in its way unbelievably impressive. The trees are now no longer merely linear, as in Ernst Gundolf's paintings,[78] the meadows are full of flowers: all around there are red peach blossoms and the lilac is beginning to bloom. But behind me the nymph Calypso slipped out of the arched grotto of her palazzo in golden garments. To escape her – for she does not fit in there – I walked faster, went off to the right, then to the left. Finally she must have seen that Odysseus was not to be had, for she turned around: but now she angrily pelted me with a thunderstorm that did not leave a dry stitch on my body, transformed my hat into a tragic mask, and chased me homeward at a gallop. But it was beautiful.

My effect on the countess is, according to Frieda, 'restraining' and 'paralysing'. From my point of view the countess is simply boring and uninteresting. Frieda herself is very talkative and open. Her blonde hair when it's let down is probably terribly 'seductive' for men, it covers her whole back which because of the hairstyle one cannot see. Yesterday she wanted to talk with me about 'erotic women' and Else especially. I realised again how much these two – I have to say it – have lied, also about you and your behaviour and I was not happy. I have only told her only a couple of the most important external events and then remarked: that I had no desire anymore to talk about it, and least of all that others talk to Else about me.

I fast moderately: 2 raw fennel and 4 oranges today, 2 apples and a kilo of oranges yesterday. Oranges without a side dish tomorrow, apples without a side dish Saturday, – then the 'Kur' is finished and then plenty of fodder.

This letter will have to wait till I have your address. It is nice to think that the strain on Mama is now behind her, my letter will have arrived, I don't particularly want to send a telegram.

I'm keen to know how it is going now in Hanover. Have you invited Karl[79] to visit us? Thousand greetings, embracing you dearest girl, from your Max.

Saturday, 18.4.1914, Ascona.

Liebes Schnäuzele,

Tomorrow I travel, so now only a hallo. Nothing new here at the moment, much conversation, difficult to summarise. I can say that it has not led directly to a conclusion and only partly to developments. Peter has joined school today. Likewise the brother in Prague has been written to. Money discussed but in a subdued way. He should become the guardian if a settlement comes about....

Pellech has mobilised Frau Hainisch and her assistant, and has given them the papers and extracted references for the court. You see the whole of the women's movement before the car of Aphrodite.

Don't be eaten up, dearest girl, but come home Monday night with me happy and healthy. Embracing you, your Max.

Heidelberg, 8.5.1915.

Lieber Schnäuzel,

So you see goodness and right and innocence triumph and all because of the appeal court judge (Senatspräsident) Lang.[80] That we appeared to others as subsidiary and blinkered, and as a result were not even taken into consideration when calling witnesses, is, given the circumstances understandable, and not insulting, if somewhat amusing. So, Frieda can be pleased. Now the case is really won.

NOTES

1. *GStA, Nachlass* Max Weber, Rep. 92, Nr 30, Bd.2, Bl. pp. 1–39. My thanks to Anthea Conreen and Klaus Friedrich for their indispensable help in translating the letters. I have retained much of the punctuation and form of the letters, which Marianne had transcribed for her selective use in her biography, rather than attempt to render them in fully formed sentences. The originals are in the Bavarian State Library. Birgit Rudhard in Heidelberg very kindly went over the translation with me and demonstrated the fallibility of some of my initial interpretations. The letters are one side of a private correspondence. Even after many readings some passages still remain perplexing.
2. Max's familiar address to Marianne. Literally it means little pig's snout.
3. Signor Giovanni Abbondio.
4. Marie Bernays was in 1906 one of the first women students admitted to the University of Heidelberg. She worked with Alfred and Max Weber on the Verein für Sozialpolitik's 1908 study on selection and suitability of the workforce in the mass production industries.
5. Eldest son (b. 1886) of the Heidelberg historian Eberhard Gothein. He was living in Peking at the time.
6. Familiar diminutive for Mädchen, i.e., Marianne.
7. Family home of Marianne's grandfather Karl Weber. They became engaged on 23rd March 1893 and went to Oerlinghausen to seek permission to marry. Max then went off to Strasbourg to visit his aunt Ida Baumgarten and also visited relatives in Heidelberg (Marianne Weber, *Max Weber. A Biography*, 1988: pp. 180–1).
8. Frieda Gross.
9. The countess is Franziska zu Reventlow, whose father-in-law was Baron von Rechenberg-Linten; see Introduction.
10. Marie Bernays.
11. A novel by Carlo Philipps, *Die fünf Stationen des Leidens* (Heidelberg: Richard Weissbach, 1811).
12. The father was Otto Gross, the son Peter.
13. Ernst Frick.
14. Frick had been jailed in 1912 (30 November) for involvement in terrorist offences; see Introduction.
15. Edgar Jaffé, economist and Weber's co-editor of the *Archiv für Sozialwissenschaft und Sozialpolitik*.
16. Mario Respini-Orelli. See B. Kubitschek, *Franziska Gräfin zu Reventlow. 1871–1918* (Chiemsee: Kubitschek, 1994), p. 442.
17. Erich Mühsam also claimed the idea as his, see *Marbacher Magazin*, 8, 1978, p.15.
18. A very formal manner of addressing each other. After the wedding Reventlow was on 'Du' terms with her father-in-law but 'Sie' with her husband, much to the former's puzzlement.
19. The countess already had a son, Rolf (b. 1.9.1897). She never revealed who the father was.
20. Elise Höller was Frieda's maid.
21. C. G. Jung analysed Otto Gross in May-June 1908 at the Burghölzli clinic in Zurich. He concluded that Otto Gross was suffering from dementia praecox

and informed Frieda. Eugen Bleuler, the director of the Burghölzli, later re-conceptualised dementia praecox as schizophrenia. See Introduction.

22. Hans Gruhle, a Heidelberg psychiatrist and a friend of the Webers. He was part of Reventlow's group and lived in Schwabing when he studied medicine in Munich from 1901–6. There he completed his dissertation under Professor Emil Kraepelin before moving to a post at the University Clinic in Heidelberg. Otto and Frieda Gross moved to Munich's Schwabing in 1905, and in spring 1907 they stayed with the Jaffés in Heidelberg.

23. *Herrn Dames Aufzeichnungen oder Begebenheiten aus einem merkwürdigen Stadtteil*, Munich: Albert Langen, 1913.

24. First published in 1909. The Tobelkind is Mina Tobler.

25. Charles-Louis Philippe, *Marie Donadieu*, Paris: Fasquelle, 1904. 'The story of a complicated *menage à trois*' notes Harry Zohn (Marianne Weber, op. cit. 1988: p. 488, n.16.)

26. A dance hall in Paris, infamous for its dancing: cancan, Argentinian tango and Brazilian maxixe. Painted by Renoir in 1876, Toulouse-Lautrec in 1890, and Picasso in 1900, and portrayed variously as bourgeois, working class and as possessing an erotic ambiance. Max and Marianne visited Paris in 1911 (Marianne Weber, op. cit. 1988: p. 501).

27. G. Lukács, *Die Seele und die Formen. Essays*, Berlin: Egon Fleischel, 1911.

28. See note 22. Reventlow had spent the best part of 1912 writing the novel in Ascona. It was a humorous exposé of the 'New Age' antics of Schwabing. Weber's airy dismissal of this work is something of a disappointment but not unexpected. The novel had an extended exposition of the 'Kosmiker's' critique of Protestantism. (The Kosmiker were a clique of aesthetes whose leader was the poet Stefan George.)

29. Ernst Bloch was especially prone to the apocalyptic during this part of his life in Heidelberg. Karl Jaspers was a friend of the Webers and a psychiatrist and philosopher.

30. Else's marriage to Edgar had become a marriage of convenience, certainly from 1910 onwards when she conducted a longlasting affair with Alfred Weber. Also in a letter from Max to Marianne, 11.3.10, Max recounts that Else could not physically stand her husband (MWG, II/6, *Die Briefe 1909–1910*, pp. 426–7).

31. Hans Gross followed through with these threats in December, 1913. They become a major theme of Weber's letters in 1914.

32. The Countess Franziska zu Reventlow and her 'husband' Rechenberg.

33. Frieda Gross was sent away to school – to the Institute Blas in Freiburg, close to the university. After Frieda's mother died (when Frieda was still a young child), she was looked after by her aunt, Sophie Riehl, who was married to Alois Riehl, professor of philosophy at the University of Freiburg. See Introduction.

34. Otto Lang was a Swiss politician and lawyer whose role was revealed in 1914, see below, note 69.

35. Quattrinis where Weber ate.

36. The proposal would have conferred residency rights for those living with, but unmarried to, Swiss nationals. Frieda, having an Austrian and Catholic marriage would have been unable to obtain a divorce from Otto, and Frick was a Swiss national.

37. Tobelchen is Mina Tobler.
38. A sort of very sweet cake.
39. Otto Lang.
40 It was Max's 49th birthday.
41. German plays off *'aufgegeben'* against *'gegeben'*. Weber is using a Kantian terminology of values that contrasts values which can be objectively given to us (*gegeben*) and those which are posited (*aufgegeben*) and open to evaluation. Marianne has to interpret Weber's response through the neo-Kantian debates on the validity of values.
42. Erotomorf – i.e. physically attractive. Reventlow's *Tagebücher* indicate that Hans Gruhle was a close and supportive friend whom she missed when he moved from Munich to Heidelberg. See also Kubitschek, op. cit. pp. 389–94.
43. Sophie Riehl.
44. i.e. Frieda had gone round to Schulze-Gävernitz's rooms and had found out what Sophie Riehl had written about her to Schulze-Gävernitz's mother. Gerhart Schulze-Gävernitz (b. 25.7.1864) was professor of national economy in Freiburg from 1893 until 1923.
45. Dr Raphael Friedeberg was a supporter of Frieda during her various difficulties. See Introduction.
46. Marianne has accompanied Max to Ascona and had then travelled back to Freiburg, staying with Sophie and Heinrich Rickert, before returning to Heidelberg.
47. As part of his case Otto Pellech submitted *Frauenbewegung und Sexualethik*, ed. Helene Lang (Heilbronn, 1909), which contained an essay by Marianne Weber. See Guenther Roth, 'Marianne Weber and her Circle' Introduction to the Transaction Edition of *Max Weber. A Biography*, Marianne Weber. Dr Otto Pellech was the Viennese lawyer employed by Frieda Gross.
48. Alois Riehl (27.4.1844–21.11.1924) was Frieda's uncle and professor of philosophy at Freiburg from 1892. Eberhard Gothein (29.10.1853–13.11.1923) was professor of national economy at Heidelberg. Heinrich Rosin (b. 1855) was an authority on administrative and insurance law. Friedrich Endemann (24.5.1857–31.10.1936) was professor of Roman and Civil Law at Heidelberg.
49. Hans Gross pursued his legal actions through the Austrian provincial court at Graz, the home town of Otto and Frieda.
50 This is now a commonly used Freudian term; for example – the overvaluing of the ego in the case of narcissism, see Charles Rycroft, *A Critical Dictionary of Psychoanalysis*, Penguin: 1968, p. 94. Otto Gross in his 1904 *Zur Differentialdiagnostik negativischer Phänomene* pointed out that both Freud and Wernicke were using the term in similar ways (E. Hurwitz, *Otto Gross. Paradies-Sucher zwischen Freud und Jung* Frankfurt: Suhrkamp, 1988: pp. 74–5). Frick's psychological state does not enable him to associate sense data in a normal way; the overvaluing of one stimulus becomes a form of dissociation (Sejunktion).
51. Weber refers to Reventlow's son, Rolf (b.1897), who was facing national service in Germany. It was still three and a half months before the outbreak of the Great War. The Countess achieved international celebrity in 1916

when she avoided frontier guards and rowed her son across Lake Constance to neutral Switzerland.

52. Otto Lang, a Zurich appeal court judge and politician. See note 69 below.
53. Professor Heinrich S. Sieveking (20.8.1871–25.12.1945), doctor of law and professor of national economy at Zurich from 1907. A student of Weber's at Freiburg, and later a contributor to the *Grundriss der Sozialökonomik*.
54. Steckbrief is a 'wanted' man poster.
55. Peterle is a love struck youth in a popular song.
56. Emil Lask (25.9.1875–26.5.1915) lectured in philosophy at Heidelberg from 1905. Frieda and Lask had a romance in 1908, but the two had not met since 1910. Lask funded Frieda's court cases. See Introduction.
57. Eva's father was Ernst Frick. Otto had agreed to declare Eva a legitimate child of his marriage with Frieda (Letter, Frieda Gross to Else Jaffé, 6 August 1911). Hans Gross knew Frick was the father. Hans's aim at this point was to threaten a legal declaration of Eva's illegitimacy in order to force Frieda to give up Peter to a guardian who would guarantee that Peter was brought up and educated in a 'proper' environment. See Hurwitz, op. cit., pp. 227–9 where the correspondence about Peter Gross between Hans Gross and the Zurich state prosecutor is quoted. Gättli, the prosecutor, refers to Peter as a 'psychisch belastete Kind.'
58. Franz Jung, the writer and anarchist, in whose flat Otto Gross was seized by the Prussian police in December 1913, argued that this was the main reason why Hans Gross wanted guardianship over his son. Gross's work of this period was published by the Berlin anarchist paper *Die Aktion*. He argued that repression of emotions and sexuality, a particular problem for women, was caused by the patriarchal structure of society whose origin lay in the child's upbringing within the family. Marriage was based on the forcible violation of the wife by the husband and the denial of any sexually emotional attachment of parents to their children. As a baby and young child Otto slept in his parents' bedroom. See Jennifer Michels, *Anarchy and Eros*, (New York: Peter Lang, 1983), pp. 40–3, and E. Hurwitz, op. cit., pp. 60ff.
59. A short story 'On the Poverty of the Spirit' published in 1912. See Edith Hanke, below, Chapter 7.
60. Helene Weber's 70th birthday. Max stayed in Ascona.
61. A reference to his fabrication of a report to excuse the Countess's son from conscription, see above 1.4.14.
62. Ernst Troeltsch, theologian and professor of philosophy at Heidelberg.
63. Elsa and Hans Ott, the sister and brother-in-law of Mina Tobler.
64. Eugen Bleuler, psychiatrist and Director of the Burghölzli Clinic in Zurich. It was at the Burghölzli that Jung psychoanalysed Otto Gross and attempted to cure him of his dementia praecox. But here Weber is visiting Bleuler to enlist him as a character witness for Frieda Gross.
65. Margarethe Faas-Hardegger and Raphael Friedeberg were charged for perjury at Frick's trial in 1912; see Harald Szeemann, ed., *Monte Verita*, 1978, p. 34.
66. This letter is added on to the previous letter of the day before.
67. Ascona.
68. Mina Tobler.

69. Otto Lang was an appeal court judge in Zurich. Frick was tried in June 1912 for some anarchist offence – probably the de-railing of a tram. He was acquitted but then re-arrested when the prosecution took the case to appeal. The appeal court dismissed the case. This is the most likely involvement of Lang. (Frick was subsequently re-arrested again by the federal prosecutor, allegedly for looking after a bomb that was used in the attack on the police station in Zurich in 1907. It was for this offence he was given a year's imprisonment at a trial in November 1912. These cases were the main subject in Frieda Gross's letters to Else Jaffé in 1912.) Weber's 'mission' to Lang was to obtain a character reference for Frieda, who had failed to inform Max of her romance with Lang.

70. Refers to the surrendering of the claim to Eva's legitimacy. To do this would mean Eva would be excluded from any will of Hans Gross, as she subsequently was.

71. Alfred had lied to Else about Max, so Max believed.

72. Alfred and Arthur are Max's younger brothers. His mother had gone to stay with the third brother, Karl, in Hanover.

73. Otto Gross was still detained in an asylum in Troppau by his father who had acquired legal guardianship over his son in January 1914. The cure was for drug addiction.

74. See above, 21.4.13.

75. Reventlow and Rechenberg had entered into a sham marriage, whereupon the father-in-law was to adjust his will to include his son. Only a certain amount of money came to Reventlow from this deception, which was deposited in a Swiss bank (Credito Ticino) that subsequently went bankrupt. Reventlow wrote a novel about the experience, *Der Hochstapler*.

76. See Marianne Weber, op. cit., 1988: pp. 513–6.

77. The envelope is stamped 14.4.1914.

78. Artist and poet (born 1881 died 1945), brother of Friedrich Gundolf.

79. One of Weber's younger brothers.

80. A year later and Frieda's suitability as a mother has been established and Weber's mission to Lang proves to have been crucial. Lang's character reference stated that Frieda 'had in all matters an unusual grasp of the psychology of the child [*für die kindliche Psyche an den Tag*]' and that the fears of Hans Gross were without foundation [*der Bergrundetheit entbehren*] (Hurwitz, op. cit., 1988: p. 229). Frieda lost the case on Eva's paternity in March 1916, when Hans took the case to appeal. When asked in court whether she was enjoying conjugal relations with Otto she would reply only that, 'I foster very happy close relations with my husband'. Frieda's maid Lisi testified that in the period in question Otto and Frieda slept apart.

Hans Gross died in December 1915. Otto managed to have the order of guardianship over him withdrawn in September 1917. Otto died of pneumonia, a destitute in Berlin in February 1920. Frieda Gross had another child, Cornelia, with Frick, who later left her to live with Margarete Fellerer. Frieda Gross remained in Tessin and died in 1950. She kept up her correspondence with Else Jaffé, whom she loved dearly.

3 Weber and Lawrence and Anarchism

Martin Green

My idea of Max Weber was shaped by the way I encountered him in writing the story of the von Richthofen sisters; and one aspect of that shaping was his being paired contrastively with D. H. Lawrence. In consequence I saw Weber's work from an oblique angle; nor did I ever know it as thoroughly as did the other people attending the 1995 Max Weber (British Sociological Association) conference. I was well aware, when I published *The von Richthofen Sisters* that I was not a Weber scholar, and not surprised that there *were* reviewers who found the book lacking in scholarly decorum.

However, recent books about both of these men have begun to pay some attention to the connection between them, and between each of them and Otto Gross. (Gross was the psychoanalyst and erotic liberator who was a strong influence on both Else and Frieda von Richthofen.) It is now tacitly admitted that a great deal has been covered up about both Weber and Lawrence – partly in the process of covering up Gross.

Before *The von Richthofen Sisters* was published (in 1974)[1] and for some time after, such connections were treated as trivial or merely romantic in their interest. But now Gross himself seems a substantial figure in cultural history; not, for various reasons, built on the same scale as his antagonists, Weber and Lawrence; but not to be dismissed as a pigmy. When I was invited to attend this conference, moreover, I realised that my thoughts had been turning back of late towards Weber – and Lawrence – though again from an apparently tangential point of view. My line of thought has carried me further into the recurrent phenomena of New Ages, especially in the linked fields of anarchism and pacifism. In the first of which, in the New Age of 1880–1914, the one which Weber and Lawrence knew, Gross was a considerable figure. And in the second, pacifism, the largest figure was Tolstoy. (His disciple, Gandhi, did not come into the general European view until the 1920s.) This was not Tolstoy the great erotic novelist, but the late Tolstoy, the Christian radical pacifist. For both Weber and Lawrence, that Tolstoy was a representative man.

So it seemed to me that I could best serve the conf
declaring my present interest, and discussing Weber
relation to various forms of radicalism, especially pac'
some extent, though not exclusively, embodied in Ot.

It will perhaps be more stimulating, though of course risк,
Gross's anarchism rather than his radicalism. But I must go on iïïu.
ately to say which kind of anarchism I mean. Of the two main kinds, one
was usually associated with Max Stirner at the level of theory, and with
terrorism at the level of practice. It was essentially violent, and engaged
often in assassination – anarchist and terrorist were often used as inter-
changeable terms. The other kind is usually associated with Kropotkin and
Tolstoy, and in the next generation with Gandhi. The theory of this kind of
ethical anarchism, sometimes called village anarchism, recommends agri-
culture, small communities, distrust of the state, and peace. The two kinds
must be seen as very different conceptually, but in individual anarchists –
and Gross is a good example – they often came blended or confused, as
we shall see.

It was of course the second or ethical anarchism which constituted a
challenge to Weber and Lawrence; because it seemed to them both attractive and dangerous. Whereas, insofar as the anarchist was a terrorist, he
ceased to interest them seriously.

In any case, the most important anarchist community for Gross and
therefore for Weber and Lawrence – its members so loosely bound
together as scarcely to deserve the name community –was Ascona, a
fishing village on the Swiss shore of Lago Maggiore, where cultural
radicals of various kinds, many of them Tolstoyans, gathered in the
period 1900 to 1920. In Ascona the ethical anarchists far outnumbered
the terrorists.

I have described Ascona in some detail in *Mountain of Truth* (1986).[2]
Here I will characterise it simply as a place where Otto Gross was
influential – as *his* kind of place – *his* place. The challenge Weber and
Lawrence met was embodied in the place – an innocently erotic Eden – as
much as in the man. In fact, in the year 1913, when the challenge was
especially acute for both men, Gross did not live there in any ordinary
sense; he did not own property or make any extended stay. But his wife
Frieda, his son, Peter, and his friend Ernst Frick, also a professed anarchist, were all to be found there. So were many others of his patients and
disciples, intermittently.

Frick had been involved in acts of terrorism in Zurich in 1907 and 1908;
and spoke of intending to blow up the whole bourgeois world.[3] Gross
himself spoke of wanting to end his life, perhaps when he was forty five

rs old, by assassinating some public prosecutor, if one was then indict-
ng Gross's anarchist comrades. (Gross made this declaration to the
doctors who examined him in 1913: a few years later, to other doctors, he
repudiated most of those confessions as romantic foolishness; records of
both examinations are to be found in the Landesarchiv, Graz.)

Such remarks would seem to show that both Gross and Frick belonged
to the first or violent branch of anarchism. But those who knew both men
disregarded their rhetoric, and described Gross and Frick as unusually
gentle and refined, and as quite inept in the practice of violence. Frieda
Lawrence, for instance, said Frick would not hurt a fly.[4] Ludwig Rubiner –
who argued with Gross over psychoanalysis – said that Gross felt his
whole calling was to drive suffering out of the world.[5] In *Sophie*, Franz
Jung depicted Sophie Benz telling Gross, 'You always want to help
people'.[6] So it is only superficially a paradox to pay attention to Gross and
Frick's traits of ethical anarchism.

Certainly Weber and Lawrence thought of Gross and Frick both as
unworldly idealists. Gross in particular was extravagantly selfless. He
gave away his money and his clothes, suffered with animals' and other
people's sufferings, devoted his whole life to his patients. He and Frick
were unable to tolerate the ordinary violence that we now call institutional.
To cite one of Gross's favourite authors, he was – seen from this angle –
another Prince Myshkin, in Dostoyevsky's *The Idiot*.

Thus Weber and Lawrence included forms of violence within their own
intentions, their own idea of virtue, and their idea of the state. Implicitly
they reproached Gross and Frick for not doing the same: they thought
men, if not women, must engage in violence on occasion, without an emotional crisis – though not, of course, without due reluctance. Gross and
Frick on occasion said similar things themselves. But – much more than
Lawrence and Weber – Gross's identity began in a profound rebellion
against the 'necessary' violence of the state; as embodied in, for instance,
respectable figures like his father.

Professor Hans Gross was a criminologist, and managed to identify
himself generally with the punishing function of society. He recommended, for instance, introducing the life-long deportation of Austrian
criminals to penal colonies. He was in fact the man who both modernised
criminology, and established it as an academic subject in the universities
of Austro-Hungary. He was also an authoritarian personality, and his only
son rebelled against him from early on and in extreme ways.

Otto Gross understood his own nervous problems in Freudian terms, as
deriving from his father's treatment of him. (Otto was for some years considered to be one of the most promising young members of the Freudian

movement.) Hans therefore seemed to many people an embodiment of patriarchal German manliness, and of the iron cage of the modernising nation-state. Otto on the other hand embodied the opposite historical tendencies – in a defiant espousal of *Mutterrecht* and anarchism. Such terms, however, are bound to suggest political theory and the history of ideas in the narrow sense, and so are not well suited to Gross and Frick. It is better on the whole to speak rather of the New Age life-style which they practised. What challenged Weber and Lawrence was not so much Gross's theories as the emotional enthusiasm, and the dramatic fate, of individuals like himself, Frick, and Frieda Gross; plus the power of these three over Else von Richthofen Jaffé and her sister, Frieda von Richthofen Weekley; women who were in their turn powerful over Weber and Lawrence.

I have discussed the relations between Else Jaffé and Weber, and those between Frieda Weekley and Lawrence; relations which had many dimensions, including the moral and intellectual. Above all, Otto Gross had been important to each woman's developing sense of self, especially in matters to do with erotic love.

Within ethical or village anarchism one can distinguish again two main tendencies. Some anarchists invested their main energies in peace, others in love – in erotic freedom. Clearly the second of the two was responsible for the fame, or scandal, that surrounded Gross and Ascona. But the first is not to be forgotten, despite its divergence from and conflict with the erotic. Pacifism was to be associated with Tolstoy, and he was one of those who most powerfully inspired the founders of Ascona, at the very end of the 19th century. Tolstoy's anarchism was positively anti-erotic. Having been one of the great erotic writers, he had turned away, towards an ascetic radicalism.

When he underwent his great change of heart, around 1881, at the beginning of the New Age, Tolstoy repudiated the message of eroticism carried by his great novels, as so much deceitful glamour. What was so wonderful about *Anna Karenina*? he asked: it was just another Guards officer having an affair with a married woman. (That was the kind of remark Lawrence could never forgive him.) Tolstoy went on to invest his energies in pacifist causes like opposing military conscription, and saving the Doukhobors, a Christian sect in Russia persecuted by the government because they refused to serve in the army. He wore a peasant blouse, ploughed and reaped with the peasants, and did his best to renounce all his privileges, as a noble and as an artist.

On the whole, the erotic branch of ethical anarchism became the stronger of the two among intellectuals after Tolstoy died, in 1910. The political kinds of anarchism – obviously the violent but also the nonviolent forms thereof – lost their power with that constituency. But there were exceptions. Gustav Landauer, another socialist-anarchist remained loyal to Tolstoy and engaged Gross in controversy, because of the latter's ideas of erotic liberation, between 1911 and 1913. Indeed, Landauer tarred all the varieties of psychoanalysis with that same brush, of erotic licence. Landauer's ideas – designed to help establish peaceful small communities – reached the kibbutzim of Israel via his friend Martin Buber. (And via Gandhi, those same pacifist and ascetic ideas of Tolstoy's also reached the Indian nationalist movement.)

Ascona was a place of refuge for men who avoided military service in their native countries, and boasted of doing so. The most picturesque example was the *Naturmensch*, Gusto Gräser, who had gone to jail for his beliefs. But conscientious objection does not seem to have been a major theme of life in Ascona. So it will be best to discuss attitudes to pacifism in a different context.

Pacifism

Radical pacifism at that time came sponsored (half-heartedly) by the Protestant churches and still less energetically by Roman Catholicism. The former engaged more of Weber's, and Lawrence's, attention, and was part of what was called, at least in America, the Social Gospel movement. (The comparable, and related, movements in England and Germany were sometimes called the Nonconformist Conscience, and the *Inner Mission*, the Home Mission.) The Social Gospel had success for instance in 1908 in America, when the Federal Council of the Churches of Christ was formed, and adopted a Social Creed, which approved Trade Unions, and protective legislation for workers, and the guarantee of workers' holidays. It was allied at several points to the new social sciences – as was the *Inner Mission*, which interested Weber.

Walter Rauschenbusch, a Baptist minister, was the member of the American movement who took most seriously the peace cause. He took the risk of leading his Social Gospel allies towards peace, against the tide of patriotic anger which swelled up when America entered the war. In 1917 he published *A Theology for the Social Gospel*, in which he wrote, 'The Great War has dwarfed and submerged all other issues, including our social problems. But in fact the War is the most acute and tremendous social problem of all... the social gospel is now being translated into international terms'. The study of peace of course led to the investigation of the causes of war, and of issues like disarmament and the rights of small nations.[7]

Weber was concerned with the Inner Mission in Germany via family members like his mother and his wife. He scorned German militarism but his appraisal of pacifism was equally abrasive. Thus he wrote to Heinrich Rickert in 1908, 'Many thanks for sending me Schmidt's political music on a toy trumpet. A horrible, nauseating sound.... *This* is how the Germans are and *that* is what they call politics'.[8] But this did not mean he was a pacifist – almost the opposite.

On the next page of Marianne Weber's biography we find him saying: 'Even with the strongest armaments we *cannot conscientiously risk* a European war *for as long as* we must expect that the leadership of our army would be interfered with by a crowned dilettante who – in diplomacy as on the field of honor – would botch *everything*. All sorts of emotional factors... are preventing this rage, which is basically justified, from being directed against the *right person*.'[9]

Quite apart from the issues that involved him, it is clear that Weber valued and cultivated a personal aura of hearty emotional force. One would guess that, because of the bitter conflict between his parents, he tried to be more forceful than his father – and men like him – in order to protect his mother's vulnerability. As a young man, he joined a student fraternity, and took part in the drinking and duelling that went with that. Pacifism would have to be a very ambiguous value for him.

In England, a generation later, Lawrence developed a comparable ambiguity about violence, and a comparable need to exert authority in self-defence. Lawrence, primarily, tried to exert that authority in domestic situations, with Frieda; Weber's field of action was politics. (The chapter of the biography just cited is called 'Activity in the World and Controversies'.) But in the contrast they make with Otto Gross, who seems not to have felt that need, Weber and Lawrence look somewhat alike.

The values and interests Lawrence learned from and with his mother at their chapel, and her Women's Cooperative Society, were Protestant and progressivist and sympathetic to the Social Gospel (not unlike Frau Weber's interests). For the Cooperative Society she wrote a paper, apparently of some length, on Robert Owen's social theories, which means a New Age and Social Gospel orientation, and a feeling for peace. But what Lawrence learned by experience as a timid boy growing up in a rough neighborhood, gave him strong but confused feelings about violence, and so about war.

In his autobiographical *Sons and Lovers* the theme of violence is subterranean, but very strong. It begins with the violence between Mr and Mrs Morel, who, without hitting each other, would shout, bang on the table, knock things over, to express anger at each other. One of the worst of these scenes occurs when the mother is pregnant with the child who will become the author. It ends with the father pushing the mother out of the house and locking the door.

She walked down the garden path, 'trembling in every limb, while the child boiled within her.'[10] When the baby is born, he has a 'peculiar knitting of the brows and heaviness of the eyes... trying to understand something that was pain.'[11] Foreseeing a difficult life for him, the mother offers her son back to God, lifting him up in her arms towards a splendid sunset.

Another quarrel between the parents leads to the mother receiving a cut on the head, and a baptismal drop of her blood falls on the baby's head. The symbols thus indicate that the child is being sensitised to violence. And he grows up hypersensitive to it, fearful of it, but attracted to it.

When he has quite accidentally broken his sister's doll, he insists on completely destroying it. He feels so guilty and hates the doll so intensely, that he builds a fire and burns it as a sacrifice.[12] His fearfulness also expresses itself in social terms. We are told he suffers the tortures of the damned when he goes to pick up his father's wages.

When the Morel family moves to a new house, it has a huge old ash-tree in front of it, which bends and shrieks when the wind is strong. The children hate this noise. 'Having such a great space in front of the house gave the children a feeling of night, of vastness, and of terror. This terror came in from the shrieking of the tree and the anguish of the home discord.... Then he heard the booming shouts of his father, coming home nearly drunk...'[13] And among the effects this has on the boy is that he sees his mother as his saviour from the father's violence. This is as powerful as the Oedipus complex in explaining his close link to her.

The mother, and the oldest child, William, are strong and fierce personalities; the word fierce is often used about William, to mean fiery and attractive. Paul is lovingly subject to both of them, feeling himself, by comparison, hyper-sensitive, maladjusted to the outside world, and a potential victim.

And his first girl-friend, Miriam Leivers, is someone even more timid and sensitive than he. This is obviously part of her attraction for him. But we are told that he also easily hated her, because she claimed him as someone like herself, nervous and insecure.

This theme of violence – which causes timidity, which in turn causes a fear of other people's suffering, which in turn causes resentment and hatred of them – runs through the whole book; indeed, through Lawrence's whole life. In the title essay of the collection, *The Death of a Porcupine*, he describes an incident from the 1920s. This anecdote focuses on his *causing* suffering – indeed death. Called on to kill a wild creature on his ranch in New Mexico, Lawrence was very reluctant. He appealed to his wife, Should he shoot the porcupine? She hesitated and said yes, 'with a sort of disgust'. 'I went back to the house, and got the little twenty two rifle. Now never in my life had I shot at any living thing: I never wanted to. I always felt guns very repugnant: sinister, mean. With difficulty I had fired once or twice at a target: but resented doing even so much. Other people could shoot if they wanted to.'[14]

We should not, I think, believe that other weapons were radically different from guns for Lawrence. In *Sons and Lovers*, Paul Morel is in danger of attack, and friends persuade him to carry a weapon, but he finds himself unable to use one or fight.[15]

Here at least the gun was to be his weapon. He tells us that by this time 'something had hardened in my soul', so that he was ready to kill; so he loaded the rifle – 'with rather trembling hands'. His bullet hit the animal but did not kill it, and so he finished it off with a blow with a stick. 'And in the moonlight, looked down on the first creature I had ever shot. "Does it seem mean?" I asked aloud, doubtful. Again Madame hesitated. Then: "No!" she said resentfully.'[16]

We notice the key words mean and resentful. Mean signals that it is a noble and Nietzschean morality Lawrence and his wife were aspiring to; while resentful – contrariwise – applies to the way they have to egg each other on. Despite their belief in violence, it goes against the grain, for both of them, to engage in it.

This theme is related to Lawrence's crucial experience of Germany. Lawrence and Frieda went to Bavaria when they left England in 1912, and he was deeply impressed by a peasant culture which seemed to him pre-Enlightenment – a culture in which behaviour and emotion derived directly from 'the unconscious'. One of his first essays was 'Christs in the Tirol', which he later adapted to be the first chapter of *Twilight in Italy*. He interprets the art of Bavarian wayside crucifixes as expressing fear and cruelty, in both makers and worshippers, but it is implicit that he admires and envies that peasant culture as something violent, strong, and authentic. (For Weber, Christianity meant something much closer to the Social Gospel.)

Both these Christs and the men who carved them were *afraid*, Lawrence thinks – with a generalised and dominant fear that was alien to the Protestant and Enlightened Englishman, D. H. Lawrence. 'They all, when they carved or erected these crucifixes, had fear at the bottom of their hearts. And so the monuments to physical pain are found everywhere in the mountain gloom.'[17]

The experience of the 1914–18 war was of course a tremendous defeat for pacifism and reinforcement of anxiety, for the countries on both sides. In 1918 Walter Rauschenbusch died of a broken heart, according to his biographer, because of the hostility he encountered from patriotic neighbours and former friends. And after 1918 intellectuals generally turned against that kind of idealism.

In 1911 Weber had intervened in a controversy in Freiburg, when an academic called pacifists silly and sentimental, and a general impugned their virility. Weber was quite uncompromising: 'In "ethics" the pacifists are undoubtedly "superior" to us .... [But] I very deliberately emphasised that politics is not and can never be a profession with a moral foundation.'[18]

He respected the position of pacifists – provided they were ready to go to their deaths for it – but insisted that 'we' must not imagine that we are pacifists ourselves. In a famous letter of 1917 he spoke of Tolstoyan nonresistance as compatible only with the life-style of St Francis, or an Indian monk, or a Russian narodnik. Only this – which is clearly out of 'our' range – would be impressive. 'Anything else is fraud and self-deception.'[19]

His attitude to the other kind of New Age, the erotic and matriarchal anarchism, was much the same. In September 1907 Otto Gross submitted an article on matriarchy to Weber's *Archiv*, but Weber rejected it summarily, as an attempt to combine the Nietzschean ethic with objective, value-free, scholarship. And in 1913 Weber argued with Frick over the '*Acosmos der Erotik*', the unworldliness of the erotic. The idea of unworldliness is usually equated with religion; but here Weber extends its reference.

D. H. Lawrence never visited Ascona, but he was living with Frieda Weekley in the climactic years of Gross's tragic story, and of Weber's involvement with Frieda Gross, the years 1912 to 1914. Such a partnership must have been at least as challenging an experience as Weber's time in Ascona, and must have made Lawrence think strenuously about Gross. Frieda Weekley had described Lawrence to her sisters and friends as a man *like* Gross and Frick; and he obviously felt some pressure to measure up to them.

We should try also to imagine the 'experience' mediated to Weber via the other von Richthofen sister. Quite apart from his love for Else Jaffé, Otto's son by Else, Peter Jaffé, was Weber's godson; and the two mothers (Else Jaffé and Frieda Gross) saw the two boys as brothers; while Max and Marianne were unhappily childless. Edgar Jaffé was Peter's legal father, Otto Gross the biological father, Max Weber the would-be father.

Not long before the outbreak of war, Lawrence walked his way alone across Italy and Switzerland, and stayed briefly in Locarno in 1914, which was walking distance from Ascona. Gross had recently been arrested, examined and found mad, and deprived of his children. Weber had recently stayed in Ascona – and taken a vigorous part in defending Frieda Gross against Hans Gross's attacks. Lawrence never mentioned the Grosses in his letters (those that have survived) but *Twilight in Italy* betrays how acutely conscious he naturally was of the connection between himself and the other man.

Talking to strangers, he identified himself as a peripatetic doctor from Graz – in other words, as Otto Gross. And when he met a group of anarchist workmen in an inn, and they expounded their political ideas to him, he could not, he says, give them the sympathetic assent they wanted from him, because he saw that they were 'idealistic'. Both he and Weber can be seen circling around Ascona and the absent figure of Gross with their minds.

Max Weber's letters from Ascona, written to his wife, show us how complex and powerful his feelings about the place, and the idea of the place, had become. In the spring of 1914 (as in the spring of 1913) he wrote home assiduously, about the Asconans and their ideas. Thus on 9 April 1914, he wrote from Zurich, 'Now is time to return "home" [that is, to Ascona] if one can so call this world full of enchantresses, grace, danger, and desire for happiness ... an oasis of purity – one cannot really describe it differently' (See 'Letters from Ascona', in this volume).

This purity was not what one would ordinarily call moral; but perhaps it was spiritual: that is, disciplined by a higher standard of sincerity and authenticity in emotion than Max and Marianne were able to live up to in Heidelberg.

Among those enchantresses the principal one was of course Friedele Gross, by general agreement a beautiful woman, with long blonde hair that hung far down her back. In her *Memoirs*, Frieda Lawrence described her as 'like an archaic Roman figure. She had the most astonishing, fine, honey-coloured hair.'[20] Even Weber's more satirical comments, on her flimsy scarves, peppered with cigarette burns, betray his fascination with her Bohemian freedoms. But Ascona meant more than that particular attraction to Weber. As his stay drew to a close he wrote more than once about the landscape and the Asconans.

On 11 April 1914, he wrote 'Here the weather is *magnificent*, so completely different from the "culture" of Lake Zurich'. He finds the Ascona landscape 'less human [*menschlich*] and without intimacy, like a study of a nude, just like Frieda's life – without background, yet not without pride and form'. What strange ambiguities resonate in that word, 'a nude'!

Weber had once or twice in these letters to Marianne depicted himself as being, in Ascona and elsewhere, like Odysseus on his wanderings: 'a castaway in a fairytale world'. In one of the last letters, dated the fifteenth of

April, he describes walking among Ascona's lilacs and peach blossoms: 'But behind me the nymph Calypso slipped out of the arched grotto of her palazzo in golden garments.... Finally she must have seen that Odysseus was not to be had, for she turned around: but now she angrily pelted me with a thunderstorm that did not leave a dry stitch on my body, transformed my hat into a tragic mask, and chased me homewards at a gallop. But it was beautiful.'

We need Otto Gross's commentary here too. One can read this fantasy in a number of ways, but one of them must surely be that Weber was acknowledging the power of the idea he found in Ascona – its power over him, the man of Heidelberg.

NOTES

1. Martin Green, *The von Richthofen Sisters. The Triumphant and the Tragic Modes of Love*, 2nd ed., (Albuquerque: University of New Mexico Press, 1988).
2. Martin Green, *Mountain of Truth. The Counterculture Begins. Ascona, 1900–1920* (Hanover and London: University Press of New England, 1986).
3. Richard Seewald, *Der Mann von Gegenüber* (Munich: List, 1963).
4. Frieda Lawrence, *Memoirs and Correspondence* (London: Heinemann, 1961) p. 83.
5. Ludwig Rubiner, *Aktion* (1913), p. 663.
6. Franz Jung, *Sophie* in *Werke*, Bd. VIII (Berlin), p. 122.
7. Walter Rauschenbusch, *A Theology for the Social Gospel* (New York: Macmillan, 1917), p. 4.
8. Marianne Weber, *Max Weber. A Biography* tr. Harry Zohn (New York: Wiley, 1975), p. 408.
9. Ibid., p. 409.
10. D. H. Lawrence, *Sons and Lovers* (New York: Viking Compass, 1958), p. 23.
11. Ibid., p. 36.
12. Ibid., p. 58.
13. Ibid., pp. 59–60.
14. D. H. Lawrence, *Reflections on the Death of a Porcupine* (Bloomington: University of Indiana Press, 1963), p. 200.
15. D. H. Lawrence, *Sons and Lovers*, p. 345.
16. D. H. Lawrence, *Reflections on the Death of a Porcupine*, p. 202.
17. D. H. Lawrence, 'Christs in the Tirol', in *Phoenix* (New York: Viking, 1936), p. 84.
18. Marianne Weber, op. cit., p. 411
19. W. J. Mommsen and J. Osterhammel, *Max Weber and his Contemporaries* (London: Allen & Unwin), p. 371
20. Frieda Lawrence, op. cit., p. 82.

4 Max Weber, Anarchism and Libertarian Culture: Personality and Power Politics

Carl Levy

Recent work on the social history of anarchism[1] has sharpened an awareness of libertarian milieus and the linkages between the intelligentsia, bohemias and anarchism. Rather than thinking of anarchism as a fundamental critique and turning away from society, studies now note that anarchists had creative impacts back on society. In Barcelona writers and academics derived inspiration from the anarchists, and in Paris the fruitful relationship has been noted between bohemias and the popularisation of new forms of capitalist consumption.

Reading Weber it became increasingly apparent to me that there was something of a similar two-way process at work. At the outset it has to be said that the extent and nature of Weber's own linkages to anarchism, syndicalism and life-style politics have been insufficiently appreciated and the range of possibilities of Weber's relationship with anarchism have yet to be spelt out. Weber clearly had a fascination for anarchists, syndicalists and libertarian life-style politics but this should not be taken as indicating that he was a 'fellow-traveller'. Instead what I aim to show is that his interaction with anarchism led him to arguments that he deployed in spheres and projects that had nothing whatsoever to do with the utopian quest for a stateless, non-hierarchical and non-coercive society.

Placing and indeed establishing the Weber and anarchism linkage is further complicated by how we should now perceive Weber. The extensive secondary literature offers accounts of Weber that would place him variously either nearer or more distanced, and either sympathetic or antagonistic to anarchism. Prominent interpreters of Weber such as Schluchter and Collins still picture Weber as the sociologist of rationalism and rationalisation.[2] Virtually all forms of anarchism challenge the progressive rationalisation of the world and its fragmentation of the individual into the separate compartments of modern living. Hence the Weber as the proponent of rationalism is placed in opposition to anarchism, and the anarchist concerns amount to virtually an irrelevance.

Hennis has vigorously contested the sociological Weber. Instead he sees Weber not as a sociologist but as a political economist, a lawyer, a historian and as a moral philosopher. Weber's work, Hennis argues, was an investigation into the nature of human personality (*Persönlichkeit*) and how this could be formed and sustained. The project of forming a life, or life-conduct (*Lebensführung*), then faces the problem of the compartmentalisation of life as it is constituted in the modern world; or in Weber's terminology the progressive separation of the spheres of life each with its own set of values. Hennis's solution to the problems of life-conduct was to appeal to Weber's sense of vocation and of professions and to invoke the spirit of an earlier status group society.[3]

Another group of Weber scholars, represented by Scaff, Goldman and Sica,[4] argue that Weber's project is a sociology of culture and that his methodology and philosophy are imbued with neo-Kantianism and a Nietzschean existentialism. This recent fashionable reading of Weber presents a wonderfully liberatory and post-modern thinker. It tries to draw on Weber's encounter with the anarchist sexual utopias of Otto Gross and Ascona. Weber's own sexuality (his relationships with Mina Tobler and Else Jaffé) is related to the successive changes made to *Sociology of Religion* and the core 'Intermediate Reflections' essay, in which the sexual and aesthetic spheres of life are increasingly given more extensive and sympathetic treatment and in which eroticism and love escape the processes of rationalisation to attain the purity of unmediated relationships.[5]

I will argue, however, that Weber's fundamental concern was not moral philosophy or the existential dilemmas of modernity and modernism but power politics, particularly and obsessively, the fate of German power. The radical flavour of Weber's quest for *Persönlichkeit* can only be understood within the contexual heritage of German liberal nationalism of the educated middle class (*Bildungsbürgertum*). Weber was socialised in the 1880s and remained a child of German liberal and Protestant assimilationist culture, as frequently noted. Weber's political liberalism originated in the *Rechtsstaat* tradition, which while believing in the rule of law, mistrusted the conception of the will of the people or the theories of natural rights and supported a centralising national state under the predominant influence of cultural Protestantism, to which Catholic and Jewish identity would be subordinated.[6]

To sum up: if recent fashionable cultural existentialist readings present a nearly 'libertarian Weber', another reading produces a Weber who is one of the last (politically ineffectual and increasingly confused) representatives of a highly cultured elite whose unspoken assumptions were threatened by the popularisation of culture and the democratisation of politics before 1914 and the spectre of the collapse of the *ancien régime* in 1918.

Therefore, Weber remains a contested figure. In the remainder of this chapter I will explore these issues through a discussion of Weber's encounters with Ernst Toller during and immediately after the First World War. Central to this encounter is his opposition of an ethic of ultimate ends (*Gesinnungsethik*) to an ethic of responsibility (*Verantwortungsethik*). Weber's relationship to Toller replicates an earlier relationship with Robert Michels, about which Mommsen and Beetham have written.[7] While a reading of the Ascona letters suggests that this well-known antinomy may be a product of Weber's mature thought (most famously argued in the two lectures 'Science as a Vocation' and 'Politics as a Vocation'), a similar dualism affected his neo-Kantianism.[8] For the building of *Persönlichkeit* is founded on intentionalist rather than consequentialist ethics (see Whimster, Chapter 1). Working within the universe of the *Bildungsbürgertum*, Weber assumed that his methods of reasoning and the foundation stones of his morality were understood by various educated audiences and it was precisely the splintering of that classical humanist 'family identity', to quote Whimster,[9] after the First World War that make the interpretations of his political interventions towards the end of his life so problematic.

Weber's German liberalism was never associated with a certain type of libertine Nietzschean will to power, nor did he have any intellectual sympathy for Benthamite utilitarianism. As Hennis and others have demonstrated, Weber's Nietzsche is a reworked version of Kant's 'ethical personalism'. Conviction politicians at the helm of state or within utopian counter-communities and movements needed *Persönlichkeit*. In order to have 'personality' one maintained a 'pathos of distance' and displayed the traditional values of the patrician: chivalry (*Ritterlichkeit*), decency (*Anstand*), abhorrence of baseness (*Gemeinheit*), and a 'natural' sense of superiority (*Vornehmheit*).[10] Weber assumed that most individuals who possessed *Persönlichkeit* would hail from his social class or the military elites who were both endowed with *Satisfaktionsfähigheit* (the right to demand and give satisfaction by fighting ritualised life-and-death duels) (See Ay, Chapter 5). Even if the Ascona letters demonstrate that a self-educated anarchist worker could be endowed with 'honorary' *Persönlichkeit*, his encounter with the university student Toller was symbolic of Weber's wider efforts at winning over the war generation of German students to his increasingly frayed form of German liberalism and his fight against any form of pacifism. It was through his pre-war encounters with anarchism, syndicalism and libertarian culture (mainly through Gross and Michels) that he thought he detected reserves of 'ethical personalism' which could serve his very different political project.[11]

But this has to be approached very cautiously. A knowledge of Max Weber's etiquette of 'personality' makes it possible to reconcile, on the one side, Weber's longing in 1919 to see the reconstruction of an effective Army General Staff[12] and, on the other, his defence in court of the revolutionary anti-militarist Ernst Toller on the grounds that his activities during the Bavarian Soviet Republic were mitigated because they were done with honourable intentions.[13] The acceptance of anarchist and syndicalist arguments and individuals within his circle has been explained by Karádi and Mommsen as examples of Weber's tolerance and intellectual curiosity.[14] But the encounter with Toller tells another story.

Ernst Toller was born into an assimilated Jewish family in Samotschin in Posen.[15] Interrupting his university studies in 1914 in order to volunteer in what he believed was a defensive war, Toller was invalided out of the army in 1916. He had fought bravely on the Western Front and was remembered as good frontline soldier by witnesses at his 1919 trial. Although he was attracted to expressionist currents (see Shields, chapter 12) before the war, he was apolitical before 1917. His conversion to anarchism occurred after he left active service and began to recuperate as a student first in Munich and then in Heidelberg. The effects of battle weighed heavily. Student friends remember him wandering off into the hills outside Munich and Heidelberg for days on end. In the summer of 1918 he was placed in psychiatric care for a short period. (Although this may have been a stratagem by his mother to save her middle-class son from the aroused suspicions of the State.)

In November 1916 Toller enrolled as student at the Faculties of Law and Economics of the University of Munich and eventually moved into digs in bohemian Schwabing. At a weekly seminar held by the professor of German literature, Artur Kutscher, he was able to listen to leading writers read their own works. It was here that he met the doyen of the Munich literary world, Thomas Mann, and was soon after invited to his home to read his own poetry. Mann must have been impressed for in 1919 he would testify favourably at Toller's trial. After spending August and September in a sanatorium, Toller was invited to the Second Lauenstein Cultural Conference organised by Eugen Diederichs. The invitation of the unknown and unpublished Toller to this gathering of the cream of the

German *Bildungsbürgertum* indicates that his performance at the literary gatherings in Munich had been very well received.

The Lauenstein meeting is important for Toller's biography because it is here that Toller met Weber and it was also at this rolling seminar cum arts festival that he began his political education. Even if Toller's radicalisation had been caused by the war, his attempts at rationalising his political thought began with Max Weber being his intellectual foil. But Lauenstein is more universally important for two other reasons. Firstly, it is perhaps the last time that representatives of the counterculture and the university came together in a peaceful dialogue. The revolutions in Munich less than two years later would see the right and left wings in bloody confrontation. Whereas pre-1914 these same fractions of *völkisch* groups, communitarians, socialists, vitalists, expressionists, the followers of the *Mutterrecht*, a new sexual ethic and pagan awakenings were marked by their common search for alternative solutions. Secondly, this is perhaps one of the last times that the pre-war elite of the *Bildungsbürgertum* could presume to talk for the nation: the ingrained etiquette of *Persönlichkeit* acted as the unspoken assumption at Lauenstein.

Weber's intellectual labour, as is known, was carried on as much outside the university as within it. It was a context which lent itself to encounters with bohemia. Max Weber's linkages to libertarian bohemias through Michels, Gross or Toller are part of a much wider force field which is discussed elsewhere in this volume. On an international comparative level the 'founders of social science' engaged in a dual encounter with both the natural sciences and literature.[16] The sociological imagination was equally influenced by the metaphors of science and literature. Hennis's assertion that Weber was a moral philosopher, political economist and lawyer rather than 'sociologist' should not be regarded as entirely novel when seen in international comparison. Indeed Collini's recent study of Weber's British contemporaries is entitled *Public Moralists*.[17] The *Bildungsbürgertum* had its functional equivalents in the 'gentleman' or the French *'honnête homme'*.[18] In all three countries cultivated, leisurely and financially independent classes encountered the same threats and promises of modernity experienced by Weber; and in all these cases the desire to preserve the innermost values of humanism intersected with encounters with democracy, socialism and, not least, bohemias.[19]

The German speaking bohemias shared a common grounding in Nietzsche or rather 'Nietzsches',[20] neo-Kantianism, *Lebensphilosophie*, the erotic movement and expressionism.[21] The specifically anarchist elements were provided by the Stirner revival through Mackay's blending of Nietzsche with Stirner,[22] the romantic libertarian Jewish intelligentsia recently charted by Löwy, and the erotic movement of Gross.[23] Indeed as

Green, Mitzman, Michaels, and Löwy, have shown, Gross's ideas and persona affected Kafka in Prague, the Dadaists in Berlin and some of Max Weber's friends and colleagues.[24]

However, these patterns of reciprocal relationship were not just the fortuitous results of charismatic and peripatetic individuals like Gross. Weber's circles intersected with circles of middle-class utopians. Within Heidelberg itself the Weber Circle was in close, and at times prickly, contact with the George Circle. More important for our argument were the more openly anarchist and libertarian circles associated with *völkisch* romanticism which affected Bloch, Lukács and Toller.[25] Through a series of middle-class left libertarian circles stretching from Gustav Landauer's *Neue Gemeinschaft* in the 1890s[26] to Kurt Hiller's *Aufbruchkreis* in 1915[27] many of the direct and indirect contacts of the Weber Circle with the libertarian bohemia were maintained. Ascona stood as the symbol of these circles.[28] Like the circles mentioned above, Ascona was not only an intellectual construct, it had a physical and geographical presence. Its meanings and functions were multifarious. As Green has shown, it served as a nature cure resort, an artists' quarter, an international and German centre of anarchism (Kropotkin, Friedeberg, Mühsam, Gross, Frick), a branch of psychotheraphy (Gross), a source of Dada and the home of modern dance (Laban). But it was also the location where the neo-conservative publisher Diederichs, the organiser of the 1917 Lauenstein Conferences, developed his *völkisch* ideas under the rubric of the new romanticism (a term suggested to him by a denizen of Ascona, Herman Hesse). Diederichs, as cultural entrepreneur and friend of Max Weber, exemplifies the strangeness of the force field of dissident politics and culture in German before the early 1920s. On the one hand he developed Nordic *völkisch* literature, and battled 'Jewish' publishers and 'Jewish' rationalism; and on the other, he published the Jewish anarcho-socialist communitarian Gustav Landauer and later leftwing expressionist playwrights like Georg Kaiser.[29] 'The real opposition', as Lunn notes, 'was not so much between *völkisch* romantics and others, but between those who developed racist doctrines and celebrated authoritarian imperial power and those who were oriented towards humanitarian and democratic goals.'[30]

The meetings organised by Diederichs at Lauenstein Castle reflected an odd mixture of the ethos of Ascona with the kitsch of German cultural nationalism. The Castle itself had been restored to mock medieval glory only in 1896 after it was brought by an 'enthusiast' and its 'proletarian' family tenants vacated.[31] Located 'on one of the gentle hills of central Germany among the blue-green fir slopes of Thuringia', as Toller wrote,[32] Burg Lauenstein was placed in one of the most culturally resonant locations for the German national imagination. The restoration of 1896 had worked its magic upon the meeting. 'The setting', Marianne Weber writes,

> was full of atmosphere. The rooms with their old-fashioned furnishing had windows looking on to wooded mountain slopes and offering several valleys. The meetings took place in the *Rittersaal* (the hall of the knights) or in the castle yard. The colourful tendrils of Virginia creepers covered the walls. From the roof the German flag waved – a symbol of superpersonal community. The old things surrounding them that had defied the tempests of times also spoke of the common roots of German civilisation, of a past in which everything and everyone had predetermined place and meaning.[33]

But Lauenstein had been the reinvention of a Wilhelmine bourgeois: the pristine world of estates and orders in which German *Persönlichkeit* could flourish was an illusion. Marianne Weber continues: 'By contrast, the feeling and thinking of the group of *modern* Germans were anything but unified; they spoke the same language but had difficulty understanding one another.'[34]

Toller only attended the second Lauenstein meeting; the first, held earlier in the spring, according to Diederichs, had been unsuccessful. The second was held in the shadow of the great war aims debate initiated by the famous Peace Resolution in the Reichstag and the split of the SPD and USPD. It seemed as if the masses, not the military and educated elites, in Wilsonian or Leninist fashion, might determine the war's outcome. The theme for the October 1917 meeting was therefore, appropriately, 'The Problem of Leadership in State and Culture'. Diederichs's brief for the second meeting is enlightening,

> The (first) Lauenstein conference was unsatisfactory, in that the creative political man was lacking.... What is needed is the New Man, whose imagination is grounded in the spirit, and who is therefore not impressed by the economic laws of life, but rather taking the Platonic view, feels that it is the spirit which also shapes economic and political life. This has nothing to do with most precepts, but rather with a chivalrous humanity, which affirms life though it believes it to be tragic. The problem is, therefore – how is this type to develop in the state, how does he achieve leadership?[35]

The invitation list included close associates of Weber: Jaffé, Sombart, Toennies; writers like Dehmel (see Shields, chapter 11), Ernst (originally associated with the anarchist oriented *Jungen* opposition to the SPD in the 1890s), Winkler, Vershofen, von Molo, and the political critics Baumer, Heuss, Grabowsky, Kampffmeyer, Scheffler, Maurenbrecher, and the anarchist Mühsam (whom Diederichs knew through Schwabing circles). Younger men included the worker poet Broger, Kroner, Uphoff and of course Toller.[36] Reflecting on the first rather disappointing meeting, Diederichs hoped that instead of merely being inhabited by the critical-intellectual type – 'this really fruitful type' – might be spotted. 'In Lauenstein', he wrote to Weber, 'we can really only play the part of the Three Kings from the Orient. I am a believer and I always live in hope of a miracle.'[37] So if the organiser of this gathering hoped to reinvigorate the natural leadership of the nation by calling on the vast and unorthodox network of contacts he had developed through his publishing ventures before and during the war, he also hoped that such a meeting would promote the development of a *geistig* revolution that he and others in the communitarian and countercultural world sensed was on the horizon at the end of the war.

But many of the manifestations of 'spirit' present at Lauenstein were not to Weber's or Toller's liking. Weber 'rejected as a serious aberration the attempt to awaken feelings of religious community during the first session by means of a medieval mystery play.[38] While Toller recalled how

poets chanted dithyrambs, and the poet Falke made his daughters dance in the moonlight before the ivy-covered walls of the castle. The quality of their dancing was of no account; they believed that the spirit of God hovered over the dancers. Through dim tapestried chambers where ancient worm-eaten furniture loomed ghost-like in the dark, they walked in the twilight feeling like medieval knights, missionaries of the Holy Ghost.[39]

The younger men and Weber had more pressing subjects on their minds. The war veterans and the younger generation were impatient to discuss the future and they seemed naturally attracted to Weber. Many of the younger members of the audience at Lauenstein were members of the *Freistudentische Jugend*, the student organisation which stood at the cusp between authoritarian and democratic communitarian and *völkisch* politics and who would invite Weber on two occasions to give famous lectures: 'Science as a Vocation' at the University of Munich on 7 November 1917 and the 'The Profession and Vocation of Politics' on 28 January 1919. Weber's position also foreshadows the multi-layered nature of his argument over the next three years. He criticised mercilessly the bombastic rhetoric of the pan-German and student conviction politicians present at

Lauenstein and demanded the democratisation of the Prussian *Obrigkeitsstaat* but he stressed that all cultural and political questions were dependent on the outcome of power politics. He stressed that an 'individual sees his own real desires clearly *only* if he tests his supposed "final" attitude by reacting to *very concrete* problems that have come to a head.' So that the universal interest in 'pacifism' or other cultural standpoints by the youth at Lauenstein would not be solved in confessional discussion under castle walls but only by answering the

> 'purely superficial preliminary question: *How will this war come to an end?* For this will determine the specific future tasks of the German character [*Wesen*] within the world. *All* final questions without exception are affected by purely political events, external though these may seem. That is why everything that is said now, and particularly by us non-participants in the war, is very nonbinding'.[40]

This conversation must be placed within the context of Weber's politics during the Great War. Until the late summer of 1918 Weber did not think Germany would be defeated. But he wanted to advance realistic war aims so that the war would end without the constant threat of French or Anglo-American revanchism. Although he disagreed with the more extreme annexationist demands of the Fatherland Party, he envisaged Germany exercising formal and informal control over much of central and eastern Europe, with a truncated Russia pushed back to its seventeenth-century borders.[41] Although many industrialists and imperialist polemicists used economic arguments to support the cause of this German empire, Weber's standpoint was usually couched in geo-political and racial-culturalist language. Weber had concluded that a vibrant German liberal capitalism was unsustainable without the co-operation of Anglo-American global capitalism. Weber's extended family ties in Western Europe and the Anglo-American world meant that he understood the dynamism behind this globalisation of capital.[42] The importance of Germany as a power-state was to protect German speaking Europe and those former dependencies of the Czarist Empire which had broken loose from Russian control after 1917–18. This line of argument was foreshadowed in his *Inaugural Lecture* of 1895 and developed throughout the Great War. It joined together his critique of pure pacifism with an idealistic gloss on the role of German power. As Lassman and Speirs note:

> Unlike the 'vulgar' nationalists, Weber does not agree that political greatness and cultural achievements necessarily go hand in hand.

He rejects the view that smaller states must in any sense be 'less valuable' from a cultural point of view. Indeed, he is thankful that there are German communities outside the Reich. In such small states (Switzerland is an example here), 'other virtues may flourish : not only the simple, bourgeois virtues (*Bürgertugenden*) of citizenship and true democracy' but the 'more intimate and yet eternal values'. It seems inevitable that Germany, as a *Machtstaat*, cannot provide the best ground for the flourishing of culture within its own borders, although the prestige of that culture may well depend upon such national power. Germany has a national responsibility to defend the culture of Central Europe against the dual threat of future Russian and Anglo-American hegemony. Writing during the First World War, it seems obvious to Weber that a powerless German state would be useless in the defence not only of German culture both within and outside the Reich, but also the cultural autonomy of Central Europe.[43]

During the war these policy objectives were accompanied by increasingly ferocious criticisms of the manner in which the imperial and military elites were running the war. Germany needed parliamentarianism so that it could create resolute popular leaders. This famous critique of Imperial Germany appeared far more radical than it actually was, and one of the reasons why Toller and other members of the wartime generation of middle-class communitarian socialists could mistake Weber for a revolutionary was the personal tone he adopted in public forums when he advanced these criticisms of the German power elite from 1917 onwards. Although he did not quite challenge the Kaiser to a duel, at the second Lauenstein meeting he only courted the sanction of *lèse majesté* so, he argued, the Kaiser and his underlings would be forced to testify in court about *the way they had mismanaged the war effort and not because they were guilty of starting the war.*[44]

Weber's major intervention at Lauenstein was entitled 'The Personality and the Life Orders'. According to Hennis's reconstruction of this unpublished lecture, the central theme of this talk, which foreshadows major themes in 'The Vocation of Science', were the well-known ground rules of the neo-Kantian *Persönlichkeit*: the tension between an external order and the demands of inner personality – fate and chance. He concluded: 'Be who you are, in any case you live in "orders" which have their own regularity, they make their demands. Gentlemen, only he who knows how to live up to the demands of the day has "personality".'[45] However, I argue, the pressing demands of the day for Max Weber were not associated with a *geistig* revolution but instead related to the effective and efficient control of the German war machine.

Toller's own recollections of Lauenstein are mixed. The twenty-four year old got up enough courage to intervene and denounce the lack of action. It was only Max Weber and the poet Richard Dehmel who impressed him. He regarded the encounter with Max Weber as a 'treasured friendship' and the position Weber took at Lauenstein became the basis for their friendly argument over the next few years.[46] The next encounter with Weber occurred in Heidelberg and can be understood under the rubric of *Persönlichkeit* and pacifism. In the next period from the autumn of 1917 to the summer of 1918 Toller became a political animal by engaging in his natural proclivity towards discipleship. He became the follower of the unlikely triad: Max Weber, Gustav Landauer and Kurt Eisner.

In the autumn of 1917 Toller transferred from Munich to Heidelberg to continue his studies. It seems likely that his major reason was to be closer to Max Weber. In Munich he had assimilated into the literary world and the bohemia of Schwabing; in Heidelberg rather than research for a putative doctorate in economics, he was probably more attracted to Weber's famous Sunday open house where his poetry moved the entire gathering.[47] He also joined a small group of pacifists and students (less than a dozen) in the rather grandiosely entitled Cultural and Political Federation of German Youth. The small group had been originally organised at a series of meetings led by Kathe Pick, a young Viennese doctoral student who would later play an important role in the Austrian Social Democratic Party.

The first action of the group was a manifesto in the *Münchener Zeitung* on 10 November 1917 in solidarity with the threats by nationalist students against the well-known pacifist Professor F. W. Förster[48] and also to demand that the University authorities lift the ban on students' rights of association and assembly that were used to prevent socialist and pacifist activity. On the broader front the League sought to counter the annexationist propaganda of the Fatherland Party and Toller and other students drafted a manifesto to be circulated to students through socialist networks throughout Germany, hoping also to recruit Max Weber as one of the sponsors because of the mutual antipathy towards this new manifestation of Pan-Germanism. In a modified form, this manifesto displayed the utopianism found in Landauer's *Call to Socialism* (1911), which Toller and other members of the group had started to imbibe. Quite naturally Weber refused to endorse it. Copies of the manifesto were sent to Förster, Heinrich Mann, Carl Hauptmann, Walter Hasenclever and Walter von Molo (late of Lauenstein). By November Toller had broadened his network to include leading Swiss exiled German and Austrian pacifist and socialist writers. Through his Swiss connections Toller became immersed in anti-war literature, but Landauer's pre-war texts shaped his anarchism.

Landauer's neo-Kantian ethical communitarian socialism appealed to Toller. 'The possibility of socialism', Landauer wrote, 'does not depend on any form of technology or the satisfaction of material needs. Socialism is possible any time, if enough people want it.'[49] In an earlier text he was more radical, reflecting the Nietzschean and Stirnerite overtones of the pre-war counterculture: 'The state is a condition, a certain relationship among human beings, a mode of behaviour between them; we destroy it by contracting other relationships, by behaving differently towards one another.... We are the state, and we shall continue to be the state until we have created the institutions that form a real community and a society of men.'[50] This apparently anti-Weber text was balanced by a position during most of the war which placed Landauer's anarchism in a strangely parallel position with Weber. Landauer was silent through much of the conflict and believed that the war was caused by the ineluctable effects of the state system, not the particular machinations of the German military and political elites.[51]

But the parallels between Weber–Toller and Toller–Landauer go deeper. Landauer's (and Kurt Eisner's) neo-Kantian moralism was the product of the same culture as Robert Michels. As we know, Weber admitted that Robert Michels was one of his closest friends until they argued over Germany's war aims in 1915.[52]

Michels's early attraction to ethical moralism was deepened by his encounter with the Marburg School of neo-Kantians. In the early 1900s Michels studied under Cohn and Natorp, but his radical critique of social democracy is to some degree derived from a well-established tradition among socialist and anarcho-socialist intellectuals.[53] From the *Jungen* of the 1890s to the young radicals of Michels's generation in the years 1904–6, dissident intellectuals lamented the lack of socialist morality and enthusiasm in the legalised and now electorally successful SPD. There was a strong neo-Kantian presence within the SPD until a new orthodoxy was created in the early 1900s, with many intellectuals, even Kautsky, expressing doubts whether the enthusiasm for human freedom and the spirit of self-sacrifice required to maintain the class struggle could be derived directly from Marxist historical materialism. By 1903–4 Michels was also attracted by the more radical anarcho-socialism of Dr Raphael Friedeberg, whom Weber would encounter in Ascona. Friedeberg's line was merely a reworking of Landauer's earlier critique of the 1890s. Indeed, in many ways Michels was closer to Landauer than Friedeberg, who emphasised a syndicalist alternative to the SPD. While Michels endorsed certain syndicalist arguments, he never believed that trade unions were self-sufficient and basic units of society (and quite naturally he also detected oligarchical tendencies within them).[54] He disagreed with Sorelian violence and the tendency of French syndicalists to denounce the role of intellectuals in radical politics.[55] But like Toller's other disciples, Eisner and Landauer, he demanded that intellectuals act as moral pedagogues to instil enthusiasm for socialism in the rank and file rather than pour its proletarian 'members as parts into a complicated machinery.'[56] If Weber had little time for the fundamentalist radicalism of Landauer–Friedeberg–Michels, the major vehicle of a more moderate neo-Kantian attack was Heinrich Braun's journal the *Archiv für Soziale Gesetzgebung und Statistik*, which to complete a circle of reciprocal influence, was bought by Edgar Jaffé in 1904, and changed its name to the *Archiv für Sozialwissenschaft und Sozialpolitik*, and became Weber's and indeed Michels's main vehicle of scholarly intervention. Underneath the shared neo-Kantian approach of Weber and these radicals, however, was perhaps the 'deepest' legacy of Friedrich Albert Lange who seemed to inform the early Weber, Braun and radical and moderate socialist intellectual revisionists.[57]

The encounters of Max Weber in Toller's life after the publication of the Heidelberg manifesto are therefore easier to understand if we conceptualise aspects of the Weber–Toller relationship as a newer version of the pre-war Michels and Weber friendship. As we have already seen, the cultural field was extremely familiar to Weber, and as I shall demonstrate the terms of the Weber–Michels argument will be repeated during Weber's attempt to win the war generation of students to an anti-pacifist and German nationalist line.

Toller's manifesto was prematurely published in the nationalist press and he had to counter accusations of treason, but this public controversy alerted the military authorities and they disbanded the League and expelled its members who were not citizens of Baden. Toller, after some adventure, fled to Berlin. In Berlin he met his last disciple, Kurt Eisner.

After a brief stay in Berlin, Toller travelled to Munich with Eisner and became deeply involved in the strike of munitions workers. The frenetic activities of the anti-war movement organised by Eisner through the USPD (in Munich) and the release of the Lichnowsky memorandum by the Spartacus League (in Berlin) were important stages in Toller's radicalisation. The Lichnowsky memorandum (like documents released later in the year by Eisner (see Ay, Chapter 5) cast grave doubts on the innocence of German motives in the summer of 1914.[58] In late January and early February he became an accomplished public speaker and handed out leaflets from scenes of his play *The Transformation* as a way to arouse anti-war feelings. It seems, however, that during the strike Toller's mindset started to change. Although the police accused him of crass revolutionary propaganda, when the leadership had been temporarily arrested and he was momentarily in charge of thousands of angry workers, he behaved moderately, declaring that the strike would continue until the arrested leaders were released and to demonstrate that the German people wanted 'a peace of understanding.'[59] This still reflected the same position he had taken after the controversy over the manifesto where he had written to local press saying that, 'for us, politics means that we feel morally responsible for the fate of our country and act accordingly.'[60] But the effect of the strike was to convert the pacifist to a pacifist revolutionary. The strike seemed to awaken Toller to the potential for fundamental social change through the use of the mass strike and the united front of the working class, in rather similar terms to the debate about the mass strike that Michels, Friedeberg, Luxemburg and even Bernstein addressed in 1904–6. But for Toller non-violent social change would usher in Landauer's libertarian community.

In early February Toller was arrested, but released in May. He had the potential charge of treason hanging over him until he was officially discharged from the army in September 1918 and all charges were dropped. Upon hearing of Toller's arrest Weber intervened and gave evidence on his behalf at the Baden military command in Karlsruhe. After his release from formal military duties in September 1918, his political activities began again in October 1918 when he spoke in Berlin at a Majority Social Democrat meeting and declared himself against Walter Rathenau's demand for a mass mobilisation in defence of the German homeland.[61]

Contemporaneously, Weber was involved in a heated debate about pacifism with a small group of students in Frankfurt. In an ensuing spirited correspondence with the pacifist Professor Goldstein, Weber revealed the ulterior motives in his relationship with Toller. Since the manifesto of the previous autumn Weber had become increasingly interested in the effects of pacifism upon the returning soldiers, convinced that the disillusion with the war would undermine the German war machine.[62] But Goldstein uncovered the *modus operandi* of Max Weber when he accused him of engaging in a dialogue under false pretences with the pacifist students in Frankfurt. Weber reviewed his position *vis-à-vis* Toller's involvement in the manifesto of 1917 and his arrest in 1918, but he recalled that both the group in Heidelberg in 1917 and the present one in Frankfurt were composed of similarly immature if seriously-minded students who (echoing Lauenstein) lacked the rational judgement of the politically possible, and

Either resist evil with force nowhere and then live like Saint Francis or Saint Claire or an Indian monk or a Russian narodnik. Anything else is fraud or self-deception. For this *absolute* demand there is only an absolute way, the way of the saint.[63]

This characteristically Weberian statement, reflects Weber's interest in Naumann's pre-war involvement in the debate over pure or qualified pacifism and his deep interest in Tolstoy (see Green, chapter 3), but it also reflects a mode of operation he used in his dialogues with Michels. In response to Michels's famous article in the *Archiv* on the oligarchical tendencies of modern society, Weber wrote:

There are two possibilities: either (1) 'my kingdom is not of this world' Tolstoy, or syndicalism thought to its conclusion,which is nothing more than the sentence 'the goal means nothing to me, the movement every-thing' translated into a revolutionary-ethical personal statement, but one that you too have certainly not thought through to its conclusion. (I shall probably write something about this sometime) or (2) affirmation of culture (that is objective culture), expressing itself in sociological condi-tions of all technique.... In the second case all talk of revolution is farce, any thought of replacing the domination of man over man by any kind of socialist society or ingeniously devised forms of democracy is a utopia.[64]

While the second half of this passage was used to criticise all forms of socialism (which would be repeated in slightly different formulations in 1918–20) and also echoes his description of modern revolution (in his reportage of the 1905 and later 1917 Russian Revolutions) as a battle of wits between two nerve-racked generals,[65] in the first half Weber is still attracted to investigating the libertarian personality: the never completed book on Tolstoy is one theme continuing to his death. But of course for Weber, ulterior motives are never far away. Scaff shows that Tolstoy's ethic of Christian brotherliness became a text that Lukács and Michels each commented on with Weber. The conversation so created is elabo-rated as a foil by Weber for his posture of realism that underlies his analy-sis of the orders of life and their value spheres.[66]

This engrained way of arguing is found in Weber's response to Goldstein. But here realism does not mean the pervasive nature of modern bureaucratisation or the growth of state power, but the specific needs of the German state in the confusing and alarming autumn of 1918. Throughout 1918 his position had evolved in response to the fortunes of the German army. In the autumn of 1917 Weber sympathised with certain socialist elements as long as this would lead to a compromise peace of all belligerents, and he spoke at a rally ('for a peace of conciliation and against the Pan-German danger') organised in Munich by rightwing Social Democrats on 5 November 1917. During the January 1918 mass strikes in Berlin, although he opposed the action he also privately sympathised with the reaction to the provocative behaviour of the German negotiators at Brest Litovsk and approved the support shown by the Social Democratic party leadership with the strike committee which helped bring the protest to a close.[67] But by the autumn of 1918 his position had hardened. With reasoning rather similar to Kurt Eisner's, Goldstein argued that in order for each German intellectual to undergo true moral regeneration, he would have to acknowledge guilt for the war. But in his response, the mention of war guilt had hit a very sore nerve. 'Our policy before the war was *stupid*', Weber wrote, 'not morally reprehensible – it certainly cannot be called that.'[68]

Indeed, Weber not only denied guilt, he was prepared to use the inherent logic of the *Gesinnungsethik* explained in his pre-war letter to Michels, to serve as a conduit of recruitment for a future irredentist war. He added that

it simply is and will continue to be a mystery to me why civil war or some other form of violence – such as any revolution employs at least, at the *very* least, as a 'means' toward an end – is supposed to be 'holy', while just self-defence in war is *not*. If the Poles were to invade Danzig and Thorn, or if the Czechs moved into Reichenberg, the first thing to do would be to establish German irredenta. I shall not be able to be the one to do this, because of reasons of health I am incapacitated, but every nationalist will have to do it, particularly the students. Perhaps you will like it better that way than 'war', but it is the same thing, and of course this is what I meant, and shall say so in public.[69]

After the shock of unexpected defeat was accepted by Weber, his main objectives were to fight against war guilt and protect German interests. Until early 1919 he did not give up on a total mobilisation of the population in a war of national defence. His chief audience during this period remained university students, but these oral and written interventions were part of a broader programme of mobilising the middle classes to defend a new German constitutional republic which would have a strong president and to prevent separatism gaining favour amongst the Bavarians and the Rhinelanders. Weber was not a very successful politician. He was not elected to the Weimar Assembly and his role at the Versailles Peace

Conference was marginal, while his audience of university students repeatedly misunderstood and disliked his line of reasoning.

The objectives of Weber's domestic and foreign policies were joined together by his concern for the future of Germany.[70] Social revolution or provincial separatism would either play into the hands of Anglo-American capital by destroying the viability of the German industrial base or by sanctioning the intervention of the Allied armies; separatism would allow France to dominate the Rhineland and possibly also Bavaria. The rapid demobilisation of the German army before the peace treaty, as demanded by pacifists and socialists, Weber argued, would allow the French army to pursue a traditional rather than Wilsonian peace. Weber reasoned that it was better to be a junior frontline anti-Bolshevik partner of the Anglo-American world rather than be under the shadow of French policy (he never envisaged Franco-German rapprochement and a West European customs union as a counter-balance). But this policy objective was prevented by Wilson's insistence upon assigning war guilt to Germany. It was the war guilt controversy that separated Weber from potential liberal and moderate socialist allies. The attribution of war guilt to Germany angered the *Bildungsbürgertum*, threatened their moral and cultural position and limited their acceptance of the new democratic regime (see Ay, Chapter 5). Yet it was a renegade from this class, the unorthodox pacifist neo-Kantian socialist literate, Kurt Eisner, who had uncovered and published evidence which showed that Germany had been the guilty party. Max Weber's final encounter with Toller occurred in a Munich temporarily ruled by Kurt Eisner and the representatives of the counterculture he had been acquainted with for the past twenty years.

Weber's final act of friendship towards Toller was as a defence witness in the trial of this pacifist anarchist follower of Kurt Eisner and organiser of the first Red Army to operate on German soil. Kurt Eisner had served as Bavarian prime minister from 7 November 1918 until his assassination on 21 February 1919. Between his death and the suppression of the regime in early May 1919, the events took on comic and tragic turns.[71] In the early stages involvement in the government included Weber's own circle: Lujo Brentano, Edgar Jaffé as Minister of Finance and Otto Neurath, chairman of the Socialisation Commission. Besides Toller, Gustav Landauer, Erich Mühsam and other representatives of Schwabing and the counterculture played key roles in the following months. Toller achieved a bewildering series of positions in a very short time.[72] On his arrival in Munich he was co-opted into the Central Workers' Council and in quick succession he became delegate to the Bavarian Worker's Council, the Bavarian Congress of Councils (of which he was elected vice-chairman), and the Provisional

National Council. Toller worked closely with Eisner and Landauer. If both were *geistig* revolutionaries who yearned for a peaceful social transformation, Eisner unlike Landauer was still a parliamentary socialist. All of them in their own way opposed the Communist group led by Levien and Leviné. Mühsam remained nominally an anarchist but supported Lenin's conception of the dictatorship of the proletariat. Landauer considered Lenin little more than a gangster and argued not for the 'dictatorship but the *abolition of the proletariat*'.[73] At first he interpreted the Bavarian Revolution as a fulfilment of his decentralised federalism which sought the dismemberment of Prussian military power and a gradual movement of people to the countryside or garden suburbs. However, although he longed to see a united front of peasants, intellectuals, artisans and industrial workers, the ironic reality was that Landauer's republic was restricted to a narrow triangle of territory around Munich and was heavily dependent on the factory proletariat. The revolution in November 1918 had succeeded due to a temporary power vacuum at the top. The disenchantment of conservative peasants with the Imperial Government's food procurement policies in the autumn of 1918 and the concurrent radicalisation of munitions workers drafted in from Saxony had discredited the old order. But this was only a temporary confluence of factors. When Eisner bowed to demands and called elections, the Majority Socialists won a healthy victory and Eisner's USPD was all but wiped off the electoral map.

Eisner was assassinated by Count Arco-Valley of the extreme right-wing nationalist Thule Society (aficionados of the swastika and one of Diederichs's associated projects) on his way to resign at the Landtag. An incident followed in which a maddened follower of Eisner shot several Majority Social Democrats in the parliamentary chamber. The Social Democrat-led Hoffmann government withdrew from Munich, which was quickly filled by more radical forces. The assassination of Eisner initiated the mass flight of workers from the SPD into the USPD and the KPD. The irony is that if Eisner had been allowed to resign, the revolution would have ended; instead his assassination saw the beginning of a second revolution.[74] Count Arco had been motivated by Weber's similar reaction of shame and anger at Eisner's release of details supporting German war guilt. If his aim was to avenge the honour of Germany, he merely initiated an even more radical phase of the revolution.

With the SPD government encamped in Bamberg, a *Räterepublik* was established in Munich on 7 April 1919. This, too, occurred due to the unintended results of social and political action. A representative of the Hoffmann cabinet attempted to draw the KPD into a coalition regime and thereby keep the SPD in charge while controlling the Communist threat.

However, neither the local SPD nor the KPD would rise to the bait, and when the *Räterepublik* was finally declared on 7 April 1919 it contained neither Communists nor Socialists. But for one week Munich and its environs were ruled by 'the Coffee House Anarchists' of Schwabing.[75] After one week of existence it was threatened with a coup by a garrison loyal to Hoffmann's government. For the last few weeks of its existence the Communists took effective control of the government. But even now this tale was bedeviled by paradox: they were dependent on the military skills to command their Red Army of a suspicious Ernst Toller.

Toller's activities before the episode of the Red Army were fairly marginal.[76] Toller was in Switzerland staying with friends after having participated in the Berne International Socialist Conference, when he heard about Eisner's assassination. With the ensuing power vacuum, he bitterly denounced the attempted SPD coalition government as a device to reintroduce parliamentarianism and from early March he became the chairman of the Munich USPD after Eisner's murder, continuing his own campaign to create a government of revolutionary councils through peaceful means. When the confused events of 5–7 April 1919 allowed Toller to participate in a Republic of Councils he was clearly ambivalent and worried but as Chairman of the Central Council, Toller became in effect the ruler of the Republic for its six days of existence.

Later, as the commander of the Red Army, Toller was initially quite successful in his defence of Munich even though he relied on extremely lax discipline, refusing to follow orders from his Communist Commander-in-Chief. Not only did he disobey orders to shoot prisoners, he allowed them to leave and some returned to fight again. Leviné and the Communists wanted to remove Toller from his command because they did not trust the USPD. The situation deteriorated on the political and military fronts and on 26 April Toller resigned his command.

The dispute between Leviné and Toller involved the issue of the ethics of ultimate ends. Toller refused to sacrifice lives in hopeless military positions and wanted to negotiate surrender, and he prevented the Red Guards from taking hostages, and he moved Arco and other prisoners out of harm's way. Two sets of ethics were in battle with each other: Toller may have shared the Communists' ends but he rejected their dogmatic belief that only present defeat could assure ultimate victory. (Leviné famously remarked that all Communist militants were on temporary reprieve.) On the other hand, the very humanitarian ideals that forced Toller into retreat and negotiation were an inevitable result of the type of revolution he wanted. He had willed the ends but not the means: in a Bavaria of armed camps Toller found it very difficult to live by the Sermon on the Mount.[77]

The final shattering blow was the murder of eight hostages from the Thule Society. After hearing of their deaths Toller tried to get them buried to prevent reprisals by the victorious Free Corps. By 3 May the whole city was in their hands and under the cover of martial law between 600 and 1200 workers, revolutionaries and innocent bystanders were executed.[78] Gustav Landauer was one of their victims. He had withdrawn from the revolution after 16 April and had stayed with the widow of Eisner in a suburb of Munich. Landauer could probably have escaped but he was saddened by the death of Eisner and his wife one year previously: he had given up.[79]

Toller hid out in Munich, only to be captured and brought to trial in June 1919. Toller's lawyer, Hugo Hasse, the USPD politician and presently victim of a rightwing assassin, followed two lines of argument to save him from the death penalty.[80] Firstly, there was no charge to answer because he was accused of high treason under a law promulgated by the Imperial Government which effectively lapsed when the monarchy was overthrown. The revolutionaries of yesterday had no grounds to put on trial today's revolutionaries. If the death penalty had been carried out on Leviné because of the attribution of dishonourable motives, Toller's defence was to demonstrate that his motives were honourable and that he had gone to great lengths to avoid bloodshed. Various character witnesses testified to Toller's idealism and courage as a soldier, and many from the literary world supported his plea. Max Weber testified to the defendant's 'entirely upright character' and claimed that Toller was innocent of political realities, recalling his Heidelberg days when he was a member of a group of young people who were completely ignorant of the realities of economics, politics or socialism, finishing with: 'only God in his wrath had made Toller a politician'. Toller, however, refused to accept Weber's attribution of a fundamentalist ethic as a mitigating circumstance. In fact, quite the contrary, Toller demanded that the court recognise he accepted full responsibility even if by this he risked the death penalty. He did not deny that he remained a revolutionary and that he still reserved the right to use force when the situation was intolerable. This mode of behaviour certainly won him Weber's respect and it seemed to express the contradiction between the ethics of conviction and the responsibility present in 'The Vocation and Profession of Politics' given earlier that year on behest of the *Freistudentische Bund*. But this similarity might just be one of superficial appearance.

The original speaker was to have been Weber who refused, but when he heard Eisner was to speak he let his name go forward as planned. As we have seen, Weber had been cultivating this group of students for at least two years because they were at the crossroads between a revolutionary and patriotic movement, which seemed to serve in Weber's mind as the model of the American club (the principle of voluntary membership and exclusiveness) rather than the outmoded student corporation. (see Turner, Chapter 9) They were an antidote to student 'zoological nationalism', and as he noted in a speech in March, he hoped that the gulf between the *Akademiker* and the mass of the German population might be attenuated through various reforms of the educational system.[81] However, like many of Weber's interventions the message is more complex than meets the eye. According to Hennis much of the 'Profession and Vocation of Politics' is neither a sociological text nor a political speech: these aspects were just a prologue to its real substance.[82] The final section deals with what comprises the genuine men and women who follow the vocation of politics. In other words, how does the personality, that charismatic personality at the heart of the vocation of the politician arise? But Hennis, too, probably misses the entire message. Weber's speech is not merely a lesson in characterology: *Persönlichkeit* is not an undefined universal, it has its specifically German characteristics. It has been argued that the much quoted famous phrase 'the polar night of icy darkness and harshness will only slowly fade' is not referring to a general condition caused by the dilemma of modern secular rationalisation. Roth has shown how these terms were used in the context of political speeches occurring contemporaneously.[83] Weber can be read to be urging the students to struggle for a 'just' and 'guiltless' peace. Who therefore was more realistic: the haunted Weber or the ethically consistent libertarian communitarians of the Munich revolution?

This returns us to the paradoxical effects of Count Arco's assassination of Kurt Eisner. Motivated by his own struggle for such an honourable peace, his deed caused the very revolution which forced Toller to become a commander of an army. Arco's assassination ultimately led to the shooting of hostages from his Thule Society which in the eyes of the Free Corps sanctioned the assassination of Landauer and the indiscriminate execution of hundreds of others. But when Arco was freed from prison after a rally of students in Munich in 1920, Max Weber came to the aid of socialist students who had been prevented from speaking against such a decision. By this time the student and bohemian community of Schwabing had been hopelessly divided and radicalised by the events of the previous year. Bavaria and Munich became a 'cell of order' in the Weimar Republic.[84]

The Munich Revolution increased the prevalence of open antisemitism. If Toller and other students of Jewish origin were arrested or deported from Heidelberg in 1917, this aspect of their background was not considered relevant. However, at Toller's trial in 1919 anti-semitism was never far away. Toller, Leviné, Mühsam, Landauer and Eisner were all Jewish even if Marianne Weber somehow places the gentile Levien and Leviné (of Jewish origins) in the camp of foreign Jewish Bolsheviks and forgets Toller (of Jewish origins and German nationality).[85] However, both Leviné (who had ties to Weber's circle through the Russian Stepun) and Toller had written early stories with heavily Jewish and messianic themes.[86]

Max Weber's own suggestion that his Jewish colleagues maintain a lower profile, however, did not save him from accusations by nationalist students of also being a Jew during his defence of the socialist students at the University of Munich in 1920. Although Count Arco's behaviour in court 'had been chivalrous and manly in every way', Weber argued, and 'his action was born of a conviction that Kurt Eisner brought disgrace after disgrace upon Germany', nevertheless, Weber concluded, if he had been minister, 'I would have had him shot.' The conclusion was clear: 'Arco's tombstone would also have exorcised Kurt Eisner's ghost'.[87] The ethics of responsibility and ultimate ends forced both Eisner and Arco to act. Max Weber's own contorted reasoning in 1920 left him exposed to criticism from all sides and exposed this lifelong German nationalist to the angered attention of more sinister competitors.

If Weber's reasoning was lost to students by 1920, Toller remembered the lessons on *Persönlichkeit* found in the 'Vocation and Profession of Politics'. His play, *Masses and the Man*, he admitted, was a product of meditation in prison on the unintended effects of the Munich Revolution.

> I had failed. I had always believed socialists, despising force, should never resort to it. And now I myself had used force and appealed to force: I who hated bloodshed had caused blood to be shed. But when in Stadelheim an opportunity for escape had presented itself, I had refused to take advantage of the plan lest my flight should cost a warder his life. What fate awaits the man, I ask myself, who tries to influence the course of the world, that is, who becomes politically active, when he tries to realise the moral precepts he recognises as just in his struggle with the masses? Was Max Weber right after all when he said that the only logical way of life for those who were determined never to over-come evil by force was the way of St. Francis, that corresponding to the most demanding standards there is only the most demanding path – that of the saint? Must the man of action always incur guilt? Always? Or, if he is unwilling to incur guilt, perish? The masses, it seems, are impelled by hunger and want rather than ideals. Would they still be able to

conquer if they renounced force for the sake of an ideal? Is man not an individual and a mass-man at one and the same time? Is not struggle between the individual and the mass decided in man's mind as well as being fought out in the social sphere? As an individual a man will strive for his own ideals, even at the expense of the rest of the world. As a mass-man he is driven by social impulses; he strives to attain his goal even if his ideals have to be abandoned. This contradiction seems to me insoluble, because I have come up against it in my own life, and I seek in vain to resolve it.[88]

But unlike Weber or the KPD who made the pre-supposition of the necessity of using violence, Toller's position was ethically consistent throughout. Toller's *Masses and the Man* is a genuine opposition between two ethics that had nothing to do with Weber's 'realism'.

NOTES

1. Günter Berghaus, *Futurism and Politics. Between Anarchist Rebellion and Fascist Reaction, 1909–1944*, (Providence, R.I.: Berghahn, 1996); Colin Campbell, *The Romantic Ethic and the Spirit of Modern Consumerism* (Oxford: Blackwell, 1987); Joan Ungersma Halperin, *Felix Fénéon. Aesthete and Anarchist in Fin-de-Siècle Paris* (New Haven, Conn.: Yale University Press, 1988); Temma Kaplan, *Red City, Blue Period. Social Movements in Picasso's Barcelona* (Berkeley, Calif.: University of California Press, 1992); Richard D. Sonn, *Anarchism and Cultural Politics in Fin-de-Siècle France* (Lincoln, Neb.: University of Nebraska Press, 1992).

2. Randall Collins, *Weberian Sociological Theory* (Cambridge: Cambridge University Press, 1986); Wolfgang Schluchter, *The Rise of Western Rationalism: Max Weber's Developmental History* (Berkeley: Calif.: University of California Press, 1981).

3. Wilhelm Hennis, *Max Weber. Essays in Reconstruction*, trans. by Keith Tribe (London: Allen & Unwin, 1988).

4. Harvey Goldman, *Power, Death and the Devil. Self and Power in Max Weber and Thomas Mann* (Berkeley, Calif.: University of California Press, 1992); Lawrence A. Scaff, *Fleeing the Iron Cage: Culture, Politics and Modernity* (Berkeley, Calif.: University of California Press, 1989); Alan Sica, *Weber, Irrationality and Social Order* (Berkeley, Calif.: University of California Press, 1988); Georg Strauth, 'Nietzsche, Weber and the Affirmative Sociology of Culture', *Archives Européennes de Sociologie*, XXXVIII (1992) pp. 219–47.

5. David Chalcraft, 'Weber, Wagner and Thoughts of Death', *Sociology*, XXVII (3) (1993) pp. 433–49; Wolfgang Schwentker, 'Passion as a model

of Life: Max Weber, the Otto Gross Circle and Eroticism', in W. J. Mommsen and J. Osterhammel (eds), *Max Weber and His Contemporaries* (London: Allen and Unwin, 1987), pp. 483–98.

6.   David Beetham, 'Max Weber and the Liberal Political Tradition', *Archives Européennes de Sociologie*, XXXV (1989) pp. 106–34; Harvey Goldman, 'Weber's Sociology and Weber's Personality', *Theory and Society*, XXII (1993) pp. 853–60; Stephen P. Turner and Regis H. Factor, *Max Weber and the Dispute over Reason and Value: A Study in Philosophy, Ethics and Politics* (London: Routledge and Kegan Paul, 1984); Mark E. Warren, 'Max Weber's Liberalism for a Nietzschean World', *American Political Science Review*, LXXXII (1988) pp. 211–22. For a more radical interpretation of Weber and the 'Jewish Question' see, Gary A. Abraham, *Max Weber and the Jewish Question. A Study of the Social Outlook of his Sociology* (Champlain, Ill.: University of Illinois Press, 1992).

7.   David Beetham, 'From socialism to fascism: the relation between theory and practice in the work of Robert Michels, *Political Studies*, XXV (1977) pp. 3–24, 161–81; Wolfgang J. Mommsen, 'Robert Michels and Max Weber: Moral Conviction versus the Politics of Responsibility', in W. J. Mommsen and J. Osterhammel (eds), *Max Weber and his Contemporaries* (London: Allen and Unwin, 1987), pp. 121–38.

8.   Goldman (1992), op. cit., pp. 35–6.

9.   Sam Whimster, 'The Secular Ethic and the Culture of Modernism', in S. Whimster and S. Lash (eds), *Max Weber, Irrationality and Modernity* (London: Allen and Unwin, 1987) p. 260. Also see Peter Breiner, *Max Weber and Democratic Politics* (Ithaca, N.Y.: Cornell University Press, 1996) pp. 198–9.

10.   Wilhelm Hennis, *Max Weber. Essays in Reconstruction* (London: Allen and Unwin, 1988) p. 150. Ralph Schroeder, '"Personality" and "Inner Distance": The Conception of the Individual in Max Weber's Sociology', *History of the Human Sciences*, IV (1) pp. 61–78; Roslyn Bologh, *Max Weber and Masculine Thinking – A Feminist Inquiry* (London: Unwin Hyman,1990) p. 106; Peter Lassman and Ronald Speirs (eds), *Weber. Political Writings* (Cambridge: Cambridge University Press, 1995) p. xxii.; Whimster, op. cit., p. 266.

11.   Whimster, op. cit., p. 271.

12.   Wolfgang J. Mommsen, *Max Weber and German Politics 1890–1920* (Chicago: University of Chicago Press), pp. 326–7.

13.   Dittmar Dahlmann, 'Max Weber's Relation to Anarchism and Anarchists: The Case of Ernst Toller', in W. J. Mommsen and J. Osterhammel (eds), *Max Weber and his Contemporaries* (London: Allen and Unwin), p. 374.

14.   Eva Karádi, 'Ernst Bloch and Georg Lukács in Max Weber's Heidelberg', in W. J. Mommsen and J. Osterhammel (eds), *Max Weber and his Contemporaries* (London: Allen and Unwin, 1987), p. 500; Mommsen (1987), op. cit., pp. 121–38.

15.   For biographical details see Dahlmann, op. cit. and Richard Dove, *A Biography of Ernst Toller. He Was a German* (London: Libris, 1990), pp. 1–40.

16.   Wolf Lepenies, *Between Literature and Science: The Rise of Sociology* (Cambridge: Cambridge University Press, 1988).

17. Stefan Collini, *Public Moralists. Political Thought and Intellectual Life in Britain 1850–1930* (Oxford: Clarendon Press, 1991).
18. Fritz Ringer, *The Decline of the Mandarins: The German Academic Community, 1890–1933* (Cambridge, Mass.: Harvard University Press, 1969); *Fields of Knowledge. French Academic Culture in Comparative Perspective, 1890–1920* (Cambridge: Cambridge University Press, 1992).
19. J. T. Kloppenberg, *Uncertain Victory. Social Democracy and Progressivism in European and American Thought, 1870–1920* (Oxford: Oxford University Press, 1986); Richard Bellamy, *Liberalism and Modern Society* (Cambridge: Polity Press, 1992).
20. Steven E. Aschheim, 'Nietzschean Socialism – Left and Right, 1890–1933', *Journal of Contemporary History*, XXIII (1988) pp. 147–68; *The Nietzsche Legacy in Germany 1890–1990* (Berkeley, Calif.: University of California Press, 1992).
21. Scott Lash, *Sociology of Postmodernism* (London: Routledge, 1990), pp. 201–36.
22. Ulrich Linse, *Organisierter Anarchismus in Deutschen Kaiserreich von 1871* (Berlin: Duncker und Humblot, 1969).
23. M. Löwy, *Redemption and Utopia. Jewish Libertarian Thought in Central Europe* (London: Athlone Press, 1992).
24. Martin Green, *The Von Richthofen Sisters. The Triumphant and Tragic Modes of Love* (New York: Basic Books, 1974); Arthur Mitzman, 'Anarchism, Expressionism and Psychoanalysis', *New German Critique*, X (1977) pp. 77–109; J. E. Michaels, *Anarchy and Eros* (New York: Peter Lang, 1983); Löwy, op. cit.; Emanuel Hurwitz, *Otto Gross. Paradies-Sucher zwischen Freud und Jung* (Zurich: Suhrkamp, 1988).
25. Löwy, op. cit.
26. Eugene Lunn, *Prophet of Community. The Romantic Socialism of Gustav Landauer.* (Berkeley, Calif.: University of California Press, 1973).
27. Lewis D. Wurgaft, 'The Activists: Kurt Hiller and the Politics of Action in the German Left 1914–1933', *Transactions of the American Philosophical Society*, LXVII (1977).
28. Martin Green, *Mountain of Truth. The Counterculture Begins – Ascona 1900–1920* (Hanover, N. H.: University of New England Press, 1986).
29. Green, op. cit., pp. 238–9; Gary D. Stark, *Entrepreneurs of Ideology. Neoconservative Publishers in Germany, 1890–1933* (Chapel Hill, N.C.: University of North Carolina Press, 1981), p. 29.
30. Lunn, op. cit., p. 344. For a recent account of this counterculture see, R. H. Dominick, *The Environmental Movement in Germany: Prophets and Pioneers, 1871–1971* (Indianapolis: University of Indiana Press, 1992).
31. Marianne Weber, *Max Weber: A Biography* (New York: Wiley and Sons, 1975), p. 597.
32. Ernst Toller, *I was a German* (New York: William Morrow and Company, 1934), p. 96.
33. Weber, op. cit., p. 597.
34. Ibid.
35. Dove, op. cit., p. 32.
36. Weber, op. cit., p. 597.
37. Quoted in Hennis, op. cit., p. 214.

38. Weber, op. cit., p. 599.
39. Toller, op. cit., p. 98.
40. Weber, op. cit., p. 599.
41. Mommsen (1984), op. cit., pp. 190–282; Guenther Roth, 'Weber's Political Failure', *Telos*, 78 (1988), p. 89.
42. Guenther Roth. 'Weber the Would-Be Englishman: Anglophilia and Family History' in H. Lehmann and G. Roth, (eds), *Weber's Protestant Ethic. Origins, Evidence, Contexts* (Cambridge Univ. Press, 1993), pp. 83–121.
43. *PW*, p. xv.
44. Toller, op. cit., p. 99. For the general background also see, Wolfgang Schluchter, 'Activity and Renunciation. Max Weber on Science and Politics as Vocations', *Paradoxes of Modernity. Culture and Conduct in the Theory of Max Weber* (Stanford, Calif.: Stanford University Press, 1996), pp. 7–47.
45. Hennis, op. cit., pp. 70–71.
46. Dahlmann, op. cit., p. 369.
47. Weber, op. cit., p. 601.
48. Dove, op. cit., p. 35.
49. Quoted in Dove, op. cit., p. 39.
50. Peter Marshall, *Demanding the Impossible. A History of Anarchism* (London: Harper Collins, 1992), p. 411.
51. Lunn, op. cit., p. 247.
52. Mommsen (1987), op. cit., p. 133.
53. Arthur Mitzman, *Sociology and Estrangement. Three Sociologists in Imperial Germany* (New York: Alfred Knopf, 1973), pp. 294–5; Corrado Malandrino, 'Lettere di Anton Pannekoek a Roberto Michels (1905)', *Annali della Fondazione Luigi Einaudi*, XIX (1988) pp. 498–501; Stanley Pierson, *Marxist Intellectuals and the Working-Class Mentality in Germany, 1887–1912* (Cambridge, Mass.: Harvard University Press, 1993).
54. David Beetham, 'Reformism and the "Bourgeoisification" of the Labour Movement', in C. Levy (ed.), *Socialism and the Intelligentsia 1880–1914* (London: Routledge and Kegan Paul 1987), pp. 114–5.
55. Francesco Tuccari, *I dilemmi della democrazia moderna. Max Weber e Robert Michels* (Bari: Laterza, 1993).
56. Pierson, op. cit., p. 189.
57. Bjarne Jacobsen, 'Looking for Weber's Deepest Roots: Friedrich Albert Lange' (Unpublished paper for the Max Weber Study Group, B.S.A., London, May, 1995).
58. Dove, op. cit., pp. 40–1.
59. Ibid., p. 45
60. Ibid., p. 36.
61. Dahlmann op. cit., p. 371.
62. Schluchter (1996), op. cit., pp. 26–7.
63. Weber, op. cit., pp. 602–3.
64. Quote in Scaff, op. cit., p. 97.
65. Lassman and Speirs, op. cit., p. 231.
66. Scaff, op. cit., p. 101.
67. Wolfgang J. Mommsen, 'Max Weber and German Social Democracy', in C. Levy (ed.), *Socialism and the Intelligentsia 1880–1914* (London: Routledge and Kegan Paul, 1987), p. 101.

68. Weber, op. cit., p. 603.
69. Weber, op. cit., p. 601.
70. Roth, op. cit., pp. 139–42.
71. Alan Mitchell, *Revolution in Bavaria, 1918–19: Kurt Eisner and the Bavarian Soviet Republic* (Princeton: Princeton University Press, 1965; Paul Pörtner, 'The Writers' Revolution: Munich 1918–1919', *Journal of Contemporary History*, III (1968), pp. 137–54; Lunn, op. cit.
72. Dahlmann, op. cit., pp. 372–6; Dove, op. cit., pp. 60–87.
73. Lunn, op. cit., p. 328.
74. Lunn op. cit., pp. 317–9. The Thule Society was one of the component organisations which formed the early Nazi Party. According to Nazi racial criteria Count Arco Valley would have been considered a Jew since his mother was Jewish! For further details see, K. P. Fischer, *Nazi Germany: A New History* (London: Constable,1995), pp. 102–15.
75. Lunn, op. cit, pp. 324–7.
76. Dove, op. cit., pp. 61–70.
77. Dove, (1990), p. 81.
78. Dove, p. 84.
79. Lunn, op. cit., pp. 336–40.
80. For an account of the trial see Dahlmann, op. cit., pp. 374–5 and Dove, op. cit., pp. 91–2.
81. Roth, op. cit., p. 146; Schluchter (1996), op. cit., p. 24.
82. Hennis, op. cit., pp. 71–2.
83. Roth, op. cit., p. 146. Also see, Schluchter (1996), op. cit., p. 18.
84. Besides the actual revolt in Munich, Gustav Landauer's activities as the commissar for 'Enlightenment and Public Instruction' during the shortlived 'Writer's Republic' left scars within the University of Munich. On 7 April 1919, one day after Weber received official confirmation of his appointment to the University, Landauer suspended classes until the summer semester. He planned to create a Revolutionary University Council, open recruitment to more working class students and fuse the scientific and philosophical faculties. He would have drastically increased the participation of students and *Dozenten* in educational and administrative decision-making. The University would have become a species of libertarian co-operative and the professors' role, Max Weber's role, would have been seriously undermined. For this episode see, Lunn, op. cit., pp. 329–31.
85. Dove, op. cit., p. 90; Weber, op. cit., p. 660.
86. Löwy, op. cit., pp. 170–1.
87. Weber, op. cit. p. 673; Roth, op. cit., p. 144.
88. Quoted in Michael Ossar, *Anarchism in the Dramas of Ernst Toller. The Realm of Necessity and the Realm of Freedom* (Albany, N.Y.: State University of the New York Press, 1980), p. 79.

5 Max Weber: A German Intellectual and the Question of War Guilt after the Great War

Karl-Ludwig Ay

Historians know that German bourgeois intellectuals (Max Weber being a prominent example) experienced the verdict of war guilt against their country as though suffering from the impact of an individual and private catastrophe. For a better understanding of this reaction it may be helpful to put Weber in his social context. As a member of the bourgeois and intellectual elite of the Kaiserreich Max Weber shared their politics and gallant upper-middle-class mentality. His social group had gained for their nation a prominent position in the world of learning, economic and egalitarian modernisation, and it was socially separated from the ordinary people by the boundary line of status honour and *Satisfaktionsfähigkeit*. Members of this educated middle-class elite (*Bildungsbürgertum*) held leading positions, they identified with their nation, they represented German scholarship, and, therefore, during the revolution of November 1918 and in the period after the country's military defeat the verdict of German war guilt was experienced by Weber's class as a collective as well as an individual condemnation. Its members felt disgraced by it, whilst the common people of their own nation held them responsible for all wartime hardships.

The example of Max Weber may help to demonstrate that the ferocious protest of the German educated middle-class elite against the verdict of war guilt was a protest against the decline and the moral stigmatisation and political isolation of their country and of their own class.

Max Weber came from a large upper-middle-class family[1] which had a significant influence on German Protestant and liberal policy and which participated actively in all branches of the liberal arts. As Guenther Roth has shown in a series of articles,[2] its members not only held important positions in the Kaiserreich but they were also involved in economic enterprises in Great Britain in particular and the Netherlands and Belgium.

In a word, Max Weber grew up in a patriotic, wealthy and cosmopolitan milieu at the heart of the wealthy upper-middle-class and among bourgeois intellectuals and academics. His social group was defined by a shared social and political mentality.[3]

One cannot overestimate the importance of this bourgeois and academic social group for Germany, because they identified directly with the Empire and they were an essential element of the social base on which imperial Germany rested.[4] The core of the academically educated bureaucracy came from this bourgeois elite group or was of noble birth. The other elite groups consisted of the old Prussian agrarian aristocracy of the *Junkers*, the aristocracy of the other German states, and the military corps of regular officers. Although commoners were practically barred from a regular officer's career (excepting the artillery and the navy), the bourgeois elite shared some of the feudal habits of this corps, especially their concept of honour. Most of the sons of educated middle-class families joined the Army for a one-year service, as *Einjährig-Freiwilliger*. This privileged route – one year instead of the three of conscription – was accessible only to young men who had completed school at a *Gymnasium* and it brought them to the highest social rank of German civil society, that of the reserve officer. Most university students and academics, including Max Weber, were commissioned as reserve officers. Their behaviour to the common people combined the social distance between officer and ordinary soldier and the rites of several centuries of academic tradition. The nobility, the military and the educated bourgeois elites accepted each other as *satisfaktionsfähig*; this is, they could demand and give satisfaction by fighting ritualised life-and-death-duels.[5] Although Weber himself never fought an actual duel he seems more than once to have been ready to take the risk.[6]

In accordance with the social situation of pre-war and wartime Germany Max Weber established a correlation between honour (*Ehre*), status group (*Stand*) or status situation (*ständische Lage*),[7] and a special group ethos created by the concept of honour that was prevalent in a homogeneous social group.[8] In a wider sense the social and political elite of the *Kaiserreich*, who consisted of the educated middle-class (*Bildungsbürgertum*), the nobility and the officers' corps, formed a larger status group for whom *Satisfaktionsfähigkeit* was common. This was the decisive social line that separated the elite from the ordinary people.

This specific sense of honour and, consequently, this social dividing line connect to the next point to be made in this chapter, the specific role the *Bildungsbürgertum* claimed to play in the life of the nation. The writer and politician Friedrich Naumann, a liberal and exceedingly patriotic

Protestant pastor, was – from the 1890s – for twenty years undoubtedly the only German politician who embodied Weber's political hopes for a modern liberal policy that was in accordance with the imperialistic, economic and social interests of the Empire. In 1913 Naumann published a popular collection of his articles entitled *On Fatherland and Freedom*. The pamphlet was immediately sold out with 50 000 copies and 8000 more were printed.[9] The frontispiece carries Naumann's portrait and the facsimile of his handwritten sentence: 'We regard the loyalty to the nation and the commitment to the transformation of the masses into human beings as nothing but two aspects of the same thing.'[10] One cannot help feeling reminded of Weber's words from the days of his early friendship with Naumann: 'We [the Germans] have transformed the Poles from animals into human beings.'[11]

Undoubtedly Naumann would not have accepted my interpretation of his words, but nevertheless I make use of my privilege as a historian. To Naumann, the masses did not yet count as human beings and so they were unable to declare their loyalty to the nation. To give a further turn to the screw, the 'nation' as a human community remained restricted to the educated elites where there existed a patriotic and a social identification of *Bildungsbürger* with Imperial Germany. The elites operated a reductionism that made the meaning of *Nation* co-terminous with *Kulturnation* and consequently with their own group. They themselves were the nation because it was they who gave shape and form to culture and scholarship, and it was they who – to quote Weber (in 1919) – were protected by the umbrella of the divine right of the German monarchies.[12]

Weber's nationalism was of a patriotic type: Improving the state of one's own country did not necessarily mean being hostile to one's neighbours. The existence of at least one statement shows he actively backed the pacifist programme of a middle-class association called *Verband für internationale Verständigung*.[13] We know that since the 1890s Max Weber had persistently condemned the post-Bismarckian policy of the Kaiser and his statesmen as irrational. We have only a handful of public statements from the pre-war period about the constitutional and the political situation of the Empire. They demonstrate Weber's patriotic and liberal criticism of the imperial government and the Kaiser where he stated, 'the welfare of our fatherland precedes everything, even the prosperity of the dynasties'.[14] But because of the dominance of feudal interests and of the bureaucracy and because of the weakness of the political parties and of the *Reichstag* and the other parliaments in the Empire, the best leaders were – in his view – excluded from political responsibility. His pre-war patriotism had nothing of the spirit of pro-German aggression against any neighbouring state and, later on, whenever he dealt with the origins of the war Weber accepted the incompetence of politicians after Bismarck as a contributing factor. Most of his numerous war-time memoranda demonstrate that his political concepts even then proceeded from the idea of a liberal and parliamentary Empire that was strong and wealthy and whose domestic policy was determined by middle-class rationality and whose foreign relations relied on a stable arrangement with all other liberal, strong and wealthy nation-states.[15]

Immediately after the outbreak of the Great War Weber reported to the army to carry out his duty for his country. As a 50-year-old reserve officer could not be sent to the Front, he was detached to help organise and administer the military reserve hospitals in the Heidelberg area for the period August 1914 to September 1915. Within a few weeks the scholar who had no managerial experience had established nine new military hospitals, and he conducted the administration and handled the military discipline of the awe-inspiring number of 42 institutions for more than one year. He was in charge of the physical and psychological health of innumerable wounded soldiers and foreign prisoners of war. His job meant a working day of 12 to 16 hours, filled not only with hundreds of administrative and directing activities but it also kept him in permanent touch with the world of the common people. His reports to his superior authorities[16] consisted mainly of complaints about poor military discipline in the hospitals and proposals to improve it through repressive measures. But one will not find that Weber had any appropriate feelings of respect or acknowledgement for the wounded who had sacrificed their health in fighting for their country. As a representative of his elite group, Weber did not reveal whether he regarded them as people in their own right or merely as human military material. This attitude becomes even more obvious in his 'General Remarks' of 1915 about his experience with the administration of the military hospitals.[17] Marianne Weber characterised it as follows: 'Many of his experiences easily fitted into the scheme of his sociological types and added fresh illustrative material to them.'[18] Hence I would regard his 'remarks' as a sociological treatise on administrative problems, discipline and need for coercion; but they were certainly no warm-hearted comment on the life and death of people.

The manner in which he dealt with the violent emotions caused by the plight of the wounded soldiers reflected his martial disposition and gallant temperament and this experience finally made him discover the common soldiers as legitimate members of his *Kulturnation*. A letter from January 1915 contains some lofty remarks about the heroic soldiers and even about the 'genuine humanity' *(Menschentum)* of those soldiers he had to deal with as a disciplinary officer, 'People who live in a highly

refined civilisation and then nevertheless are equal to the horrors of war
out there ... who *despite* this come back like that, as *thoroughly decent*
as the great majority of our people – such people are genuine human
beings ....[19]

And as a social scientist he coped with the emotions stirred by the fate
of the suffering soldiers around him by transferring them to the level of
scientific thought, thus creating the new sociological category of the
'extraordinary' (*Außeralltäglichkeit*).[20] At Christmas 1914 he gave a
speech to the patients. They knew they would have to leave for the
battlefield soon after recovering. A few lines of this speech have been
saved in Marianne Weber's *Biography*.

> In everyday life death comes to us as something uncomprehended, as an
> irrational fate from which no meaning can be derived. We simply have
> to accept it. But every one of you knows why and for what he dies if it
> falls to his lot. Those who do not come back will be seed corn of the
> future. A hero's death for the freedom and honour of our people is a
> supreme achievement that will affect our children and children's chil-
> dren. There is no greater glory, no worthier end than to die this way.
> And to many death gives a perfection that life would have denied him.[21]

These words delivered under the Christmas tree recall the solemn
description of mass-slaughter in the 'Intermediate Considerations' essay,
'Death on the field of battle differs from death that is only man's common
lot. Since death is a fate that comes to everyone, nobody can ever say why
it comes precisely to him and why it comes just when it does.... Death on
the field of battle differs from this merely unavoidable dying in that in
war, and in this massiveness *only* in war, the individual can *believe* that he
knows he is dying "for" something.'[22]

The real everyday life in the hospitals was less heroic. It did not alter
Weber's attitude towards the war and it did not mitigate his fundamental
criticism of the Kaiser, the government, and the political ideologies. For
the whole time of his service Weber did not make a single public statement on politics and war and peace.[23] But maybe his experiences did
influence his political estimation of the common people. In the course of
the Great War Weber's own political ideas were converted from his old
middle-class liberalism and parliamentarianism to the programme of a
constitutional democracy. For him there no longer existed any reason for
the traditional concept of the political inferiority of the ordinary people. In
the spring of 1917 he demanded equal suffrage for every soldier even in
the state of Prussia.[24]

Obviously this new political respect for the common soldiers deferred to the newly discovered humanity of the 'human material' of the German army,[25] and, as well as his war-time liberalism, it was not shared by most of the German bourgeois intellectuals. But nevertheless he himself always felt bourgeois and he felt that this elite along with the agrarian aristocracy and the officers' corps formed the nation itself.

Grasping this fundamental trait of the mentality of the educated middle class, and so Max Weber's, helps to understand the shock they received from the egalitarianism that accompanied the military collapse and the Revolution of 1918 and from the verdict of German War Guilt formulated in the Versailles Treaty. That shock was not only connected with the loss of their elite status but with a wider complex of problems that focus on the question of war guilt.

Since the 1890s Europe had witnessed a process of increasing rivalry between the great powers and the allied blocs. In addition there was the hostility between the numerous peoples in the Austro-Hungarian Empire. These tensions culminated in the murder of the Archduke and heir to the Imperial Throne, Franz Ferdinand, in Sarajevo in the summer of 1914 and in the subsequent crisis in July. It was not until the 1960s that Fritz Fischer's famous book revealed how the imperial German military elite and the government had made use of the crisis to precipitate war.[26] Before Fischer's publication neither the allied governments nor educated Germans could know or even assume that German political will had unleashed an unprecedented catastrophe on Europe and the world. This complicates the discussion of Max Weber's, as well as other German intellectuals', knowledge of the facts of German responsibility for the outbreak of the Great War.

The publication of volume 16 of the *Max Weber–Gesamtausgabe* has informed Weberians about Weber's activities as a member of the German peace delegation to Versailles in 1919 and it has made clear to them what had already been known to historians: that German bourgeois intellectuals, like Max Weber, understood the verdict of German war guilt – as finally formulated in the Versailles Treaty of 1919 – not simply as an unjustified political act against a defeated country but one aimed to make the German nation stand disgraced and stained in the eyes of the world. Therefore the Treaty was characterised as a peace of disgrace (*Schandfrieden*).[27]

This chapter seeks to demonstrate how and why German intellectuals (Max Weber being a prominent example) experienced this verdict as though suffering from the impact of an individual and private catastrophe. For this purpose it will concentrate on three further issues:

1.   Germany's ranking in the modernisation of the western world before
     1914 and the self-confidence of German bourgeois intellectuals that
     stemmed from this,
2.   the influence of the First World War on the moral and social situation
     of this group,
3.   the mental catastrophe wrought by the military collapse, the
     Revolution and the Armistice in November 1918 and the Versailles
     Treaty of the following year (28 June).

1.   The first point leads to the question how Auschwitz was possible, how
a nation in the heart of Europe could become so cruel and barbaric for the
12-year period of Hitlerism. This question has provoked various answers.
One of them is to draw a straight line of a special German development
from Luther to Bismarck and to Hitler. Another explanation of German
National Socialism is offered by the widely adopted thesis of a German
separate path (*Sonderweg*). This notion of a separate deviating path necessarily presumes a regular highway along which the other western nations
proceeded and that Germany and German elites refused. In Randall
Collins's recent critical summary of this thesis, German society was 'often
considered non-democratic and militaristic because of failure to undergo
its own modernizing revolution; as a late modernizer, it had been antagonistic to other Advanced Societies and prone to the anticivilizing impulses
manifested in Nazism'.[28] The theory of the specific German modernity
deficits was as elegant as it was successful. A very fruitful consequence of
this was the Allied policy of Re-education after the defeat of Hitlerism.
Nevertheless the *Sonderweg* theory was a matter of ideology and undoubtedly also had unforeseen and less beneficial consequences. It obstructed a
clear view of historical reality. Germany's position in the history of
western modernisation during the nineteenth century was obscured by the
theory of modernisation lag. By the same token it also obscured the social
and intellectual German context of avant-garde intellectual giants like
Einstein, Freud, Thomas Mann, Marx, Mommsen, Nietzsche, Roentgen,
Weber and so on.
  But these people had a context. As part of the international community of science and scholarship and alongside bourgeois capitalism and
high officials of their own country, the middle-class intellectuals for-
warded the modernisation of Germany. As Collins demonstrates,
Germany in the nineteenth century was among the world leaders of modernisation. Collins isolates four indices of modernisation as found in
Great Britain, the US, and to a lesser degree France. As expressed in the
abstract to his article,

1. *Eve and the Future: Eve*

2. *Eve and the Future: First Future*

3. *Eve and the Future: The Serpent*

4. *Eve and the Future: Second Future*

5. *Eve and the Future: Adam*

6. *Eve and the Future: Third Future*

7. *A Love: Happiness*

8. *On Death, Part I: Death as Saviour*

On 2 dimensions, bureaucratization and religious secularization (especially in education), Germany led the modernization process since the 18th century; on the 3rd, capitalist industrialization, long-term differences were relatively minor; on the 4th, democratization, Germany did not lag as much as Anglo-oriented theory claims, as we see by examining separately the expansion of parliamentary power and the voting franchise in each country.[29]

2. We should, therefore, accept that Germany contributed very much to Western modernisation, and a great deal of this contribution consisted of the achievements of the social elite group of German intellectuals. No doubt they were aware of the foreign 'philosophers, mathematicians and scientists', cited by Collins, who attended 'German universities to keep up with advanced ideas', and of the estimated 10 000 American students who studied in Germany in the late nineteenth century. The German professors ranked highly in the international community of science and scholarship and they were proud of their role as modernisers and contributors to world civilisation. This was expressed in the notorious lines of Emanuel Geibel in 1861,

Macht und Freiheit, Recht und Sitte,
Klarer Geist und scharfer Hieb
Zügeln dann aus starker Mitte
Jeder Selbstsucht wilden Trieb,
Und es mag am deutschen Wesen
Einmal noch die Welt genesen.[30]

When, around 1900 less able leading German politicians claimed *a place in the sun* for their country[31] and led Germany into political isolation, a feeling of being different from the rest of Europe emerged, a tendency from which Max Weber's milieu did not remain untouched. Wolfgang Mommsen has shown the short step from a new *German Idea of Freedom* to the so-called *Ideas of 1914*, which consisted of the illusionary feeling of consent throughout all classes of the nation in the nationalistic and militaristic euphoria at the outbreak of the War.[32]

For our purposes there is no need to inquire into the origins of the Great War. The only essential issue for our line of argument is the German invasion of Belgium and Luxembourg. This was the first military action of the war. For Germany's enemies it constituted the grounds for Germany's responsibility for the war. The Germans on their part insisted that the conflicting long-term political and military interests of all European great

powers had caused the war and therefore their isolated country was innocent. But this line of reasoning was weakened by the German invasion of
the neutral states of Belgium and Luxembourg, and it was ruined by their
military machine. The resistance of the population of the invaded countries slowed down the progress of the army on its way to France, and the
army broke this resistance by the use of terror and atrocities against civilians. Already in the first weeks of the war French scholars and allied propaganda were able to prove that German soldiers had killed mothers and
their children and damaged masterpieces of architecture when proceeding
through the Belgian city of Louvain.[33]

The invasion of Belgium and the moral disaster of the massacre became
a major topic in the war of propaganda which accompanied the fighting on
the battlefields from the very beginning of the war.[34] No doubt it was the
exclusion of their country from the civilised world as a topic and a result
of this propaganda that was felt so keenly by the German academic elite
who saw themselves as personifying Germany and World Culture. They
felt immediately compelled to deny both a special German responsibility
for the war and the committing of immoral cruelties against civilians –
and they had to justify the invasion of Belgium. The first of a long series
of memoranda issued by German professors appeared on 4 October, 1914.
It had been signed by 93 of Germany's most renowned and internationally
respected scholars, scientists, writers and artists. It included Lujo
Brentano, Paul Ehrlich, Fritz Haber, Ernst Haeckel, Gerhard Hauptmann,
Friedrich Naumann, Max Planck, Max Reinhard, Wilhelm Roentgen,
Gustav von Schmoller and so on,[35] many of whom belonged to Weber's
sphere. And many more memoranda followed showing that national hubris
and political blindness were about to reach epidemic proportions.
Numerous members of the intellectual elite revelled in dreams of Germany
taking part in ruling the world alongside the other great imperialist
powers.[36]

Like most people in the belligerent countries Weber acknowledged the
invasion of Belgium had been the crucial step into war. But for him and
for most Germans this aggression had been an act of defence and therefore
justified. Beyond this explanation of the campaign through Belgium
Weber produced a further justifying argument. He denied the very existence of Belgium's neutrality. Because her borders with France were not
fortified he assumed her to be a secret ally of the western powers.[37] If this
line of reasoning is completed, it follows that the Belgian civilians who
had resisted the invasion had invited being treated as 'franc tireurs' and
combatants, and so killed. Consequently there had been no massacres and
war crimes in August 1914 but only legitimate military targets. Weber was

most certainly convinced of the truth of his argument. Admittedly he never published any articles on the German massacres in Belgium, but he considered accusations of barbarous atrocities committed by German troops as sheer propaganda.[38]

Before the late summer of 1918 Weber never doubted that Germany would win the war. But he refused to dream. The fulfilment of all the imperialistic and annexionist aspirations would provoke the everlasting and aggressive hostility of the allied western powers towards Germany and it would provoke war after war. Therefore he pleaded for modest peace conditions to be imposed by a finally victorious Germany on its enemies.[39] Furthermore he continued candidly to regard the West, England and America, as a model for further constitutional development of the Empire. In his war-time studies on the Economic Ethics of World Religions he acknowledged a universal scholarly community through his respectful use of English and French authors. Without explicitly saying it, Weber was shocked by the spectre of Germany's isolation from the West. By the end of the war this isolation had become reality.

3. My third point will consist of a short description of the mental catastrophe wrought by the military collapse, the Revolution and the Armistice in November 1918, and by the Versailles Treaty in the following June.

After four years of death, fear, hopes, inflation and hunger, which hit families of all classes in all the countries involved, the end of the war, of the imperial splendour of Hohenzollern rule and of the dominance of the traditional elites came with the sudden military collapse of Austria and Germany in October 1918. It was accompanied by a strong and growing popular demand for peace and by the revolutionary period from November 1918 to the spring of 1919. Defeat and revolution resulted from the people's hunger for peace, no matter at what price. In this situation most of the loyal middle-class intellectuals were no longer able to understand essentially what was happening. They did not realise the depth of people's desire for peace and they were blind to the broad movement for the removal of the old order of state and society. Numerous individual reports demonstrate that most of them were profoundly surprised when they learned from their newspapers on 8 and 10 November that there had been revolutions in Munich and Berlin. Without seeking the learned advice of the leading academics the people had adopted socialist revolutionary leaders and toppled the German monarchs from power and made Germany a democratic state.

The bourgeois intellectuals had collectively lost their moral leadership of the nation. As a result of their ideological role in boosting morale in a war that was now lost, their identification with the nation had terminated; they now appeared as responsible for all the hardships of the war as well as the continuing international isolation caused by the economic and political blockade after the armistice. In the first weeks of the revolutionary period they seemed for a while to be treated as public parasites[40] – such was the fall from grace of the proud middle-class intellectuals who had been so confident of their importance.

At this sharpest of turning points most of this group 'got their feet back on the ground',[41] including Weber.[42] On the same day (4 November) that the revolt of the sailors in Kiel began and Kurt Eisner announced the Revolution in Bavaria, Max Weber in a speech before Munich liberals publicly pleaded against peace at all costs and against a Socialist Revolution:[43] 'The bourgeois order has a tenacious hold on life....' He was right but at the time the political opinion of his class carried little weight. During the first phase of the revolutionary period in Germany socialism seemed to be victorious. In an astonishing turn Weber now declared his convictions were nearest to Socialism.[44]

Weber did not remain resigned to the military defeat and revolutionary change for long. To legitimise and to formalise the revolutionary turn to democracy, the German political parties and the revolutionary government of the Empire[45] planned to give the country a new constitution. Like other academic liberals such as Edgar Jaffé, Hugo Preuss, Gustav Radbruch, Ernst Troeltsch, who all took on political posts, Weber for the months November 1918 to January 1919 was always at the point of taking on a leading political or administrative function in order to contribute to the reconstruction of Germany as a respected parliamentary republic.[46] He tried for nomination as a candidate of the liberal middle-class party, the German Democratic Party (*Deutsche Demokratische Partei*), for the January elections to the constitutional assembly (*Verfassunggebende Nationalversammlung*) in Weimar. He failed, but nevertheless he took an active part in the election campaign of his party, and in December he was at least invited to take part in the preparatory deliberations for a new constitution for the Reich.[47]

Wolfgang Mommsen has summarised Weber's activities and ambitions during the post-war period and especially during the election campaign in a few lines: firstly, the making of a democratic constitution for the new republic; secondly, the mobilisation of the German middle classes for a progressive and democratic policy; thirdly, the rejection of the accusation that only Germany was responsible for the war, an accusation which he considered false and unfair.[48] As can be seen the emphasis was not primarily on the need for an immediate peace at all costs but on the conditions for a settlement. That is, he defended the war even after it was lost. In doing this he was defending the mentality of middle-class interests against the common desire for peace and the mass movement of the Revolution.

In his last speech before the Revolution he said, on 4 November 1918, 'There is at least one condition for the stability of peace: its appearance must allow all peoples involved a sincere and innermost submission.'[49] The stability of the peace was dependent on its honourable appearance and the appearance of peace was regarded as a question of honour. One needs to remember Weber's gallant notion of honour belonged to a man who on more than one occasion was on the brink of fighting a duel.[50]

When Weber made this speech he could not foresee that a leading politician, the revolutionary Bavarian Prime Minister Kurt Eisner, who had been one the leading protagonists of peace and reconciliation between the nations during the war, would on 23 November publish papers that seemed to imply German responsibility for the war. For Eisner confessing German guilt was a means of reconciliation with allied statesmen and in addition was meant to mitigate their conditions for peace. Eisner also hoped for a further effect: the revolutionary German people would see who was responsible for the disastrous war and for their misery: the Kaiser and the imperial government, the military, the capitalists, the bureaucracy, and the bourgeois intellectual elite; in other words, people like Weber. During the revolutionary period, then, the question of war guilt came to have a specific social and political aspect.

The actual effect of Eisner's publication on the peace negotiations may be disregarded here. But its internal effect is of great interest because it provoked an extremely emotional campaign among bourgeois intellectuals against any verdict of war guilt.[51] Nearly from its very beginning, this campaign accompanied the allied deliberations about the conditions for peace with Germany and Austria; it was also to poison the Weimar Republic from its inception until its finish,[52] and it marked the real start of the German deviation into the *Sonderweg*. At the same time the Reich and the German-speaking remainder of Austria were the only defeated and totally isolated occidental states, their elites left feeling humiliated and stigmatised by the verdict of war guilt. Only Germany, and Russia in the east, remained isolated and without reconciliation after the war. The *Sonderweg* came to an end 25 or 30 years later when, firstly the Hitler Empire was smashed in 1945 and, secondly, when the Cold War, after 1946, created new political alliances ending the international isolation of both parts of a then divided country; and last but not least, by the German recognition of German guilt.

In 1929 Weber's liberal and democratic colleague and friend Hermann Oncken explained the reason for the above-mentioned campaign in a radio broadcast: 'We struggle against the paragraph on war guilt [in the Versailles Treaty] which has been forced upon us, because it is virtually the moral core of the peace treaty.'[53] And Oncken did not fight alone.[54] A semi-official Special Centre for the Research of the Origins of the War edited a specialised monthly on the 'war guilt question' as well as a bibliographical survey.[55] The Union of German Booksellers published its own 175-page guide of the vast literature on the same subject.[56]

When Weber reacted to Eisner's publication (see above) he found himself in the mainstream of his academic colleagues. His venomous tirades against the revolutionaries show he had realised Eisner's intentions. Weberians may be shocked by his chauvinist hopes for national resistance to his country's humiliation by the military victors. Obviously Weber's social class and his notion of honour were violated by the question of war guilt. The day after Eisner's publication he sent a famous letter to Friedrich Crusius about the then current political situation. He called the revolutionary regime an *Ochlokratie* – mob rule, and he denounced the 'political and social masochism of those pacifists lacking all sense of dignity, even now grubbing about with great relish in sentiments of "guilt".'[57]

But one phrase in the letter shows Weber himself shared – and also fought – those sentiments in his nightmarish dreams of guilt when he pondered on – and refused the idea that the defeat might have been a trial by ordeal:[58] '*Success* in war had not been – to my inner self – proof of something like a trial by ordeal, and the God of Battles had very well been "on the side of the larger battalions".' The letter abounds with 'we' and 'us': 'We must let the raging class struggle take its course till it spends its fury', or, '110 years ago we showed the world that we – and only we – were able to be one of the leading civilised races even under the rule of a foreign oppressor. This is what we shall now do once again!' Who did he mean by 'we'? We may suppose Weber was insisting on something like an exclusive identity between the *Bildungsbürger* and the nation, both of them condemned through the judgement of the military defeat and the tribunal of Versailles.

On a sheet of notepaper whose purpose is unknown he raved about the same subjects. Among other notes it contains the following:

'Lost – the greatest war in history! I Not *militarily* but *politically*. Too many enemies I By doing wrong? – So now I slap them on the mouth! I A dog's sense of honour. Trading off dignity for advantages.I'[59]

Maybe these notes served as a first rough sketch for his last contribution to the election campaign, an article entitled 'About the question of "War guilt"', which was printed 17 January 1919 in the *Frankfurter Zeitung*.[60]

The point of interest in this article is to see how Weber, even then, insisted on his war-time analysis of the European political constellation from which the war had originated, how he unswervingly declared that Germany had had reasonable war objectives, and the emphasis he placed on dignity and honour. Germany had been pronounced guilty with the help of the Eisner publication and without fair trial by the Versailles tribunal of allied powers. And this 'guilty', he explained, would be the weapon to bend German provinces to foreign rule and to load uncounted reparations onto Germany's shoulders in order to subject her forever. He did not use the word, but today's readers may be strongly reminded of the – later – popular term, *Schandfrieden*. Ironically, the day after the publication of this article, while Kurt Eisner was on an election campaign, the Bavarian Government decided to call Weber to Lujo Brentano's chair at Munich University.

War-time and post-war inflation had consumed the fortune of Weber's family. After the death of his widowed sister Lily he had to maintain her orphaned children. Exhausted by long years of starvation he had to earn a living for his now larger family. The official document stating his appointment to the professorship in Munich is dated 6 April 1919 – the last day before Bavaria became a Soviet Republic. And in May, after the revolutionary Bavarian Soviet Republic had been bloodily suppressed, he joined the German delegation to Versailles. The defeat of his country, the Bavarian revolution, the inflation, public and personal economic decline and, consequently, the collapse of the traditional elites, of his own class and of the traditional system of values in common with his days on the Versailles delegation and the Versailles Treaty, induced a mood of frustration and melancholic resignation.

It was probably during these days in the spring of 1919 that he gave expression to those sentiments when in revising 'The Profession and Vocation of Politics' he wrote: 'Only someone who is certain that he will not be broken when the world, seen from his point of view, is too stupid or too base for what he wants to offer it, and who is certain that he will be able to say "Nevertheless" in spite of everything – only someone like this has a "vocation" for politics.'[61] These were the concluding words of his last and greatest text about politics and they express his mood of resignation. He was not strong enough for his vocation for politics.

After Versailles Max Weber returned to his books[62] and retired from the life of active politics for the last 16 months of his life. In the winter of 1919 until 1920 he began to rewrite his book on Economy and Society. In his revised chapter on status situation (*ständische Lage*) we find not one word about honour.[63]

NOTES

1. See the genealogical tables which can be found in each volume of the *Briefe* of the *Max Weber Gesamtausgabe* (hitherto vols 5 and 6 for the period 1906–1910 (Tübingen: Mohr, 1990 and 1994).

2. Guenther Roth, 'Introduction' and 'Weber the Would-Be Englishman: Anglophilia and Family History' in: H. Lehmann and G. Roth, (eds), *Weber's Protestant Ethic. Origins, Evidence, Contexts* (Cambridge Univ. Press, 1993), pp. 1–24 and 83–121; 'Between Cosmopolitanism and Ethnocentrism: Max Weber in the Nineties', in: *Telos* 86, (1994), pp. 1–15.

3. The German term for this group is *Bildungsbürgertum*. 'The enigmatic character of the *Bildungsbürgertum* is not only determined by origins, occupation, political and religious views, income situation and property; rather it is shaped by a sociality which is defined primarily by another characteristic, namely a commonality grounded in education whatever all other differences. The specific prestige which is thereby obtained is defined from within by convention and successfully claimed to the world. From this characteristic stems the equality within the group and the exclusivity from the world. The claim to special social prestige is legitimised by the assumed representation of values and behavioural orientations that may claim general social significance. The standards of their own life-conduct are considered to be exemplary; analogously to 'noblesse oblige' it is 'education demands.' M. R. Lepsius, 'Das Bildungsbürgertum als ständische Vergesellschaftung', M. R. Lepsius, ed., *Demokratie in Deutschland. Soziologisch-historische Konstellationsanalysen* (Göttingen: Vandenhoeck & Ruprecht, 1993), pp. 303–14.

4. See F. Ringer (1969), *The Decline of German Mandarins. The German Academic Community, 1890–1933* (Cambridge/Mass.: Harvard Univ. Press, 1969); 'Sociography of German Academics 1863–1938', *Central European History*, 25, (1992), pp. 251–80.

5. U. Frevert, *Ehrenmänner. Das Duell in der bürgerlichen Gesellschaft*, (Munich: C. H. Beck, 1991), *passim*, especially pp. 11 ff.

6. Frevert, ibid., 'Honour as a key concept of a status society still had validity for Weber and he paid it great attention in both his scientific work and in his personal life. He saw himself publicly as someone capable of duelling and did not allow any occasion in practice to divert him from this habit.' p. 12.

7. See the chapter written before the war, 'Class, Status, Party' ("Klasse, Stand, Parteien") in *Economy and Society* (New York: Bedminster, 1968), p. 932: 'In contrast to classes, Stände (*status groups*) are normally groups [WuG: "Gemeinschaften"]. They are, however, often of an amorphous kind. In contrast to the purely economically determined 'class situation,' we wish to designate as *status situation* every typical component of the life of men that is determined by a specific, positive or negative, social estimation *honour*. This honour may be connected with any quality shared by a plurality, and of course, it can be knit to a class situation: class distinctions are linked in the most varied ways with status distinctions'. The corresponding post-war chapter about 'Status Groups and Classes' (*Stände und Klassen*) runs as follows: '"Status" (*Ständische Lage*) shall mean an effective claim to social esteem in terms of positive or negative privileges', (ibid., p. 305, and Wu G, pp. 534–5) and much else, but nothing related to the concept of honour.

8. See Max Weber, '*Die Börse, I. Zweck und äußere Organisation*' (Göttingen: Vandenhoeck & Ruprecht, 1894), p. 47: 'Above all he [the small speculator] hinders the formation of a uniform class of stock exchange traders defined by general social background, upbringing, education and experience who would then be in a position to recruit "honour courts" from their own membership and would then have the energy to have an educational influence and whose verdicts would be respected. At no time will the verdicts of an honour court, which is constituted from the social mishmash that is now the public of our exchanges, find respect; this is because the sheer prerequisite of a uniform concept of honour [*'ein einheitlicher "Ehrbegriff"'*] is lacking.'

9. Friedrich Naumann, *Das Blaue Buch von Vaterland und Freiheit. Auszüge aus seinen Werken*, and *Von Vaterland und Freiheit. Auszüge* (Königstein i.T. / Leipzig: Langewiesche, 1913).

10. 'Das Bekenntnis zur Nationalität und zur Menschwerdung der Masse sind für uns nur zwei Seiten derselben Sache.'

11. *MWG, I/4*, p. 626–7, 'Man hat gesprochen von einer Herabdrückung der Polen zu deutschen Staatsbürgern zweiter Klasse. Das Gegenteil ist wahr: wir haben die Polen aus Tieren zu Menschen gemacht.' (November 1896)

12. *MWG, I/16*, p. 418 (2 January 1919 in Heidelberg).

13. Soon in *MWG, I/8*, Anhang.

14. This was said, 30 November 1908, in response to Georg Jellinek's comments on the Daily Telegraph affair. Weber's address will be published soon in *MWG, I/8*.

15. *MWG, I/16*, passim.

16. *Erfahrungsberichte über Lazarettverwaltung*, critically edited in *MWG, I/15*, pp. 26–48; partly trans. in Marianne Weber, *Max Weber. A Biography* (New Brunswick, N.J.: Transaction, 1985), pp. 537–50.

17. Ibid.

18. Marianne Weber, op. cit., p. 536.

19. Marianne Weber, op. cit., pp. 522 ff. The German original is as follows: 'Menschen, die inmitten einer raffinierten Kultur leben, die dann trotzdem draußen dem Grausen des Krieges gewachsen sind (was für einen Senegalneger keine Leistung ist!), und die dann *trotzdem* so zurückkommen, so *grundanständig*, wie die große Mehrzahl unserer Leute, – das ist echtes Menschentum ...'). M. Weber, *Max Weber. Ein Lebensbild* (Tübingen: Mohr, 1926), p. 531.

20. *FMW*, p. 335; the term *Außeralltäglichkeit* can be found in the German version of the *Intermediate Reflections* near the phrase quoted below in note 23 ('Zwischenbetrachtung. Theorie der Stufen und Richtungen religiöser Weltablehnung', *MWG, I/19*, p. 493).

21. Marianne Weber, op. cit., p. 527.

22. *FMW*, p. 335; see also the original version: 'Und von jenem Sterben, welches gemeines Menschenlos ist und gar nichts weiter, ein Schicksal, welches jeden ereilt, ohne daß je gesagt werden könnte, warum gerade ihn und gerade jetzt ... – von diesem ... unvermeidlichen Sterben scheidet sich der Tod im Felde dadurch, daß hier, und in dieser Massenhaftigkeit nur hier, der Einzelne zu wissen *glauben* kann: daß er "für" etwas stirbt.' *MWG, I/19*, p. 493.

23   Except for the reports on discipline in military hospitals (*MWG, I/15*, pp. 26–48), there is only one – then unpublished – text in the respective *MWG* volume dating from before the end of 1915 (see note 39). See also W. J. Mommsen, *Max Weber and German Politics* (Chicago: Chicago University Press, 1984), pp. 190 ff.

24.   See Max Weber's articles *Ein Wahlrechtsnotgesetz des Reichs. Das Recht der heimkehrenden Krieger* (March 1917) and *Das preußische Wahlrecht*, (April 1917), *MWG, I/15*, pp. 217–21, and pp. 224–35.

25.   During the Great War the soldiers of the German army were commonly referred to as 'Menschenmaterial'. Article 'Material', *Etymologisches Wörterbuch des Deutschen* (Munich: Deutscher Taschenbuch Verlag, 1995), p. 847

26.   F. Fischer, *Germany's Aims in the First World War* (London: Chatto & Windus, 1967) and below, note 51 and 52. For a short survey of the German discussion about the question of war guilt see also N. Ferguson, 'Public Finance and National Security: The Domestic origins of the First World War Revisited', *Past and Present*, 142, (1994), pp. 141–68.

27.   See the evidence in the final part of this paper.

28.   R. Collins, 'German-Bashing and the Theory of Democratic Modernization', *Zeitschrift für Soziologie*, 24/1, (1995), pp. 3–21.

29.   Collins, op. cit., p. 3.

30.   E. Geibel, '*Deutschlands Beruf*', (1861) first print in Geibel's *Heroldsrufe* (1871), and in his *Gesammelte Werke*, Vol. 3, (1883), p. 214.

31.   Chancellor Bernhard von Bülow in the Reichstag, 6 December 1897, said, 'We will not force others into the shade but we also demand our place in the sun.'

32.   W. J. Mommsen, 'Die "deutsche Idee der Freiheit". Die deutsche Historikerschaft und das Modell des monarchischen Konstitutionalismus im Kaiserreich', *Staatswissenschaften und Staatspraxis*, 3, (1992), pp. 43–63. In brief see also Th. Nipperdey, *Deutsche Geschichte 1866–1918*, vol. 2: 'Machtstaat vor der Demokratie', (Munich: C. H. Beck, 1992), pp. 778 ff.

33.   J. Horne and A. Kramer (1994) 'German 'Atrocities' and Franco-German Opinion, 1914: The Evidence of German Soldier's Diaries', *The Journal of Modern History*, 66, (1994), pp. 1–33.

34.   Horne and Kramer, op. cit., see also K.-L. Ay, *Die Entstehung einer Revolution. Die Volksstimmung in Bayern während des Ersten Weltkrieges* (Berlin: Duncker & Humblot, 1968), p. 43.

35.   Horne and Kramer, op. cit., p. 5.

36.   See F. Fischer, op. cit.; Chr. Jansen, *Professoren und Politik. Politisches Denken und Handeln der Heidelberger Hochschullehrer 1914–1935* (Göttingen: Vandenhoeck & Ruprecht, 1992); K. Schwabe, *Wissenschaft und Kriegsmoral. Die deutschen Hochschullehrer und die politischen Grundlagen des Ersten Weltkriegs* (Göttingen: Vandenhoeck & Ruprecht, 1969).

37.   See Weber's article 'Deutschland unter den Europäischen Weltmächten' (9 November 1916), *MWG, I/15*, pp. 161–94, especially pp. 176 ff., and the newspaper-reports from 1 August 1916, about his speech 'An der Schwelle des dritten Kriegsjahrs', *MWG, I/15*, pp. 656–89, especially p. 676.

38.   See Weber's statement on 4 February 1919 during the first session of the Heidelberg *Arbeitsgemeinschaft für Politik des Rechts* (*Heidelberger*

Vereinigung), concerning the 'Abwehr der "Greuel-Propaganda"' of the allied powers, *MWG, I/16,* p. 207.

39. This follows clearly from his then unpublished article (spring, 1915) about the problems of making peace; *MWG, I/15,* pp. 54–67.

40. See K.-L. Ay, *Appelle einer Revolution* (Munich: Süddeutscher Verlag, 1968).

41. This was the usual term for the hostile arrangement with the Revolution and democracy – 'sich auf den Boden der Tatsachen stellen'.

42. See W. J. Mommsen, 'Einleitung', *MWG, I/16,* p. 3.

43. Speech in Munich on 'Deutschlands politische Neuordnung', *MWG, I/16,* pp. 363 ff.

44. *MWG, I/16,* p. 379. Three weeks after the revolution, Weber declared himself to be scarcely distinguishable from the numerous economically literate members of the social democracy (1 December 1918 in Heidelberg). A few days later Weber's period of fellow-travelling was over.

45. The first article of the Weimar Constitution is, 'Das Deutsche Reich ist eine Republik. Die Staatsgewalt geht vom Volke aus.' The term 'Reich' is a relic and a reminder of the name and the splendour of the 'Holy Roman Empire', which was quite the opposite of modern annexionistic or imperialistic states. In modern times the name as such has never indicated a programme of aggressivity or militarism.

46. For Weber's positions and activities see W. J. Mommsen, *Max Weber und die deutsche Revolution 1918/19* (Heidelberg: Stiftung Reichspräsident-Friedrich-Ebert-Gedenkstätte. Kleine Schriften 18, 1994).

47. See the record of the deliberations (9–10 December 1918) about the Constitution of the Weimar Republic including Weber's proposals, *MWG, I/16,* pp. 56–90.

48. W. J. Mommsen's 'Einleitung', *MWG, I/16,* p. 4.

49. 'Das Mindeste für einen dauerhaften Frieden ist, daß er so aussieht, daß alle beteiligten Völker sich aufrichtig innerlich fügen können.' See note 43.

50. See the opening section of this chapter.

51. For the discussions in Germany on the *Kriegsschuldfrage,* M. Dreyer and O. Lembcke, *Die deutsche Diskussion um die Kriegsschuldfrage 1918/19* (Berlin: Duncker & Humblot, 1993); U. Heinemann, *Die verdrängte Niederlage. Politische Öffentlichkeit und Kriegsschuldfrage in der Weimarer Republik* (Göttingen: Vandenhoeck & Ruprecht, 1983).

52. 'Dieser wirklichkeitsblinde Nationalismus wurde zu einer der schwersten Belastungen der Weimarer Republik. Der Kampf gegen den 'Versailler Schmachfrieden' und die 'Kriegsschuldlüge' geriet zur Lebenslüge eines Nationalismus, der über den Geburtsmakel der Republik, den verlorenen Krieg, nie hinwegkam.' D. Langewiesche, 'Nation und Staat in der jüngeren deutschen Geschichte', *Historische Zeitschrift,* 254 (1992), p. 375.

53. Cited in Chr. Weisz, *Geschichtsauffassung und politisches Denken Münchner Historiker der Weimarer Zeit. Konrad Beyerle, Max Buchner, Michael Doeberl, Erich Marcks, Karl Alexander von Müller, Hermann Oncken* (Berlin: Duncker & Humblot, 1970), p. 238.

54. Among works by well-known authors were J. Ebbinghaus, *Kants Lehre vom ewigen Frieden und die Kriegsschuldfrage* (Tübingen, 1929); H. Kantorowicz, *Gutachten zur Kriegsschuldfrage 1914,* ed. I. Geiss,

with an introduction by G. W. Heinemann (Frankfurt a.M.: Europäische Verlags-Anstalt, 1967); M. von Montgelas, *Leitfaden zur Kriegsschuldfrage* (Berlin, 1923).

55.   *Literatur zur Kriegsschuldfrage* (Berlin: Zentralstelle für die Erforschung der Kriegsursachen, 1926). The title of the monthly was *Die Kriegsschuldfrage. Monatsschrift für internationale Aufklärung.*

56.   *Die Kriegsschuldfrage Ein Verzeichnis der Literatur des In- und Auslands betreffend die Geschichte des imperialistischen Zeitalters* (Leipzig: Börsenverein deutscher Buchhändler, Ausschuß der Deutschen Gesellschaft für Auslandsbuchhandel', 1925).

57.   'politisch-sozialer Masochismus würdeloser Pazifisten, die bis jetzt wollüstig in "Schuld"-Gefühlen wühlen'; M. Weber, *Gesammelte Politische Schriften* (München: Drei Masken Verlag, 1921), p. 482.

58.   'als ob der Krieg*erfolg* innerlich etwas bewiese wie ein Gottesgericht, und als ob der Schlachtengott nicht "mit den größeren Bataillonen" wäre. [...] Den wütenden Klassenkampf müssen *wir* austoben lassen ... *Wir* haben der Welt vor 110 Jahren [in the Napoleonic wars] gezeigt, daß *wir – nur wir –* unter Fremdherrschaft eines der ganz großen Kulturvölker zu sein vermochten. *Das* machen *wir* jetzt noch einmal!' Ibid.

59.   'Größten Krieg der Geschichte *verloren.*| Nicht *militärisch* sondern politisch. Zu viel Gegner | Durch Unrecht? – so jetzt! | Auf den Mund schlagen! | Hundeehre. Erhandeln von Vorteilen durch Würdelosigkeit |'; *MWG, I/16,* pp. 160 ff. See also the *Editorische Bericht*, ibid., pp. 158 ff.

60.   *MWG, I/16,* pp. 179 ff.

61.   *PW*, p. 369. The sentence cannot be found in Weber's original notes for his speech (28 January 1919, *MWG ,I/17, pp. 138–55* but only in its – obviously enlarged – printed version (ibid., pp. 157–252). This booklet of 65 pages (it takes approximately 3 to 4 hours to read the complete version to an audience) which was published at the end of June, 1919 ('Editorischer Bericht', *MWG, I/17,* p. 134), a few weeks after Weber's return from the Versailles conference.

62.   *Wirtschaft und Gesellschaft* (1921–22) and *Gesammelte Aufsätze zur Religionssoziologie* (1920–21).

63.   See above, note 7.

6 Sexual Revolution and Anarchism: Erich Mühsam

Ulrich Linse

A Portrait of Mühsam

Mühsam was a leading figure in the world of what may be termed post-terrorist anarchism, an anarchism that belonged more to the parlour than the barricades. Mühsam was an amateur artist and writer whose artistic output passed through the phases of naturalism, expressionism and social realism and avoided the de-politicisation of the aesthetic in favour of pronounced ideological biases.[1] His work was rooted in emotional rebellion and opposition to bourgeois society and the authoritarian establishment.[2] Before the war Mühsam spent his time in the bohemian cafes and cabarets of European cities, especially those of Munich and Berlin, and the libertarian subculture of Ascona. At the turn of the century he came into contact with a workers' anarchism, which was anti-nationalist and anti-social democratic, and the alternative 'real' socialism of Gustav Landauer. Mühsam believed it his political duty to create an intellectual and material home for social outcasts and those belonging to the under-class. (His journal carried the name of his programme, *Cain. A Journal for Humanity*.) His activities within Landauer's Socialist Federation were unsuccessful, as were his endeavours during the First World War to bring about an anti-militaristic front and to initiate a mass anti-war movement. He propagandised for the dissolution of the Wittelsbach monarchy, and like other German writers he took part in the revolutionary radicalisation in Bavaria.[3] In the spring of 1919 he was actively involved in a legal capacity in the Foreign Office of the first brief Soviet Republic in Munich, which is sometimes incorrectly termed 'anarchist'. The outcome of the activities was 15 years imprisonment on charges of high treason, but he was released in an amnesty (together with Hitler) in 1924. He settled in Berlin and with his monthly publication *Fanal* he vehemently opposed the Weimar Republic because of its adherence to the old author-itarian style of the Wilhelmine state. His plays were staged in Piscator's theatre in Berlin. Motivated by the Bavarian revolutionary experience and

129

repression Mühsam the anarchist then tried to unite the 'revolutionary proletariat' in a united front and, amongst other things, was active in the communist 'Red Cross' for political prisoners. In 1933 he published his political testament 'How to liberate society from the state. What is communist anarchism?' that was a combination of Bakunin, Landauer, Kropotkin and Lenin. His – failed – objective was to free the German anarchists from their sect-like obsession and political self-isolation. He himself remained a political loner, as well as a marginal literary figure. His own contribution to anarchist theoretical development (in direct opposition to his anarchist and syndicalist comrades in Germany) was based on his Bavarian experiences. For him the soviet was a realisation of anarchist administrative principles which for him legitimised the dictatorship of the proletariat. The National Socialists arrested him for his own 'protection' and he was murdered by the SS after being tortured in the concentration camp at Oranienburg in 1934. His unshockable wife Krescentia 'Zensl' Elfinger (1884–1962), a Bavarian farmer's daughter and a waitress, whom he had married in 1915,[4] managed to bring parts of his work into the Stalinist Soviet Union where his name and work were misused for propaganda purposes. After his re-discovery in the wake of the anti-authoritarian student revolt of 1968 in West Germany, he also gained partial recognition in the DDR.

Two 'Anarchists' and a Woman

The imprisonment and threatened certification of Otto Gross and the consequences for his wife Frieda (with the possible loss of custody over their two children) caused the lives of Max Weber and Erich Mühsam to overlap for a brief period of time. In a letter to Emil Lask in November 1913 Weber complained that Frieda had unfortunately discussed this matter with 'such sad dimwits, like that Mühsam and his gang' who for Weber were synonymous with 'anarchist riffraff'. Another letter (25 December 1913) to Lask, who had been a former lover of Frieda, throws more light on the matter.[5] In this Mühsam is no longer described as a dimwit, but is singled out from those 'spineless characters', 'fools', and 'windbags', to whom Mühsam had passed on information from Frieda that included a letter written by the doctor in charge of the Austrian asylum where Otto Gross was being held. Weber criticised Mühsam for not being aware that these others would misuse the case for their own purposes. 'It was quite clear that these spineless dimwits, who soil the good name of "Revolution" with their bragging heroics on paper, would misuse this solely for their own advancement.' Lask received this message, obviously to pass on to Mühsam: 'In my opinion, it is Mr. Mühsam's duty to do all he can, to get that lot to keep their gobs shut.' This angry letter at least bestows upon Mühsam a special role within the ranks of the hated 'windbags' (these included the writers Franz Jung, Ludwig Rubiner, Blaise Cendrars and Simon Guttmann!) despite having published jointly a short appeal on behalf of Otto Gross in a special edition of the Munich based 'Revolution' – so disparaged by Weber.[6] These letters make clear the special role occupied by Mühsam as Frieda Gross's confidant, bound as they were by a common hatred of the state. In Weber's opinion she should have remained silent or found a more reliable – and chivalrous – confidant like himself.

Weber was blinded by his anger. Mühsam had in fact tried to remain discreet and had only made an issue of the affair in his own magazine *Cain. A Journal for Humanity* as a result of indirect pressure exerted by the Berlin group, led by Franz Pfemfert, whose journal *Aktion* had published an appeal for Otto Gross.[7] In the January issue of 1914 Mühsam ended his reticence which he justified: 'Unlike *Aktion* I am of the opinion that matters which are not yet definite should not be discussed publicly. As long as there is hope that an injustice can be rectified without outside pressure I do not feel the need to complicate matters by shouting about them.'[8] But now he thought it was necessary to voice an opinion on the matter, lest he be accused of indifference.

Weber's rivalry with the anarchist Mühsam culminated in Weber's offer to Frieda Gross to 'give her all possible help, including the most outright force' (*äußerste Gewaltsamkeit*).[9] This anticipated Mühsam's own later public threat to launch 'a very active campaign' to free Otto Gross from the mental asylum in which he had been confined by his father.[10] The remarkable legal efforts made by Weber to protect Franziska zu Reventlow's son Rolf from military service in Germany in spring 1914, would have met with Mühsam's approval.[11] In 1910 the public prosecutor in Munich had accused Mühsam and his associates 'of trying to persuade as many conscripts as possible not to join the army and to flee to Switzerland … [Mühsam's friend Johannes] Nohl had persuaded the mechanic Pemsel, who should have joined the 3rd Pioneer Battalion on 21 October 1908, not to join and supplied him with money for his escape to Switzerland.' (Indictment). (At the beginning of the war the Countess Reventlow took the anarchist course of self-help and rowed her son across Lake Constance to Switzerland and safety.) Weber the academic and Mühsam the writer had more in common than Weber would have wished to acknowledge. There are no known statements by Mühsam about Weber.

What the reader of Weber's letters cannot know, but could perhaps suspect, is that Mühsam's radical approach did not stem solely from his anarchistic solidarity with Otto Gross (with whom he had been friends since 1907) but rather the fact that Frieda Gross (after having made a pact of sexual freedom with her husband in spring 1907) had become his lover. Despite numerous sexual adventures in the meantime he still thought back to their 'blissful honeymoon period' when he had gone to Augsburg with Frieda.[12] On New Year's Eve in 1911/1912 he wrote in his diary: 'Friedel, Friedel! This year begins with thoughts of you and this year like all the years for the rest of my days will end with thoughts of you – and I shall live in eternal misery.'[13] And on New Year's Eve in 1915 he wrote: 'Friedel has become like a dream to me, a sweet and tender dream, which I shall continue to dream for the rest of my days.'[14] Two years later, re-reading the reporting of his trial in 1910 (see below), in which he had been derided for his 'grotesque appearance', he consoled himself in May 1912, 'And in spite of this quite a few women – and probably not the worst – have been very, very fond of me. A person who Frieda has loved can't possibly be so ugly!'[15] Mühsam who himself was always in financial difficulty was at this time still giving Frieda money for her son Peter, who had been born during the year of their relationship.

It is obvious, that concerning Frieda and Otto Gross and their Ascona friends, Weber was entering dangerous territory, where his hatred of anarchism and his feelings of chivalry have their counterpart in his own fantasies of violence and sexual competitiveness. The despised pseudo-revolutionary 'idiot' and bohemian, and fourteen years his junior, whom he nevertheless also refers to as 'Mr. Mühsam', embodied a mixture of anarchism and sexual revolution of which Weber in his Ascona visits of 1913 and 1914 knows but dares not partake.

Although Weber never personally met Mühsam in Ascona (Mühsam was a regular visitor between 1904 and 1909) he will have read Mühsam's brochure 'Ascona' published in 1905 in Locarno. This mentions the 'exceptional Germans' living there, and concluded that Ascona was pre-destined to become 'a meeting place for those who due to their individualist tendencies are unsuited to ever becoming useful members of capitalist society'.[16] So Weber's encounter with an Asconan anarchism according to Mühsam's viewpoint is one which belongs to the utopian and not the revolutionary syndicalist variety as represented by Robert Michels.[17] (see Levy, above.) It was an anti-capitalist (or even pre-capitalist) defiance by Mühsam who saw himself as the advocate of the lumpenproletariat.

Indeed the people with whom Weber enjoyed particularly friendly relationships in Ascona were also the close friends of Mühsam and in agreement with his anarchist sexual revolutionary endeavours. These included not only Frieda and Otto Gross (according to police records Otto and his girlfriend Sophie Benz belonged to Mühsam's close circle of friends in Munich), but also the Countess Reventlow (whom Mühsam apparently personally introduced to Otto in Munich),[18] and particularly Frieda's boyfriend at that time Ernst Frick with whom Weber discussed anarchism of the deed (*Tat-Anarchismus*). Mühsam had already met Frick in 1904/5 as editor of the Zurich anarchist publication *Weckruf*, and according to police evidence Frick was one of Mühsam's closest associates in the anarchist scene in Munich in 1909.[19] It is very likely, that he was one of the main members of the group led by Mühsam who were involved in smuggling saccharin from Switzerland to Austria in order to finance their 'Action Group' ('*Gruppe Tat*') whose aim was to bring about 'Propaganda of the Deed' by means of bomb attacks, break-ins and robbery, politely termed as 'expropriation'. It is clear, then, that Weber was mixing with the world of erotic women whose beliefs were grounded in anarchism and the active anarchists who were the very embodiment of Mühsam's world. Edgar Jaffé and Raphael Friedeberg also belonged to their joint circle of friends.

In the bohemian circles of the major cities as well as its refugee outpost in Ascona there was 'a passionate struggle for a new way of life for the entire future of mankind'. Closely related to this was 'the natural attitude of social joyousness of those who anticipated the cultural times', which Mühsam then incorporated into his erotic play *The Open Marriage* (*Die Freivermählten*).[20] Mühsam should be regarded as a significant yet hidden primary reference point for Weber during this period.

If we take the period of Imperial Germany Weber and Mühsam appear as pole and counter-pole: Belief in the state and democracy vs. anarchy and the absence of government; a belief in nation and war vs. internationalism and anti-militarism; political reformer vs. revolutionary; spokesman for the bourgeoisie vs. spokesman for the 'drop outs' and vagabonds; established academic vs. the bohemian intellectual on the margins in the cafes and cabarets; discipline vs. rebellion; objectivity vs. passionate subjectivity; establishment vs. drop out; Heidelberg vs. Schwabing. These opposite tendencies were in fact to lead to a confrontation between both men. Due to Mühsam's failure to appear at the second Lauenstein (see Levy) conference in the summer of 1917, the revolutionary anti-militarist and the nationalist opponent of pacifism did not meet until a public meeting in Munich on 4 November 1918. Mühsam opposed Weber's reformist and legal course of action in favour of unconditional peace and revolution.[21] The upholder of the principle of responsibility stood irreconcilably against the radical 'literati'.

Of course these two men also had many things in common: both dedicated their lives to the theory and praxis of power, both had antagonistic relationships with their fathers, both came from middle class backgrounds and experienced financial dependence on their parents, and both were concerned about their lack of attractiveness to the opposite sex and sexual impotence. Both suffered because they systematically abused their bodies (which brought them to the sanatorium of Ascona, or 'salatorium' as Mühsam joked), and they both suffered from emotional breakdowns and underwent psychiatric and psychotherapeutic treatment. Mühsam underwent psychoanalysis with Otto Gross and wrote enthusiastically about it to Sigmund Freud, saying that his literary productivity had not suffered as he feared and that, moreover, his artistic sensibility and ability to take an objective appraisal of his own work had been increased.[22] He discontinued the treatment because Otto asked about his sexual relationships (and perhaps his relationship with Frieda?).[23] Both sought solutions from the restrictions of the Wilhelmine era and looked for these in the 'erotic movement' of that time.[24]

Anarchistic Sexual Revolution

Mühsam had worked amongst other things as an assistant pharmacist and came from a Jewish middle class background in Lübeck. He began his journalistic career in 1902 in the bohemian cafe society of Berlin among the literary circles. He was a member of the 'New Community' of the brothers Heinrich and Julius Hart. His political 'career' started among the worker-anarchist groups of Berlin and Munich. His first pseudonym was 'Nolo' (I refuse).[25] It was an expression of his opposition to a domineering father as well the demands of Wilhelmine society placed upon a budding member of the educated middle class. But his peripatetic and unsettled bohemian life (he only settled in Munich after 1910) and his need to borrow money alienated him from working class anarchists. In 1908 the Prussian secret police stated that apart from attending a few political meetings 'he was not closely involved with the anarchist movement. He leads an irregular life doing nothing in particular. His former comrades were now ignoring him almost completely.' His second attempt to join the anarchist movement by becoming a member of the Socialist Federation (*Sozialistischen Bund*), which had been founded by Gustav Landauer in 1908, and organising on his behalf the 'lumpenproletariat' in a Munich branch, was also doomed to failure due to his restless nature. Moreover, only very few of those people he had invited to the first meeting, which included 'representatives of the working class, students, artists and women' (prostitutes had also been approached), had little enthusiasm for the 'new approach to socialism'. Mühsam was not an organiser or clubby sort of person during this period of time, rather he was a human being involved in an experiment in living. Despite extreme internal and external pressures he tried to bring about a 'life of freedom' that was no longer bound by the political and social moral restrictions of the time. This also meant a more liberal attitude to sexuality.

Both the working class anarchists and Landauer's Federation disagreed completely with Mühsam's 'sexual politics' (if such a pompous term may be used). The central question for organised labour was the abortion issue (the struggle against Paragraph 218 of the Penal Code) and free access to contraception. The socialists considered sexual matters were of private concern and refused to raise them to the level of an anti-militaristic 'refusal to give birth'. It was only the working class anarchists – excluding Mühsam[26] – who saw in the issue a potential political weapon.[27] The working class whole-heartedly supported bourgeois respectability with regard to marriage and family life and only a minority of the working class anarchists adopted the notion of 'free love' in the sense of polygamous relationships. Gustav Landauer was also a traditionalist with regard to the institution of marriage and like Pierre-Joseph Proudon, he opposed 'Pornocraty', as a result of which he and Mühsam had a serious falling out.[28]

Mühsam, the bohemian, was completely in favour of polygamy, which he elevated to the level of a without rule (an-archic) and domination-free form of sexuality. He conducted a provocative anti-bourgeois 'ostentatious bohemian promiscuity'[29] and was involved in superficial love affairs living out this fantasy as far as possible. Thus the erotic daydreamer wrote the following: 'I may be sitting next to Puma, desperately wanting to kiss her, and yet at the same time be thinking about Frieda, wanting to be with her and reaching out into space to touch her hand. There again, only a word or movement or even a glance from Uli can arouse an absolute passion in me, and then only five minutes later I meet with Vallière, drowning her hands with kisses and capturing her breath whilst looking at my watch up to the moment when I leave her abruptly in order to meet Lotte. Perhaps it is stupid and impractical of me not to hide all this, but I cannot help it. I may be in bed with Lotte, making passionate love to her, and at the same time be in raptures about Moggerl.'[30] Our self-proclaimed lover was, however, often without luck with women and at times grateful if he found a willing chamber maid. Venereal disease was an inevitable outcome of his life style. Mühsam had reason enough, however, to express his gratitude in his autobiography to those 'excellent girls from Schwabing who lived life without inhibition or prejudice and who knew how to give love in the same way'.[31] Indeed he saw his teachings on sexuality as an ideological exaggeration of bohemian love life: 'The forms of love were taken up by the artistic bohemia free of anxiety and unburdened by theory. They were for me in their numerous expressions a model of artistic behaviour – the testing of fundamental views of the world by personal experience, and in the public realm an example for the possibility of a world of freedom.'[32]

Like other writer-rebels he combined his bohemian erotic adventures with the new sexual ethics of Otto Gross to develop a libertarian sexual doctrine.

> Based on his professional activities as a sexual psychologist Gross believed in a morality founded on absolute promiscuity. I had reached the same conclusions as him, but coming from a different angle. The anarchist theory of society I support strives for a social interaction of human beings based on the utmost personal freedom. I believe that it is only internal and voluntarily held obligations that are valid and that every imposed moral constraint not only debases those adhering to them but also those who enforce and live by these constraints. Freedom for all necessitates freedom for every individual and vice versa: freedom does not exist unless there is freedom for all. For this reason the battle against authoritarian power can only be fought in parallel with the battle against authority in one's personal surroundings; above all against one's own craving for authority that controls one's own beliefs and desires and so draws one ever closer to authority. I concluded furthermore that a person seeking to impose power on just *one* human being, wishes to impose power on all. He who acts out the role of the gendarme in the personal sphere will develop those tendencies in himself, and a person who allows themselves to be treated as a slave at home, will allow there to be slavery everywhere and has lost the potential of finding freedom. All traditional forms of virtue are based on command and obedience, on ruling and serving, and this finds its most poignant expression in the generally accepted and rarely criticised form of sexual morality. From the very start of my activities in social propaganda, I strongly attacked the principal of monogamy and the officially protected institution of marriage, particularly the misinterpretation of the idea of faithfulness (*Treue*) as meaning being physically faithful to one partner alone.
>
> Otto considered this ethically superior form of exclusivity in love to be the main factor in emotional repression, and therefore an impure source of many forms of self torment and a mutual poisoning of each

others lives, resulting in hysteria and terrible psychogenic effects. I believe this to be the original source of lack of freedom, imposed on human beings by themselves and by the world around them. We are in complete agreement about sexual jealousy and consider this to be a particularly disgraceful form of jealousy, although this had been sanctified by authoritarian upbringing and the moral teachings of the church.[33]

Mühsam reminisced, 'I believed and (still do believe) marriage to be an institution protected by society and one that imposes personal constraints on the individual. Monogamy as an act of faithfulness is I believe a falsification of morality, and to acknowledge sexual jealousy as a valid emotion is to support the worst possible authoritarian tendencies. To equate love with mutual surveillance is to go against nature, deeply anti-libertarian and serves reactionary interests – a kind of slave morality.... For myself I believe that being set free from the chains of sexual love is an organic part of the programme leading to the liberation of humanity from all forms of servile pressure.'[34]

Of course, it must be mentioned here that Mühsam and Gross were themselves at times overcome by sexual jealousy – the object of their jealousy being none other than Frieda Gross. Mühsam recorded in his diary his conversations with Gross which he hoped would favourably influence Frieda: 'Of course it must be even more important for me now, than even at the time when I lost my beloved, and his maliciousness may have influenced her attitude towards me. Yesterday, when we were saying goodbye, he asked for my forgiveness about this matter. During the time I was together with Gross, I was constantly being reminded of Frieda and it had affected me terribly. It was because he was witnessing so closely the happiest time of my poor wretched life, and it was he, who later condemned me most harshly in front of Frieda.'[35] From the same source in 1912 we discover that Otto had brought about the separation of Mühsam and Frieda by misusing information that he had gained during his psychoanalysis of Mühsam. When Otto Gross reminded him about this, Mühsam wrote, 'I was deeply enraged.' He went on to add that Otto Gross had believed that Mühsam had tainted Frieda's character, and because of this, Otto had felt so angry that he had wanted to kill Mühsam. 'I was aware of this', writes Mühsam, 'and it was at the end of 1908 that I constantly felt that my life was being threatened. One day I eventually confronted Gross about this, and explained to him that I couldn't protect myself from murder, but that one ought to do the decent thing and not act treacherously. The murder plan had by then, however, been abandoned. We talked all this through yesterday and he apologised profusely.'[36]

In his play *The Open Marriage*, written in 1911 and published in 1914, the central character was an emancipated 'amorous woman' based not on one of the 'enchanting girls' he had known in Munich or Vienna but on the beautiful 'Alma', who was a mixture of Frieda Gross and Franziska zu Reventlow.[37] Alma is a polyandrous woman whose love is described by the poet in the play as 'sublime', 'infinitely sweet, for she has the experience of many lovers'.[38] Alma says of herself, 'There are men who hate me because I left them. I love them all, and always will. Faithfulness does not reside between the legs.'[39] Referring to her current lover Frieda-Franziska goes on to say, 'I have been as little unfaithful to him as I have to any other man. I have too much respect for my experiences than to sully them with notions of unfaithfulness. I believe that I have never been truly unfaithful to any man.'[40] She accepts, as did Frieda Gross, that marriage and erotic relationships were irreconcilable – so analogous to Reventlow's opposition of eroticism and love. The moral demise of the amorous women is brought because she 'loses the status of lover and takes on the position of a wife.'[41] The character of the poet backs her up with the dictum: 'Faithfulness makes women boring and habit devalues them.'[42]

Alma wanted to be the lover of men in an 'open marriage' and not be legally restricted as a wife.[43] When her boyfriend, aware that she is expecting his child, voices his claims of ownership: 'Alma! My only one! My beloved! We are having a child', she replies tartly, 'I am having a child.'[44] Mühsam oscillated between Gross–Bachofen theory of mother-right (Mutterrecht) and the ideology of the radical wing of the contemporary bourgeois women's movement (led by Helene Stoecker) which believed that motherhood was the ultimate fulfilment of the liberated woman. Alma dreams about this child which was conceived in a relationship of free love: 'My child will not grow up in a bourgeois family. Its earliest impressions of life should be a sense of freedom. If its parents display mistrust and tell it what to do, the child will be shy and withdrawn like all children from "proper" homes. Should he be a boy, he will be a rebel, and if a pretty girl – for I shall not have an ugly child – then she will never have to question the natural privilege of beauty: the freedom to explore the pleasures of life.'[45]

During Weber's discussions in Ascona with Frick and Frieda Gross about a future society free from sexual jealousy where 'free love' truly exists,[46] Weber is not only indirectly discussing this matter with Otto Gross, but also with Mühsam. In *The Open Marriage* Mühsam reproaches his contemporaries: 'You bring up women as monogamous because you want to be more sure of your wife should you lose control of yourselves in front of her. Your jealousy is based on laziness. Jealousy, the most infantile form of envy, is the most pathetic excuse for your cowardice; for you fear the superior competition of those men who allow a woman the right to decide her own destiny.'[47]

Mühsam believed himself to be one of those 'superior competitors' and his masculinist ideology[48] becomes very clear when he publicly takes on the battle of supporting homosexuality against Paragraph 175 of the Penal Code. (Homosexuality was illegal in Germany until 1969). His very first independent publication in 1903 was entitled 'Homosexuality. A report on the moral history of our time.'[49] His close friendship with the homosexual Johannes Nohl, the son of a famous professor of education and the black sheep of the family, probably 'enticed' him into this subject. He had disputed the content of the pamphlet in a 'public letter' shortly after publication – only, however, to the extent of having adopted without question the views of Magnus Hirschfeld and his 'humanitarian-scientific committee'. (They held the view that homosexuality was a biological condition and not due to social conditioning.) Mühsam believed that social-ethical reasons were sufficient to demand the abolition of Paragraph 175. He would not relinquish this demand: 'I continue to support the aims of the pamphlet and using every means possible to fight the ridiculous, unjust law, which makes a mockery of cultural awareness by making sexual love between men illegal.'[50] 'Actions', he wrote with anarchism in mind, 'in which two consenting adults have engaged without hurting each other, should be of no concern to anybody else.'[51] This basic belief is later more generally reiterated in *The Open Marriage*: 'Only that which endangers sociality (*Sozietät*) can be termed immoral, not the activities of two consenting adults.'[52]

It is highly questionable whether Mühsam himself had been involved in a homosexual relationship with Nohl.[53] He later wrote in his diary that his close relationship with Nohl had grown out of the fact that 'apart from him I had nothing.'[54] What they had in common was loneliness, rebellion against their fathers, and the enjoyment of a roving life. At Mühsam's trial in Munich in 1910 he was portrayed as a 'pederast' which had serious consequences for his career as a writer. He found himself boycotted from working on newspapers and in the end was forced into bringing out his own publication entitled *Cain. A Journal for Humanity* (*Kain. Zeitschrift für Menschlichkeit*). 'The fact that I have denied being a homosexual', he complains in a letter written after the trial 'is of no consequence, the rumour carries more weight than my own denials. The rumours are hardly surprising. I have repeatedly and publicly spoken out against Paragraph

175; there are several homosexuals in my close circle of friends, and I have never taken their ironic affections for me seriously enough to protest, because I do not regard homosexuality as being criminal. I now know that the claim that someone is a pederast is not a disparaging remark, but rather a seriously damaging attack upon the person concerned.'[55]

In spite of this even Mühsam's writings contain elements of defamation. His masculinist ideology placed 'love between men' into the realms of idealised love, rather than sexual love (which takes place between men and women!), and 'lesbian love' is downgraded as being aesthetically inferior.[56]

In his play *The Open Marriage* the character of the poet, who is Mühsam, reproached the 'Puritans' – all those people 'who defend a strict sexual moral code' – 'as quite uncritical people, who wish to uphold their monopoly on sexuality using fidelity'[57] It was exactly this bourgeois-asceticism and the general obligation to a sexual morality which rejected the new erotic code that Max and Marianne Weber publicly supported. After having encountered the love life of Frieda Gross, Weber, as well as Mühsam were 'ready to defend a woman's right to a polygamous existence.'[58] They reached quite different conclusions as a result of their dealings with Frieda Gross of course. Weber would have found Mühsam's play totally incomprehensible. It was rooted in libertarian anti-parliamentariansm and overestimated the erotic and anarchist movement's ability to bring about a social revolution and change people's private lives. It rejected the main aims of the bourgeois as well as the social democratic women's movement, namely the right to vote, in favour of a women's right to chose and above all to have control over her own body.[59] For Weber 'women's liberation in the public sphere' – i.e. in politics, law or economics – 'was the prerequisite for emancipation of her private life'.[60] Mühsam's total belief in sexual reform as the key to solving the women's question and his mistake of equating sexual liberation with women's liberation is radically different to Weber's reform programme of bringing about an equality of the sexes balanced by a renewal of emotional, sexual and erotic relationships.[61]

It must be noted that Weber could achieve this balance only through a dividing up of his personal relationships; however the price paid by Mühsam for his sexual promiscuity was certainly no less. Like the Countess Reventlow, who was unable to form close relationships with men during her lifetime, Mühsam could not 'form a long-standing relationship with a woman who would liberate him yet at the same time be devoted to him'.[62]

Translated by Anthea Conreen

NOTES

1. U. Linse, 'Die Anarchisten und die Münchner Novemberrevolution', in Karl Bosl, ed., *Bayern im Umbruch* (Munich and Vienna: Oldenbourg 1969); U. Linse, *Organisierter Anarchismus im Deutschen Kaiserreich von 1871* (Berlin: Duncker & Humblot); U. Linse, 'Die Transformation der Gesellschaft durch die anarchistische Weltanschauung. Zur Ideologie und Organisation anarchistischer Gruppen in der Weimarer Republik', *Archiv für Sozialgeschichte*, 11, (1971) pp. 289–372; H. Hug, *Erich Mühsam. Untersuchungen zu Leben und Werk* (Glashütten im Taunus: Auvermann, 1974); G. W. Jungblut, *Erich Mühsam. Notizen eines politischen Werdeganges* (Schlitz: Slitese, 1984); L. Peter, *Literarische Intelligenz und Klassenkampf. Die Aktion 1911–1932* (Cologne: Pahl Rugenstein, 1972); W. Fähnders and M. Rector, *Linksradikalismus und Literatur. Untersuchungen zur Geschichte der sozialistischen Literatur in der Weimarer Republik* 2 vols, (Reinbek bei Hamburg: Rowohlt, 1974); W. Haug, *Erich Mühsam. Schriftsteller der Revolution* (Reutlingen: Trotzdem, 1979); R. Kauffeldt, *Erich Mühsam. Literatur und Anarchie* (Munich: Fink, 1983); E. Mühsam, *Revolutionär und Schriftsteller* (Lübeck: Schriften der Erich-Mühsam-Gesellschaft, 1990); W. Haug, 'Die Beziehungen von Anarchismus und Expressionismus am Beispiel Erich Mühsam', *Internationale Wissenschaftliche Korrespondenz zur Geschichte der deutschen Arbeitbewegung*, 28, (1992), pp. 511–22.

2. H. Kreuzer, *Die Boheme. Analyse und Dokumentation der intellektuellen Subkultur vom 19. Jahrhundert bis zur Gegenwart*, (Stuttgart: Metzler, 1968); A. Mitzman, 'Anarchism, Expressionism and Psychoanalysis' *New German Critique*, 4, 7, (1977), pp. 77–104; W. Fähnders, *Anarchismus und Literatur. Ein vergessenes Kapitel deutscher Literaturgeschichte zwischen 1890 und 1910* (Stuttgart: Metzler, 1987); A. Kleeman, *Zwischen symbolischen Rebellion und politischer Revolution. Studien zur deutschen Boheme zwischen Kaiserreich und Weimarer Republik* (Frankfurt and Bern: Lang, 1985); D. Schiller, 'Bohème und Revolution. Erich Mühsam 1901–1911', *Weimarar Beiträge*, (1989/90) pp. 1277 ff.

3. K. Kreiler, *Die Schriftstellerrepublik. Eine Studie zur Literaturpolitik der Rätezeit* (Berlin: Guhl, 1978); H. Viesel, ed., *Literaten an der Wand. Die Münchner Räterepublik und die Schriftsteller* (Frankfurt: Büchergilde Gutenberg, 1980).

4. R. Rocker, *Der Leidensweg von Zensl Mühsam*, (no place: 1941); Z. Mühsam, *Zensl Mühsam. Eine Auswahl aus ihren Briefen* (Lübeck: Schriften der Erich-Mühsam-Gesellschaft, 1990).

5. Letters, Max Weber to Emil Lask – 25.11.1913, 25.12.1913, GStA.

6. E. Hurwitz, *Otto Gross. Paradies-Sucher zwischen Freud und Jung* (Zürich: Suhrkamp, 1988).

7. Ibid., pp. 18–24.

8. Ibid., pp. 28ff.

9. Letter, Max Weber to Frieda Gross, 24.11.1913, GStA.

10. E. Hurwitz, op. cit., p. 29.

11. Max Weber to Marianne Weber, see p. 54

12. E. Mühsam, *Tägebücher 1910–1924*, ed. C. Hirte (Munich: Deutscher Taschenbuch, 1994), p. 44.

13.   Ibid. p. 76.
14.   Ibid., p. 135.
15.   Ibid., p. 81.
16.   E. Mühsam, *Gesamtausgabe, Vol. 3, Prosaschriften* I (Berlin: Verlag Europäische Ideen, 1978), p. 103.
17.   W. Röhrich, *Revolutionärer Syndikalismus. Ein Beitrag zur Sozialgeschichte der Arbeiterbewegung* (Darmstadt: Wissenschaftliche Buchgesellschaft, 1977).
18.   E. Mühsam, 'Liebe, Treue, Eifersucht. Die Ansichten der Gräfin Franziska zu Reventlow', *Die Aufklärung*, ed. M. Hirschfeld, 1, (1929), pp. 315ff.
19.   Indictment.
20.   E. Mühsam, *Ausgewählte Werke, Bd.1 Gedichte, Prosa, Stücke*, ed. C. Hirte (Berlin: Volk und Welt, 1978), p. 667. See U. Linse, 'Die Freivermählten: Zur Literarischen Diskussion ubër nichteheliche Lebensgemeinschaften um 1990' ed. Helmut Scheuer, *Liebe, Lust und Lied – Zur Gefühlskultur um 1900* (Kassel, forthcoming).
21.   Weber, *MWG I/16*, p. 361; G.W. Jungblut *Erich Mühsam. Notizen eines politischen Werdeganges* (Schlitz: Slitese, 1984), p. 109.
22.   E. Mühsam, *In meiner Posaune muß ein Sandkorn sein. Briefe 1900–1934*, ed. G. W. Jungblut (Vaduz, Liechtenstein: Topos, 1984), pp. 98–101.
23.   E. Mühsam, (1929), op. cit., p. 315.
24.   M. Green, *The von Richthofen Sisters* (New York: Basic Books, 1974).
25.   E. Mühsam, (1978) op. cit, pp. 6ff.
26.   H. Van den Berg, '"Frauen, besonders Frauenrechtlerinnen, haben keinen Zutritt!" Misogynie und Antifeminismus bei Erich Mühsam', *Internationale wissenschaftliche Korrespondenz zur Geschichte der deutschen Arbeiterbewegung*, 28, (1992), p. 507.
27.   U. Linse, 'Arbeiterschaft und Geburtenentwicklung im Deutschen Kaiserreich von 1871', *Archiv für Sozialgeschichte*, 12, (1972), pp. 205–71.
28.   E. Mühsam, (1994) op. cit., pp. 14, 29ff.; Mühsam, *Gesamtausgabe. Bd.3. Prosaschriften I* (Berlin: Verlag Europäische Ideen, 1978), pp. 666ff.; Van der Berg op. cit., pp. 489ff.
29.   Van der Berg, op. cit., p. 85.
30.   E. Mühsam, (1994) op. cit., p. 46.
31.   E. Mühsam, *Ausgewählte Werke* (1978), p. 568.
32.   E. Mühsam (1994) op. cit., p. 66.
33.   E. Mühsam (1929) op. cit., p. 315.
34.   E. Mühsam, *Gesamtausgabe. Bd 3. Prosaschriften II*, pp. 666 ff.
35.   E. Mühsam (1994) op. cit., p. 42.
36.   E. Mühsam (1994) op. cit., p. 95.
37.   E. Mühsam, *Ausgewählte Werke*, p. 386; R. Faber, *Franziska zu Reventlow und die Schwabinger Gegenkultur* (Cologne and Vienna: Böhlau, 1993), pp. 174–6.
38.   E. Mühsam, *Ausgewählte Werke Bd 2*, (Berlin: Volk und Welt, 1978), p. 373.
39.   Ibid., p. 384.
40.   Ibid., p. 383.
41.   Ibid., p. 386.
42.   Ibid., p. 373.

43. Ibid., p. 385.
44. Ibid., p. 387.
45. Ibid., p. 411.
46. Letter, Max Weber to Marianne, 14.4.1913, DStA, see above, p. 47.
47. E. Mühsam, op. cit., p. 393.
48. G. L. Mosse, *Nationalism and Sexuality. Respectability and Abnormal Sexuality in Modern Europe* (New York: Fertig, 1985).
49. E. Mühsam, *Gesamtausgabe Bd 3*, op. cit., p. 9–47.
50. E. Mühsam (1984) op. cit., 1, pp. 26ff; 2, pp. 731ff.
51. E. Mühsam *Gesamtausgabe* (1978), p. 44.
52. Mühsam, *Ausgewählte Werke Bd* I (1978), p. 406.
53. In spite of the view of Martin Green, *Mountain of Truth* (Hanover and London: University of New England Press, 1986), p. 126.
54. E. Mühsam, 1994, op. cit., p. 59.
55. E. Mühsam 1984, op. cit., I, p. 128.
56. E. Mühsam, *Gesamtausgabe*, pp. 21 and 39.
57. E. Mühsam, *Ausgewählte Werke*, 1, pp. 406ff.
58. E. Mühsam, *Gesamtausgabe, 2*, pp. 667; cf. Max Weber, *MWG II/5*, pp. 464 and 529.
59. E. Mühsam, *Ausgewählte Werke*, 1, p. 394.
60. I. Gilcher-Holtey, 'Max Weber und die Frauen', *Max Weber. Ein Symposion*, ed. C. Gneuss and C. Kocka (Munich: Deutscher Taschenbuch, 1988), p. 149.
61. Ibid., p. 150; Van der Berg, op. cit., pp. 480, 490ff.
62. C. Hirte, *Erich Mühsam. 'Ihr seht mich nicht feige'*. (Berlin: Verlag Neues Leben), p. 119.

7 Max Weber, Leo Tolstoy and the Mountain of Truth

Edith Hanke

Early in 1913, and again in 1914, Max Weber travelled to Ascona, in fulfilment of a promise of legal assistance previously given to Frieda Schloffer-Gross, wife of Otto Gross. As can be seen in Sam Whimster's essay and Max Weber's letters from Ascona (see above), this friend of both Max and Marianne sorely needed some support in her struggle for the custody of her son Peter. And so it might seem purely coincidental that Max Weber found himself stranded for several weeks in these 'realms of the fabulous'.[1] This German scholar found himself among dropouts, philosophers of life, and existential reformers; among people who had, either deliberately or out of necessity, placed themselves in opposition to the bourgeois order and had broken with it.

Ascona was a place where Leo Tolstoy, who at that time had established a reputation as a leading cultural critic, found an audience ready for his ideas. In 1879 the author of *War and Peace* had undergone a conversion and become a Christian penitent and moralist.[2] Starting from a reinterpretation of the Sermon on the Mount, he developed into a relentless critic of the institutions of state, society and the Church. By the second half of the 1880s he had found a rapidly expanding audience for his writings in Germany and as a critic of modernity he was soon ranked alongside Nietzsche. Both prophesied the coming end of Western Christian civilisation, but their premonitions sprang from quite different sources. For those contemplating the intellectual merits of rival worlds, Tolstoy stood for a radical ethical fundamentalism and pacifism, for vegetarianism, pedagogical reform and agrarian communities. This last played a special role in Ascona. The founders of 'Monte Verità' sought advice in 1900 from Albert Skarvan, a Hungarian military doctor and Tolstoyan.[3] Influenced by Tolstoy's teaching, Skarvan had refused military service and hence suffered prison, exile and the forfeit of his doctoral title. Before settling in Switzerland he was received by Tolstoy in Jasnaja Poljana. Skarvan's support for agrarian communism made a strong impression on Karl Gräser, one of the seven founding members of the community and who had suffered a fate similar to that of Skarvan. In the event, the practical entrepreneurship of Henri Oedenkoven and Ida Hofmann prevailed, and the homeopathic sanatorium which they developed was relatively successful. Separate from this group was the Hungarian 'Tolstoy man' Vladimir Straskraba-Czaja, who ran, together with his family, the vegetarian inn 'Die Heidelbeere'.[4] This one-time engineer had given up his career and dedicated himself in Switzerland entirely to the teachings of Tolstoy, disseminating them in the *Locarno-Ascona-Bote*. During the winter of 1910 he brought out a special edition to commemorate Tolstoy's death. Following this all trace of him disappears.

It is very unlikely that Weber came across any of these Tolstoyans on his visits to Ascona. But in his legal dealings with Frieda Gross he did become acquainted with the Swiss anarchist Ernst Frick. Since 1911 Frick had lived in Ascona with Frieda and her son Peter, together with their own daughter, Eva Verena. Max Weber's interest in Ernst Frick was at first purely a legal matter. The personal integrity of Frick was a matter of some importance to him in the light of the imminent hearing concerning custody of Peter Gross. This relation with the 'client' altered during conversations between Weber and Frick which took place in 1913 while Frick was in custody, and then during 1914 in Ascona. Weber developed a strong interest in Frick's fate and gave him his advice – this much is quite evident from the regular letters to Marianne. Conversations between the two men revolved around fundamental ethical questions, culminating in Weber's remark that, for Frick, 'Tolstoyan asceticism was the only possible path that one could take.'[5] Max Weber's interest in Frick, the Swiss anarchist, took on in this way a new dimension: how is it possible for men to live outwith a modern world in which capitalism and the bourgeois world-view hold sway? How can such a lifestyle be justified? It seems that there was for Weber only one answer to this question: 'Tolstoy's resolute path'.[6] The passage from correspondence cited above shows that Max Weber saw Frick in the light in Tolstoy's ideal, and sought to measure him by it.

Ernst Frick is one of those who has remained in the shadows on the 'Mountain of Truth'. Surviving references to him are sparse, and he has left little personal trace. I will try below to throw some light upon his biography, and then consider the degree to which Frick did in fact represent a Tolstoyan anarchism. Finally, we will consider why Max Weber saw 'Tolstoy's resolute path' as the unique model for Frick's life.

1. Ernst Frick

Contemporaries portray Ernst Frick as a 'lanky, gaunt Swiss', and as a 'gentle, shy man who retained his youthfulness into old age.'[7] Although of humble background, he gave the impression of being 'extraordinarily cultivated and well-educated.'[8] The artist Richard Seewald, who lived for many years near Ascona, was especially struck by 'his unparalleled frugality'; he contented himself daily with just 'a piece of bread, a cup of tea or a glass of cheap country wine.'[9] Born in Zürich in 1881, Frick's occupational record seems quite questionable: sometimes he is a railway worker, machinist or foundry worker, then a painter; but mainly he is the 'Swiss anarchist' who was kept by women. Apparent contradictions are resolved if we place these occupations in chronological order. Frick was first a worker and trade union member in Zürich.[10] We first encounter his name in a political context on 28 May 1904 on the masthead of the anarchist newspaper *Der Weckruf*: 'Letters and financial contributions to Ernst Frick, Ottostraße 17, Zürich III.'[11] The paper had been founded in 1903 as an outpost of the Franco-Italian *Réveil-Risveglio*, which was published in Geneva by the Italian printer Luigi Bertoni (1872–1947). *Réveil-Risveglio* represented the radical wing of the French and Italian trade union movement, which in Western Switzerland had became part of an established anarchist tradition. This German-language parallel edition of *Réveil* was a means for the diffusion of anarcho-syndicalism in the German-speaking part of Switzerland. The editor was the Hungarian emigrant and follower of Tolstoy, Matthias Malaschitz (1871–1904).[12] During the short period that Malaschitz was editor the fortnightly paper advocated antimilitaristic and syndicalist anarchism, frequently resorting to the words of Nietzsche and Tolstoy for theoretical underpinnings. After the death of Malaschitz editorial control was assumed by Robert Scheidegger and Ernst Frick, which implies that they were part of the paper's inner circle. In August 1904 Frick stepped down for a year and left control to Scheidegger, who then worked, or served as nominal editor, first with Erich Mühsam, and then with the brothers Max and Siegfried Nacht. Frick had editorial control from September 1905 to May 1906. Under his leadership two substantive themes were emphasised: firstly the struggle for 'direct action' and the General Strike, and secondly the struggle against militarism. In contrast to the early years of the paper, under Frick it became politicised and radicalised, which in part at least can be explained by developments in the Swiss Trade Union Congress. In 1906 the Congress had rejected 'direct action' and opted for a reformist parliamentary road in collaboration with the Social Democrats.[13] The revolutionary syndicalism of *Der*

Weckruf made it a rallying point for all radicals, and its print-run quickly rose to 4000 copies.[14] The paper also advocated conscientious objection, putting its own collaborators in the vanguard of the movement. Robert Scheidegger was sentenced to five months in prison for his public refusal of military service,[15] and Ernst Frick received fifteen days detention for his refusal to take part in a reservists' exercise.[16] The 'Antimilitarist Supplement' reported on these and similar actions. Passages can be found in these pages from Tolstoy's pacifist writings, and amongst the recommended books mention was regularly made of his pamphlet 'To Soldiers and Young People', which was obtainable 'from the publisher of the *Weckruf*'.[17] The history of *Der Weckruf*, and Frick's propagandistic phase, ended on 1 May 1906 with its call to revolution.

Martin Green in his study of Monte Verità reports that Frick visited Ascona for the first time in 1906, so that he could receive medical treatment from Raphael Friedeberg.[18] Opinions vary as to whether he was suffering from tuberculosis or not. Green presumes that he made contact with Otto Gross in Ascona and then went to Schwabing. During the years 1906 to 1911 Frick turns up in Munich and in Zürich, but it is quite unclear how he supported himself. Contemporary accounts offer us three possible explanations. Leonhard Frank in his autobiographical novel depicts Frick as the leading initiator of a raid on the premises of a Munich meat trader. The thieves got away with only seven marks, Frick putting the money back with the remark that with such a sum one could not undermine this pillar of the state.[19] That ended the robbery. In addition to this, Frank writes of an earlier robbery by Frick which was carried out not for his own enrichment, but for purely ideological motives.[20] He is reputed to have been an extreme critic of money; and so we can discount robberies and break-ins as a likely basis of income.

The second possibility was mentioned by Leonhard Frank, and appear to be quite plausible. Frick is supposed to have lived and worked in Germany under a false name,[21] and in the evenings attended meetings or stayed alone in his room. Here, surrounded by the writings of Bakunin and Kropotkin, he is thought to have written long letters to anarchist comrades in Spain and Italy urging them to perpetrate political murders.[22] In Frank's fictionalised account he is suspected of murder in the course of a robbery, which he regards as an honour but, at the same time, seeks to keep those around him in the dark and so keep this moment obscure and mysterious. Others, mindful of this aspect of his character, never thought that Frick had committed a criminal offence; Richard Seewald for instance gave the affair a humorous twist and suggested that if he had been part of one, then at most he had acted as look-out.[23] Frick's role in a bombing in

Zürich during the night of 3 June 1907 is just as murky. The bombing was itself only a diversion, the real object of the action being the freeing of a Russian who was about to be extradited.[24] Ernst Frick and his comrade from the *Weckruf* period were under suspicion, taken into remand and then released for want of evidence. Five years later the case was revived since Robert Scheidegger, in the meantime interned in Austria for smuggling saccharin, made a statement denouncing Frick and implicating Margarethe Faas-Hardegger, a co-defendent and union secretary. She had originally provided Frick with his alibi. Frick and Faas-Hardegger were arrested in March 1912.[25] On 30 November the Swiss Federal Criminal Court sentenced Frick to twelve months imprisonment for possession of explosives, and for the premeditated derailment of a tram in October 1908 (Frick had assaulted the driver, a strikebreaker).[26]

But let us get back from terrorist anarchism to the question of Frick's means of support posed above. The third possibility, a condition politely referred to by Max Weber as that of an '*homme soutenu*',[27] was put rather more baldly or even cynically by Emil Szittya, who was well-acquainted with life in Schwabing and Ascona: he stated that Frick had lived off women for years, first of all from working women, then from intellectual women, until finally he was left 'stranded' with Frieda Gross.[28] Frick, under the influence of Otto Gross, seems to have become an adherent of erotic anarchism; or, at the very least, Gross's psychoanalytic doctrine would have legitimated Frick's free and shifting intimate relationships. Frick lived together with Gross's wife from 1909, Otto Gross having himself facilitated the relationship. This partnership was itself not without tension and hardly 'monogamous', as Max Weber expressed it.[29] Ernst Frick and Frieda Gross moved to Ascona with the children Peter and Eva Verena in 1911. The move seems to have distanced Frick from the anarchistic movement, and he lived chiefly off Frieda's money. He left Frieda in 1919 or 1920, who in the meantime had borne him three daughters, and went to live with the Austrian Margarethe Fellerer (1886–1961). In the mid-1930s she became a well-known portrait photographer.[30] Frick made a career for himself as a painter. In 1924 he was a founding member of the Ascona group of artists who called themselves 'The Great Bear', prominent amongst whom was Marianne von Werefkin.[31] Frick's paintings were exhibited in Zürich, Basel and Berlin; his home however remained in Ascona, where he died in 1956.

2   Ernst Frick and Tolstoy's Ethic

How can the manner in which Ernst Frick conducted himself be related to Tolstoy's ethics? One link can be made through a particular form of anarchism named after Tolstoy himself. In 1900 Paul Eltzbacher, a legal philosopher and former student of Rudolf Stammler, published a book which included a systematic treatment of Tolstoy's anarchism, which he characterised as idealistic, refractory and anomic.[32] The meaning of these categories must be outlined here briefly, because anarchism was itself only a part of Tolstoy's doctrine.

Tolstoy's entire ethics centred upon inner conviction, and advocated individual reformation.[33] He therefore supported individual conscientious objectors, or for example a pacifist sect whose emigration from Russia was paid for with the proceeds from the sale of *Resurrection*. He hoped that sagacity, individual acts, and, especially, self-denial on the part of the rich, the educated and those in government, would lead to the collapse of a state and economic system resting upon the exercise of force. Tolstoy did not develop an alternative legal or social order; instead he placed faith in the New Testament imperative of altruism being sufficient guide for harmonious human existence. This represents the anomic aspect of his teaching, and is evidenced by his behaviour during the 1905 Revolution when, although hoping for the collapse of Tsarism, he remained true to his doctrine and cautioned both sides that they should not use force in their struggle against evil. Eltzbacher characterised Tolstoy's advocacy of peaceful revolution as refractory. During his final years Tolstoy maintained the firm conviction that observance of God's laws was of paramount importance, whatever the future consequences might be. Tolstoy's ethic of love treated the immediate present as the exclusive standard of propriety in the evaluation of an action, integrating an action with its result as well as with its ethical and theological evaluation.[34] This ethico-religious, idealistic core of Tolstoy's anarchism looked too much like political quietism to many revolutionaries, who, disappointed, simply rejected his teachings.

Very few adopted Tolstoy's doctrines in their pure undiluted form. Tolstoyans were distinguished instead by their ethical pacifism, and the religious foundations of Tolstoy's beliefs were treated as no longer relevant, and simply ignored. This disjunction in Tolstoy's influence is clearly evident in the way that German-speaking socialists and anarchists adopted his ideas. Orthodox socialists found Tolstoy's teachings barely accessible, for they completely rejected his ethico-religious 'superstructure'. The only part of Tolstoy's doctrines with which they were in agreement was his substantive critique of capitalism. A more intense engagement with Tolstoy's work could be found among ethical or idealist socialists and anarchists, such as Kurt Eisner, Gustav Landauer, the early Erich Mühsam and Ernst Toller. But even these circles made heavy weather of the genuine religious foundations of Tolstoyan anarchism. Nonetheless, Tolstoy remained an important ethical landmark.

The anarchistic milieu in which Ernst Frick moved during his involvement with the *Weckruf*, and then later in Schwabing, were to some extent marked by an ethical and Tolstoyan perspective. As noted above, in its early days the *Weckruf* was moulded by the Tolstoyan Matthias Malaschitz. Like his immediate teacher Eugen Heinrich Schmitt, Malaschitz was a representative of a religiously-coloured, ethical and pacifist anarchism. Ernst Frick was also in contact with Gustav Landauer through Margarethe Faas-Hardegger. A letter of Landauer's from October 1908 indicates that Frick was a member of the Socialist Association that had recently been formed in Bern.[35] This group published the *Sozialist* in Berlin and Bern from 1909 to 1915. Both editors, Faas-Hardegger and Landauer, were adherents of Guild Socialism and distanced themselves from an organised and authoritarian socialism. Sensibility, education and culture played an important part in their idea of socialism. True, Faas-Hardegger's work as a union secretary was much more closely involved in practical issues than was that of Landauer; her critique of capitalism did not therefore lead her to a denial of all technical achievements.[36] Landauer by contrast lived quietly, supporting himself by translation and other publications. He was the theorist of the enterprise and concerned with the intellectual foundations of a new libertarian socialism. He printed in the *Sozialist* mainly translations from Proudhon, Kropotkin and Tolstoy. The major elements of his anarcho-socialism were strongly influenced by Tolstoy; and so if we can identify the effect that these had for Landauer we can at the same time shed some light on Frick.

We can assume that Landauer had a comprehensive knowledge of Tolstoy's work. He had read *War and Peace* while in prison during 1899, and from 1900 he gave regular lectures on Tolstoy, initially in the circle around the Hart brothers,[37] who were of major importance for the German Naturalist movement. Landauer not only printed Tolstoy's political pamphlets in *Sozialist*, but he also published excerpts from his literary writings, letters and diaries.[38] In Frick's case we can only assume probable acquaintance with the antimilitary pamphlet 'To Soldiers and Young People', which he published in the *Weckruf* during his period of tenure. Such Tolstoyan influence as was discernible in the *Weckruf* focused exclusively on conscientious objection; and it can also be assumed that Frick and his co-defendent Scheidegger founded this principle on the idea of a 'class conscious revolutionary proletariat',[39] and not upon Christianity or some other form of human awareness. Frick's use of Tolstoy was extremely selective, whereas Landauer's reading was much more extensive. This is most apparent from the Tolstoy memorial issue of the *Sozialist* that Landauer produced. His own piece in this issue lends insight into the personal significance that Tolstoy had for him.[40] He places emphasis on Tolstoy's supersession of the contrast between rationalism and belief, or as Landauer put it, 'scepticism and mysticism'. Landauer felt unable to subscribe to the Christian postulates of Tolstoy's ethics, presumably because of his Jewish background. He would in any case have rejected on intellectual grounds any other system of dogmatic religious belief. In this fashion he arrived at a secularised 'innerworldly mysticism'.[41] This was to form the emotional tie between people. Although this represents a deviation from Tolstoy's teaching, it is testimony to Landauer's own thinking. Ernst Frick on the other hand seems at the religious level to have adhered unquestioningly to the Nietzschean belief that 'God is dead'.[42]

In his obituary Landauer addressed himself to the central aspect of Tolstoy's pacifist ethics. This lay in a congruency of means and ends, or in Landauer's own formulation, 'the aim, non-violence, is also the means by which this goal is achieved.'[43] Ernst Frick was of quite a different disposition: he was disposed to violence if we are to ascribe any credibility to the fictionalised account of robberies, and also assuming that the sentence for the armed attack on the Zürich police barracks was not based upon fabricated evidence. This means that he saw crime as a legitimate means in the struggle against injustice. In this connection a comment made by Frick about the Tolstoyan Otto Buek in the context of a minor controversy in the *Weckruf* during 1906 is illuminating. Buek was a Russo-German living in Berlin who had been denounced by an anonymous correspondent for carrying on anarchist agitation while quite undisturbed by the police.[44] In a reader's letter of 15 February 1906 Buek responded to the accusation that he was a suspected police spy as follows:

> My activity is of a non-political nature and confines itself to purely academic philosophical research, as well as the translation of Tolstoy's writings and the dissemination of his ideas. My cultural path is one of ideal-ethical self-education.[45]

His support for a General Strike and direct action should not, continued Buek, be confused with some 'vulgar conception' of anarchism. This idealist-quietist form of anarchism was dismissed by Frick as being 'moderated by the Tolstoyan way of thinking'.[46] This makes it clear that Frick was firmly behind the *Weckruf*'s revolutionary and active programme of class struggle. That also squares with the literary accounts according to which the works of Bakunin and Kropotkin were to be found on Frick's bookshelves. Both were exponents of the 'propaganda of the deed'. Neither of them ruled out criminal activities or the use of force in pursuit of revolutionary goals.[47] By contrast, Landauer remained faithful to Tolstoyan pacifism and his own concept of self-realising socialism until February 1919.[48] This latter idea was based upon the conviction that it would be possible to foster socialist conceptions under capitalist conditions within communes or settlements formed by like-minded people. Violent upheaval was not therefore Landauer's way. Because of this, he was accused during the First World War, as Tolstoy had been earlier, of passivity and a reluctance to engage in positive action.[49] Landauer initially hailed the Bavarian revolution, which at first went quite non-violently, as a victory for the spirit of Tolstoy.[50] As Commissar for Education he took part in the construction of a new society, but soon became caught up in the maelstrom of political radicalisation, and finally became a tragic victim of the counter-revolution. Even today, the destruction of the Bavarian revolution represents not merely the failings of idealistic amateur politicians, but also the collapse of the Tolstoyan ideal of an ethical pacifism.

Gustav Landauer took a rather traditional line when it came to erotic matters outwith the political sphere. He regarded marriage and family as voluntary forms of cohabitation and gave them a definite place in his overall view of ethical association. Landauer did not defend the radical asceticism of Leo Tolstoy's *Kreutzer Sonata*, but he joined with the Tolstoy translator Ludwig Berndl in polemicising against the so-called 'new ethics' as represented by Sigmund Freud and Otto Gross – 'one of the worst kind of Freudians'.[51] He saw in the new tendency a 'product of degeneration and banality', since it reduced love to 'the satisfaction of certain muscular needs'.[52] It can safely be assumed that Ernst Frick had at this time completely assimilated psychoanalytic doctrine, since he was from 1906 to 1911 a close friend of Otto Gross and one of his 'followers'. Leonhard Frank confirms that Frick participated in discussions in the Café Stephanie in Schwabing concerning 'the uninhibited superman, free of complex', discussions which naturally centred upon Otto Gross.[53]

To sum up: it is true that some trace of Tolstoyan antimilitarism can be detected in Ernst Frick, but besides that we find a compound made up from Bakunin, Kropotkin, Nietzsche and Freud (or rather Gross). We do not know whether Ernst Frick ever succeeded in making sense of all this, or whether he remained just 'very confused by his anarchist, philosophical and psychoanalytic reading.'[54]

3. Max Weber's Conception of Tolstoy and Ernst Frick

Max Weber met Ernst Frick in 1913 in prison, and then again in 1914 shortly after his release, while he was still deeply marked by his internment and sentence. It seems that Frick's spell in prison was a period of intense reflection on his own life, and on its future. Max Weber's letters to Marianne Weber show that their discussions centred on questions of *Lebensführung*, on the question of ethical conduct in general, and erotic life in particular.

On 31 March 1914, Max wrote to Marianne as follows:

> Anyway he would like to realise 'goodness' and 'brotherly love' (*Nächstenliebe*) through the acosmicism of the *erotic*. I had already told Frieda why that is not possible, and she admits that the only possible path was that of Tolstoyan asceticism, towards which he constantly tends. This is where he will end up, if he still has the strength for it.[55]

This passage shows that Frick did not advocate an unbounded eroticism, but instead sought to connect eroticism with ethics. Contemporaries record that intimate relationships in Ascona were arranged according to unarticulated rules, and that Frick embodied this form of ethical regulation.[56] Besides this, it seemed to morally trouble Frick that, in the forthcoming custody hearing, it was Frieda's relationship with him, an unemployed anarchist, which would be the decisive reason for the loss of her son Peter.

Frick was therefore confronted with the problem that he wished, in Weber's words, 'to realise goodness and brotherliness through the acosmicism of the *erotic*', but the threat of failure loomed. Weber sought to make clear to him, through his play with the word acosmic, why brotherly altruism and the radical pursuit of eroticism were mutually exclusive. This antithesis stands in the history of Weber's work between his letter to Else Jaffé of 13 September 1907, in which he presents a critique of Otto Gross's doctrines, and the revised version of the 'Intermediate Reflections' essay from 1919–1920.

In 1907 Weber wrote that he would have respected Gross's idea of a consistent 'acosmic' love if Gross had discarded the futile inclusion of ethical theories and of Nietzsche.[57] This assessment is generalised in the 'Intermediate Reflections': the erotic takes its own course. It is acosmic, that is, world-denying, for it sets itself against the everyday order of western rationalism. Moreover, since it only simulates the feeling of human attachment and dedication, a major conflict arises with the ethic of brotherliness.[58]

Weber had described the latter at the first German Sociology Congress in 1910 as an amorphous expression of love antagonistic to sensuality, likewise dubbing this as 'acosmic'.[59] As a typical example of this 'acosmic orientation' he cited Russian literature, but in particular Tolstoy. And so even in 1910 Tolstoy was for Max Weber synonymous with an ethic of unworldly brotherly altruism (*Brüderlichkeitsethik*).

The 'Intermediate Reflections' essay runs through the tensions existing between world-renouncing salvational religions and individual cultural spheres; and close examination shows that Weber always introduces Tolstoy's ethics as the example of an unworldly brotherliness. Of course, at the time he was visiting Ascona Weber had yet to write the 'Intermediate Reflections', but he had already worked out his basic ideas in the section 'Religiöse Ethik und "Welt"' for his sociology of religion.[60] Consequently, we can assume that during 1913 and 1914, when Weber was in discussion with Frick, he had in mind a pre-formed theory which set up an insuperable opposition between the erotic and Tolstoyan ethics, consigning both in addition to a place quite remote from this 'world'. The degree of severity in this polarisation in the letters concerning Frick can only be explained by this intellectual context.

In addition to this, Max Weber found rationally-conceived projects for living intellectually fascinating, as he indicated in 'Intermediate Reflections';[61] he had a high personal regard for them if they were consistently pursued. He was therefore personally impressed by 'Tolstoy's rigorous consistency', as reported by the sociologist Paul Honigsheim in his recollections of Heidelberg.[62] During the same period (the years 1911 and 1912) Weber conceived plans to write an essay on Tolstoy's ethics, and a Tolstoy book which would preserve 'all reflections of the most personal experiences'.[63] Tolstoy embodied for Weber, alongside Jesus, Francis of Assisi and Kant, an idealistic and formidable heroic ethic, whose worth lay in consistent, and not half-hearted, emulation. Weber's warning to Frick finds an echo in *Science as a Vocation*:[64] find *your* demon. In the case of Frick, this means to choose between the 'acosmicism of the erotic', or the acosmicism of brotherliness and goodness, i.e. Tolstoy's ethics – and once the choice is made then live it out consistently, otherwise you become a laughing stock, a dishonourable figure.

Weber sought to apply principles derived from his own theoretical studies to the life of Ernst Frick, and how far he was prepared to go with this becomes clear in the passage following the one quoted above. The letter of 5 April 1914 leads up to a fundamental ethical problem:

Prison has had such an effect on him [Frick] that he cannot leave off brooding on the significance of goodness. He has been driven to distraction by the insight that the *outcome* of virtuous action is so often quite irrational and results in evil when one behaves 'virtuously', so much so that he questions whether one *ought* to act virtuously: an evaluation of moral action in terms of its *consequences* and not its intrinsic worth! For the time being he cannot see that there is a mistake in this, so I will see to it that he gets a copy of *The Brothers Karamazov*, and then later Lukács' dialogue [on the Poverty of the Spirit], in which the problem is dealt with.[65]

Lukács' short story *On the Poverty of the Spirit (Von der Armut im Geiste)* was published in 1912, and in it he works through the consequences of the suicide of his friend Irma Seidler. On moral grounds he had refused to marry her, and so felt responsible for her taking her own life. The good intention of saving her from a lifetime with him had demonstrably fatal consequences. The other recommended book, Dostoyevsky's *The Brothers Karamazov*, deals with the absurdity of being. (See Charles Turner, chapter 8.)

For Weber, the irrationality of an action stemmed from the fact that the modern world had fragmented into competing value orders, so that the majority of life spheres were either ethically neutral, or positively hostile to an ethical order – but in any case they were not dominated by an ethic of goodness and human kindness. Ethical action thus for the most part created irrational paradoxes which completely perverted good intentions.

The entire set of problems were dealt with by Weber in connection with 'the question of value judgements.' In the revised 1917 version of the essay on value freedom he formally distinguished two contrasting principles of action, congruent with the distinction between *Gesinnungsethik* and V*erantwortungsethik* which can be found first properly formulated in *Politics as a Vocation* from 1919. An action is either legitimated by the autonomous value of the act, derived from 'pure will' or *intentionality*, or alternatively, through acceptance of the consequences for the foreseeable possible or probable *consequences* of an action.[66] The use of the terms 'pure will' and intentionality indicate that Weber was relying upon Kant for the philosophical definition of *Gesinnungsethik*. In Kant, *Gesinnung* has a central place in the elucidation of the categorical imperative. Here the principle or the form of moral action is founded in *Gesinnung* ('inner conviction'), quite independently of the result of the action or any other influences on the action.

As in Kant, in Weber we are dealing with a categorical definition of types of action, which at this abstract level do not yet convey any sense of the content or value of a given ethic. From a systematic viewpoint, Tolstoy's ethics are intentional (*Gesinnungsethik*) because of the underlying principle of action. Initially this is a completely value-neutral ordering. Weber's appreciation of an ethic of intention becomes more substantial if the passages from Tolstoy are placed in relation to the political sphere.

Tolstoy turns up for the first time in Weber's writing in connection with his two chronicles of the Russian Revolution of 1905. Tolstoy appears here as an advocate for the peasants, promoting the abolition of property in land and hoping that everything else will eventually fall into place. Tolstoy regards all liberal-democratic values, such as 'Constitution and Freedom of Personality', as 'Western abominations'.[67] Since Weber saw a chance for individualism in the political struggle taking place in Russia, Tolstoy's apoliticism became antagonistic to his own interests. It is against this background that we find the first contrast between an ethic based upon 'outcomes' and one based upon 'duty'.

> Once that which is recognised to be a positive 'duty' is done, then, because *all* values other than ethical ones have been excluded, that biblical injunction comes into force again which has become ingrained not only in the soul of Tolstoy but in the entire Russian people: 'Resist not evil'.[68]

Weber defined the political in terms of power; this implied that purposeful political action based on any pacifist ethic was an impossibility, since such ethics were rooted in the renunciation of force as a means to a given end. This formulation makes clear that Weber rejected the application of a pure ethic of duty or of intention in the political sphere. The judgement applies not just to Tolstoyan anarchism, but to syndicalism. As far as Weber was concerned this movement was not serious about political success. This view was repeated in several letters to his younger colleague Robert Michels, arguing that any talk of a 'strike ethic' must be based on an ethic of intention, since hitherto strikes had only had negative consequences for the entire movement.[69] Strikes were only capable of unfolding 'the flame of pure intention' and keeping it alight.[70] Practical success cannot be expected from this approach. And so Max Weber presented Robert Michels with a choice: to choose between rejection of the world – 'My realm is not of this world' (Tolstoy, or an unswerving syndicalism) – or the affirmation of the given culture.[71] It can be imagined that Weber presented the same argument to the syndicalist Ernst Frick, seeking to shake his 'religious faith in a future society free of envy.'[72]

In the midst of the World War, at a time when pacifists were increasingly inclined to invoke Tolstoy, Weber employed Tolstoy, the man whose ethic was based upon conviction, as a weapon against those who were lukewarm and half-hearted. Gesine Nordbeck, the Swiss pacifist, incurred his especial wrath for placing Christian law above the duty to one's fatherland. Weber explained to her what he understood by 'our responsibility before history' and sketched the basic outlines of the tasks facing the German Empire.[73] He then cautioned her to leave the Gospel out of the argument, or use it completely consistently. 'And along that path there are only Tolstoy's ethics, nothing else.'[74] This would mean doing without all the great cultural achievements, 'beauty, honour, virtue and eminence.'[75] We encounter similar formulations in *Politics as a Vocation*. Here we find the attempt to use the Sermon on the Mount for political ends decisively rejected. Weber considered the fate of the German state to be at stake during the war, and this goes a long way to explain the ferocity of his rejection. His formulation of an ethic of responsibility in *Politics as a Vocation* became therefore a defensive response to an ethic of conviction which became tinged with an ethic of political naïveté, an association which persists to this day. In spite of this, its converse, the ethic of responsibility, should not be associated with an ethic of pure power, of a *Realpolitik*. It is an ethic based upon the knowledge that politics rests upon the exercise of force and power, and so anyone seeking to achieve something must take this into account.[76] In this context responsibility demands moderation in the exercise of this means, and anticipation of possible consequences. In contrast to the ethic of conviction or of intention, Max Weber consciously linked the ethic of responsibility to the conditions of modern culture. In a quite Nietzschean sense, it demands a strong personality, capable of establishing and maintaining values, who can give sense to a meaningless and ethically-neutral world. This personality-type is itself a tragic figure, bereft of resort to any set of beliefs or any church, existing in a constant tension between the demands of this 'world' and 'the demands of the day'.[77]

Weber's rigorous and sober analysis of the modern condition led him to the conclusion that Tolstoy's ethics and the anarcho-erotic ideas of Ernst Frick did not belong to this 'world'. There was however a place for them: far away, among virtuosi, on the Mountain of Truth.

Translated by Keith Tribe

NOTES

1. Letter of Max Weber to Marianne, 9 April 1914; see chapter 2.
2. See Edith Hanke, *Prophet des Unmodernen. Leo N. Tolstoi als Kulturkritiker in der deutschen Diskussion der Jahrhundertwende* (Tübingen: Niemeyer, 1993).
3. See Robert Landmann (i.e. Werner Ackermann), *Ascona. Monte Verità. Auf der Suche nach dem Paradies* (Zürich: Benziger, 1973), pp. 21ff.
4. See H. Szeemann (ed.) *Monte Verita. Berg der Wahrheit. Lokale Anthropologie als Beitrag zur Wiederentdeckung einer neuzeitlichen sakralen Topographie*, (Milan: Electa Editrice, 1980), p. 62. The characterisation of Straskraba-Czaja as a 'Tolstoy man' goes back to Hermann Hesse and in all likelihood was a reference to him. I must thank Hermann Müller, a Gräser specialist, for this piece of information as well as numerous other references to the Tolstoyans on Monte Verità.
5. Letter of Max Weber to Marianne, 31 March 1914, see chapter 2.
6. Max Weber, 'Between Two Laws', *PW*, p. 78.
7. Observations respectively from L. Frank, *Das Ochsenfurter Männerquartett. Roman*, (Munich: Kindler, 1965), p. 40; and R. Seewald, *Der Mann von Gegenüber. Spiegelbild eines Lebens* (Munich: List, 1963), p. 173.
8. This was the first impression that Frick made on Hans Gross when visiting Graz in 1909; recorded in E. Hurwitz, *Otto Gross. Paradies-Sucher zwischen Freud und Jung* (Frankfurt a.M.: Suhrkamp, 1988), p. 233.
9. Seewald, *Der Mann von Gegenüber*, pp. 169, 173.
10. Szeemann, *Monte Verita*, p. 44.
11. For a history of *Der Weckruf* see M. Nettlau, *Geschichte der Anarchie* Bd. 5.1, (Vaduz: Topos, 1984), pp. 305–6.
12. Malaschitz died on 5 June 1904; see the obituary in *Der Weckruf* 2 Jg. No. 8 (25 June 1904), p. 1.
13. The decision was made at the meeting of the Congress during Easter 1906; see F. Thies, 'Streiks und Lohnbewegungen', *Handwörterbuch der Schweizerischen Volkswirtschaft, Sozialpolitik und Verwaltung* vol. 3.1 (Bern: Verlag Encyklopädie, 1911), p. 813.
14. See 'An die Freunde des *"Weckruf"*', *Der Weckruf* 3 Jg. No. 18 (October 1905), p. 4.
15. R. Scheidegger, 'Offener Brief an die Militärdirektion des Kanton Zürich', *Der Weckruf* 3 Jg. No. 15 (August 1905), Antimilitarist Supplement p. 1; see for a report of the sentence 'Robert Scheidegger vor dem Kriegsgericht' *Der Weckruf* 3 Jg. No. 18 (October 1905) Supplement 'Der Antimilitarist', p. 1.
16. See the notice in *Der Weckruf* 3 Jg. No. 16 (September 1905), p. 4.
17. *Der Weckruf* 3 Jg. No. 18 (Oktober 1905) Supplement, 'Der Antimilitarist', p. 2; No. 23 (December 1905) Supplement p. 1; references to Tolstoy's pamphlet, which was published in Berlin in 1905 and immediately confiscated, can be found between October 1905 and April 1906. Holzmann, an anarchist and collaborator on *Der Weckruf*, contributed an afterword to the pamphlet.

18. M. Green, *The Mountain of Truth. The Counterculture Begins. Ascona 1900–1920* (London and Hanover: University Press of New England, 1986), p. 131.
19. L. Frank, *Links wo das Herz ist* (Munich: Nymphenburger Verlagshandlung, 1952), p. 40.
20. Frank, *Links wo das Herz ist*, p. 18; Frank, *Das Ochsenfurter Männerquartett*, p. 109.
21. This claim is lent support by a statement from the Munich City Archives (Letter of 23 January 1995) to the effect that they have no registration documents under the name of Ernst Frick.
22. Frank, *Das Ochsenfurter Männerquartett*, pp. 109–12; Frick is portrayed as the 'Swiss gunmaker' referred to in Seewald, *Der Mann von Gegenüber*, p. 172.
23. Seewald, *Der Mann von Gegenüber*, p. 172.
24. For this information I must thank Dr Robert Dünki, Zürich City Archives (letter of 8 March 1995). See also the notice in *Der Weckruf* 5. Jg. No. 58 (1 May 1907), p. 4, which relates that two Russian revolutionaries were interned in the Zürich Police Barracks awaiting delivery to 'the Czar hanging from the gallows'. This makes it likely that Frick did in fact participate in their escape.
25. See 'Aus der Zeit', *Der Sozialist* 4 Jg. No. 7 (1 April 1912), p. 56; for Scheidegger's betrayal see in particular E. Szittya, *Das Kuriositäten-Kabinett*, (Konstanz: See Verlag, 1923), pp. 101–3.
26. Hurwitz, *Otto Gross*, p. 202.
27. Letter of Max Weber to Marianne Weber, 7 April 1914, see chapter 2.
28. Szittya, *Das Kuriositäten-Kabinett*, p. 151.
29. Letter of Max Weber to Marianne Weber, 7 April 1914, see chapter 2.
30. Szeemann, *Monte Verita*, p. 115.
31. W. von der Schulenburg, 'Die Schule von Ascona', in *Das Werk. Schweizer Monatsschrift für Architektur, freie Kunst, angewandte Kunst* 20 Jg. (1933), p. 184.
32. P. Eltzbacher, *Der Anarchismus*, (Berlin: Guttentag, 1900. Eltzbacher became a correspondent of Tolstoy's because of his work on the book.
33. Hanke, *Prophet des Unmodernen*, pp. 16ff.
34. See J. N. Davidov, 'Max Weber and Leon Tolstoy: Verantwortungs- und Gesinnungsethik', in J. N. Davidov, P. P. Gaidenko, *Russland und der Westen. Heidelberger Max Weber-Vorlesungen 1992*, (Frankfurt a.M.: Suhrkamp Verlag, 1995), p. 69.
35. Letter of Gustav Landauer to Margarethe Faas-Hardegger, 27 October 1908, in M. Buber (ed.) *Gustav Landauer: Sein Lebensgang in Briefen*, vol. 1, (Frankfurt a.M.: Rütten und Loening, 1929), p. 220.
36. See Mark Harda (pseud. M. Faas-Hardegger), 'Liebe ist aller Wurzel Lust', *Der Sozialist* 1 Jg. No. 1 (15 January 1909), p. 4.
37. Hanke, *Prophet des Unmodernen*, pp. 137ff., 147.
38. Between 1909 and 1913 16 translations from Tolstoy were published in *Der Sozialist*, among them the first publication of Tolstoy's 'Speech against the War'.
39. Scheidegger, 'Offener Brief', *Der Weckruf* 3 Jg. No. 15 (August 1905) Beilage, p. 1.

40. G. Landauer, 'Lew Nikolajewitsch Tolstoi', *Der Sozialist* 2 Jg., Nr, pp. 179–81, 23–24 (15 December 1909).

41. P. Despoix, 'Von der Bühne zur Geschichte: Gustav Landauer', *Internationales Archiv für Sozialgeschichte der deutschen Literatur* 15 Jg. (1990) pp. 146-68. See also my essay 'Das "spezifisch intellektualistische Erlösungsbedürfnis". Oder: warum Intellektuelle Tolstoi lasen', in G. Hübinger, W. J. Mommsen (eds) *Intellektuelle im deutschen Kaiserreich* (Frankfurt a.M.: Fischer, 1993), pp. 158–71.

42. Frank, *Links wo das Herz ist*, p. 18.

43. G. Landauer, 'Lew Nikolajewitsch Tolstoi', p. 180.

44. Anon., 'Wir denunzieren', *Der Weckruf* 4 Jg. No. 3 (February 1906), p. 4.

45. O. Buek, *Der Weckruf* 4 Jg. No. 4 (March 1906), p. 4.

46. Ibid., p. 4.

47. K. Diehl, 'Anarchismus', in L. Elster, A. Weber, F. Wieser (eds) *Handwörterbuch der Staatswissenschaften* vol. 1 (Jena: Gustav Fischer: 1923), p. 282.

48. Cited in R. Kauffeldt, 'Die Idee eines 'Neuen Bundes' (Gustav Landauer)', in M. Frank, *Gott im Exil. Vorlesungen über die Neue Mythologie*, 2. Teil (Frankfurt a.M.: Suhrkamp Verlag, 1988), p. 149.

49. For example, Ernst Toller asked himself early in 1918 'why this fervent revolutionary keeps so quiet'; *Eine Jugend in Deutschland*, Gesammelte Werke vol. 4 (Munich: Hanser 1978), p. 104.

50. G. Landauer, *Aufruf zum Sozialismus. Revolutionsausgabe* (Berlin: Paul Cassirer, 1919), p. VIII.

51. Landauer in a comment on the article by Ludwig Berndl, 'Einige Bemerkungen über die Psycho-Analyse', *Der Sozialist* 3 Jg. No. 13 (1 July 1911), p. 104.

52. G. Landauer, 'Tarnowska', *Der Sozialist* 2 Jg. No. 7 (1 April 1910), p. 50.

53. Frank, *Links wo das Herz ist*, p. 18.

54. As testified by Frieda Gross in her statement to the 'Lunatic Inspector' for the Canton of Zürich, related in Hurwitz, *Otto Gross*, p. 228.

55. See above, p. 54.

56. Seewald, *Der Mann von Gegenüber*, p. 173.

57. Letter of Max Weber to Else Jaffé, 13 September 1907, in M. R. Lepsius, W. J. Mommsen (eds) *Briefe 1906–1908*, MWG II/5, (Tübingen: Mohr (Paul Siebeck), 1990), p. 402.

58. Max Weber, 'Intermediate Reflections', translated as 'Religious Rejections of the World and their Directions', *FMW*, p. 348.

59. Contribution to discussion of Ernst Troeltsch's paper 'Das stoisch-christliche Naturrecht und das moderne profane Naturrecht', *Verhandlungen des Ersten Deutschen Soziologentages vom 19–22 Oktober 1910 in Frankfurt a.M.* (Tübingen: J. C. B. Mohr (Paul Siebeck), 1911), p. 200.

60. 'Religious Ethics and the World', *ES*, pp. 576–610.

61. *FMW*, p. 324.

62. P. Honigsheim, 'Max Weber in Heidelberg', in R. König, J. Winckelmann (eds) *Max Weber zum Gedächtnis* (Cologne: Westdeutscher Verlag, 1963), pp. 240ff.

63. For the essay see the introduction to W. J. Mommsen (ed.) *Max Weber: Zur Russischen Revolution 1905. Schriften und Reden 1905–1912*, MWGI/10,

(Tübingen: J. C. B. Mohr (Paul Siebeck), 1989), p. 24; for the book, see Marianne Weber, *Max Weber. A Biography* (New Brunswick, N.J.: Transactions, 1988), p. 104.

64. Max Weber, 'Science as a Vocation', *FMW*, p. 156.
65. See chapter 2.
66. Max Weber, 'The Meaning of "Ethical Neutrality" in Sociology and Economics', *MSS*, p. 16.
67. Max Weber, 'Bourgeois Democracy in Russia', *The Russian Revolutions*, translated and edited by G. C. Wells and P. Baehr (Cambridge: Polity Press, 1995) p. 141, n. 194.
68. Ibid., p. 52; see in this connection 'Politics as a Vocation', in W. G. Runciman (ed.) *Max Weber. Selections in Translation* (London: Cambridge University Press, 1978), pp. 216–7.
69. Letters of Max Weber to Robert Michels, 19 February 1909 and 12 May 1909, *MWG II/6* (Tübingen: J. C. B. Mohr (Paul Siebeck), 1994), pp. 60–1, 125.
70. 'Politics as a Vocation', *Max Weber. Selections in Translation*, p. 218.
71. Letter of Max Weber to Robert Michels, 4 August 1908, *MWG II/5*, p. 615f.
72. Letter of Max to Marianne Weber, 14 April 1913, see chapter 2.
73. 'Between Two Laws', *PW*, p. 75.
74. Ibid., p. 78.
75. Ibid., p. 78.
76. 'Politics as a Vocation', *Weber. Selections in Translation*, p. 223.
77. Max Weber, 'Science as a Vocation', *FMW*, p. 156.

8 Weber and Dostoyevsky on Church, Sect and Democracy

Charles Turner

if, with the Romans, we understand being alive as synonymous with *inter homines esse* (and *sinere inter homines esse* as being dead), then we have the first important clue to the sectarian tendencies in philosophy since the time of Pythagoras: withdrawal into a sect is the second-best cure for being alive at all and having to live among men[1]

Hannah Arendt

When we received our commissions we were ready to shed our blood for the honour of our regiment, but scarcely any of us knew anything about the meaning of real honour, and if anyone had known it, he would have been the first to jeer at it[2]

Fyodor Dostoyevsky

Among historians of ideas, any number of 'elective affinities' have been sought between Weber and his predecessors or contemporaries. Here I suggest another: between Weber's formulations of the relationships between church, sect and democracy and certain themes in Dostoyevsky's writing. Dostoyevsky was not a central influence on Weber, but we do know that he had read and discussed *The Brothers Karamazov*, making explicit reference to it on more than one occasion.[3] We know from Honigsheim that scarcely a week passed without Dostoyevsky's name being heard at the Webers' Sunday gatherings.[4] What Weber 'took' from Dostoyevsky is perhaps no more than what he tried to take from any great novelist: an awareness of the tragic irreconcilability of opposed value positions and a corresponding ability to do equal justice to rival world-views. As one who was religiously 'unmusical', nowhere would his admiration have been greater than in Dostoyevsky's treatment of lives lived according to, or in defiance of, religious precepts.[5]

I will refer mainly to Ivan Karamazov's poem, 'The Grand Inquisitor', which deals with the foundations of ecclesiastical authority in terms of the ethical demands that secular institutions can and should make on their members. I will argue that Weber thought in these terms in making his distinction between church and sect. 'Church' and 'sect' represent the outer edges of the continuum of associational life, the one recommending a mode of membership and pattern of conduct valid for all regardless of and not dependent upon individual capability, the other demanding an *intensity of devotion* from its members which distinguishes the sect sharply from its institutional environment. The church, as an enterprise (*Betrieb*), is compulsory, universalistic, and demands relatively little from its members. The sect, an association (*Verein*) grounded in a principle of voluntary membership, is particularistic, and demands much more.[6] Weber's work contains a conception of democracy animated by the tension between the *ethical slackness* of a church member and the *intensity* of the sectarian.

The distinction between church and sect has been interpreted in a number of ways. Firstly, church and sect have been seen as solutions arrived at by religious communities to the problem of organisation which follows from the ordeal of determinate existence in the world.[7] Secondly, the Puritan sects have been seen as central to Weber's account of the breakthrough to the modern world.[8] Thirdly, recent commentators such as Alexander have linked the church–sect theme to democracy in America, emphasising with de Tocqueville the importance of *voluntaristic* forms of association as a foundation for modern democracy.[9]

While this is an enticing connection to draw, I agree with Wilhelm Hennis that Weber remained thoroughly European. De Tocqueville viewed the 'decentralising' force of voluntary associations in America in the mirror of 'intermediate powers' in *ancien régime* Europe, while Weber remained lukewarm about the advent of democracy in post-imperial Germany. (See Ay, Chapter 5.) Alexander misses the German/European context in which his political writings were produced, a context that included the politico-historical legacy of aristocratic and absolutist regimes and fierce debates over culture and ethics.[10] Weber described sects as apolitical or even anti-political forms of association. The distinctive feature of his theory of democracy is the attempt to combine two concerns which modern political science and sociology frequently keep separate: an almost Hobbesian definition of the state, and the question of how a human life should be led.[11] It is his deep concern for the latter problem, and not an elitist disdain for democracy as such, that is the basis of his scepticism toward democracy as a formal set of procedures. In his articles on democracy and parliament he was concerned about the political education, maturity and judgement of all citizens, not only leaders.[12] If Weber happened to admire the energy and vitality generated by sect-like voluntary associations, he did so because he perceived in them the foundation of a modern, non-egoistic form of business ethics, particularly in America. But as a northern European protestant he was suspicious of political theory which attributed political status to organisations or associations existing below the level of that which monopolises the legitimate means of violence.[13] But against a Hobbesian background he then asks whether there *is* a single set of *substantive human qualities* that might be common to, or diffused throughout, a population. It is this capacity to raise ethical questions in the context of an apparently realist conception of political life which sets Weber apart from both the tradition of Hobbes and Carl Schmitt, and from the tradition of apolitical thought about politics which was such a distinctive feature of 19th century Russian intellectual life and that was the bane of Wilhelmine politics.

Troeltsch

In a footnote to the essay on protestant sects (which is in fact an essay on American business clubs) Weber noted that 'his' distinction between church and sect had been adopted by Troeltsch in his *The Social Teachings of the Christian Churches*.[14] Here the church-sect distinction is formulated in a characteristically Weberian way, that is to say to the church's disadvantage. Discussing the early Christian community's need for a firmer 'sociological point of reference' regarding the perceived inescapability of the world, Troeltsch describes Catholicism's failed attempt to base the church on a distinction between its divine and human elements, between the priesthood as mediator of salvation and the church's 'other activity'.[15] What takes place instead is 'the real secularisation of the Church, in which the central point of religion is materialised and externalised, and delivered up into the hands of the secular art of organisation. This secularisation affected the other spheres of life, science and art, and the life of the state and of society, far less.'[16] Moreover, when the church's character as an organisation was combined with its status as the basis for 'the ecclesiastical unity of civilisation', the ethical standards demanded of individuals *qua* members of such a church were set at a relatively low level, in contrast to 'the radicalism of the christian social ethic, and the tendency to form small groups in which it is possible to carry this radicalism into practice'.[17]

But in the lecture presented to the German Sociological Association in 1911 when discussing the difficulty of transferring this ideal to the profane world, Troeltsch identifies not two but three solutions: church, sect – and mysticism.[18] While a *church* institutionalises grace and compromises with the social and ethical orders of a sinful world, the *sect* turns grace into 'a recognisable power of Christian life praxis',[19] and is thereby the coming together of 'mature and conscious Christian personalities' in which preaching and sacrament are bound up with the subject and his activity. Church and sect are related to one another as compulsory organisation to voluntary community. In *mysticism*, however, emphasis falls on the imme-diate presence and inwardness of religious experience and feeling, a feeling which cannot be satisfied with the objectivity of cult, dogma and institution. The appropriate sociological form for a radical individualism devoid of the ties of profane community is hermeticism, or a community of monks. Where it does not assume a sociological form, it remains a uni-versalistic, acosmic ethic of love or brotherliness.[20] (See Hanke, Chapter 7.)

In the discussion which follows Weber insists that, in reality, the three types of 'response' which Troeltsch outlined 'interpenetrate'. As an illus-tration Weber refers to Russia. We can ask of any of the great churches, in what infallible power is ultimate authority vested? For the Catholic church, it is the Pope, for the Lutheran, it is 'the word' and those whose calling it is to interpret it. By contrast, argues Weber, Russian Christianity 'was and is today, as a specific type, to a high degree the Christianity of antiquity.'

> In the orthodox church there lives a specifically mystical belief that brotherly love, the love of one's neighbour, those uniquely human rela-tionships which appear to us so simple … form a way, not to some sort of social effect – which is quite irrelevant – but to a knowledge of the meaning of the world, to a mystical relationship with God.[21]

This, Weber insists, is the key to an understanding of novels such as *The Brothers Karamazov*. The reader's impression that the course of events described there verges on the chaotic and meaningless does not arise from the fact that such novels were written for newspapers, but is grounded

> in the secret conviction that a life shaped by politics, society, ethics, lit-erature, art, or the family, is meaningless compared with the under-ground life which extends beneath it and is embodied in Russian literature's most quintessential forms, a life which is so difficult for us to grasp because it rests upon wholly primitive Christian foundations. It is the conviction that that which Baudelaire called the soul's sacred prostitution, love for one's neighbour, regardless of who he is, that this

amorphous, formless relationship of love furnishes access to the portals of the eternal, the timeless, the divine.[22]

For Weber, this religiosity, in its disdain for form and for the idea that the world or the self exist to be shaped and moulded by human endeavour, stands at the opposite pole to Calvinism, in which proof of election is sought *within* the orders and powers of the world, and in which internal individual discipline provides for a continuity of individual practice.

Now in formulating the difference Weber was not merely formulating an opposition between the basic principles of two types of Christianity, but referring to and employing an opposition which Georg Simmel would later describe as *the* conflict of modern culture: life versus form.[23] This is unsurprising, since at the time *Lebensphilosophie* was popular in Germany, and Weber was himself keen to resist its influence and instead appeal to values, form, the inescapability of impersonal bureaucracy, and that hardness towards the self which recalled the spirit of Luther.[24]

It is in this context that a comparison with Dostoyevsky both makes sense and is made difficult. To elevate values and form above life, as does Weber, is to encounter the dilemma that while the worth of political science is its ability to raise ethical questions, an ethics which is without social mediation makes little sense. Values and form were the principles through which Weber insisted that the relationship between ethics and action was indirect.

In Dostoyevsky, by contrast, the transition from the one to the other is smoother, and the relationship between psychology and sociology, or religion and politics, one of mutual implication. The gap between doctrine and practice, idea and reality, and the tension between spheres of conduct, which are the central tenets of Weberian science and Weberian politics, are obliterated in Dostoyevsky; and it is this which lends intensity to the greatest passages in his novels. Witness Shatov or Stavrogin in *The Devils,* Prince Myshkin in *The Idiot*, Raskonlikov in *Crime and Punishment*. Consistency of conduct, of *Lebensführung*, however much Weber prized it and was fascinated by it as it appeared in Dostoyevsky's creations, was something for which a German Protestant could only strive and which he was in constant danger of failing to achieve. When the burden of achieving that consistency in an increasingly complex and differentiated world seemed intolerable, Weber's thoughts would frequently turn to the Russians he knew in Heidelberg, and to the nihilists and anarchists of Dostoyevsky's novels, demanding and achieving consistency, but doing so by renouncing rather than dwelling in the midst of the complexities of institutional existence.[25]

It is important to be clear that Weber's attraction to the intensity of the *Russian* nihilist and anarchist was at the same time his disdain for its *German* equivalent. Weber wanted to believe that while Russia's political underdevelopment, its failure to achieve a liberal state, and its relative lack of social differentiation made possible an apoliticism which retained its political relevance, the process of rationalisation and *Vergesellschaftung* which Germany had recently undergone, together with its Lutheran and pietist traditions, made a-political or pre-political or anti-political politics an irrelevant and inappropriate form of social ethics. But at the same time one cannot avoid the impression that his interest in Russian examples of 'consistency of *Lebensführung*' was also prompted by the disquieting thought that Germany and Russia might not be as far apart as he implied. Germany too suffered from a dearth of genuine, mature statesmen ready to act politically within the confines of a rationalised and bureaucratised world and from a plethora of 'amateur social politicians',[26] on the one side, and apolitical literati, on the other side, advocating, if not practising, the 'politics of the street'.[27] Weber wanted to believe that Germany's political institutions could be made 'modern' and robust enough to turn the statements of the literati into irrelevant 'prattlings' he claimed they were. In revolutionary Munich he would see just how fragile was the distinction between Russian backwardness and Germany modernity.

The Grand Inquisitor and the Constitution of Authority

Weber was moved and agitated by the sorts of enthusiasts and fanatics who populate Dostoyevsky's novels, but it is unlikely that anything would have surpassed for him the 'The Grand Inquisitor' passage from *The Brothers Karamazov*. Put in Weberian terms this account of a meeting in sixteenth century Seville between a Catholic cardinal and Christ (who is never named or even speaks) is a justification for the routinisation of charisma, and an explanation of why the primitive brotherliness of the early Christian community had to be transformed into the universal, bureaucratic organisation of the western Church.

It contains an *anthropological* justification for worldly authority which Weber hinted at but never provided, and explores the basic difference between two beliefs: that all human beings are good and strong and capable of leading the life led by Christ, and that they are all weak and incapable of doing so. Christ's mistake, and the reason that, recognising him in the streets of sixteenth century Seville, the people are prepared to see him arrested at the inquisitor's behest, is not a failure to solve what Marxists call the 'problem of organisation'. The mistake lies in the false assumption that the people values the bread of heaven above material security, that they are capable of a 'Russian' acosmic brotherliness in the face of their better knowledge of each other's wickedness, and that, granted freedom of conscience, they will know how to, and desire to, exercise it. 'I swear,' says the Grand Inquisitor, 'man has been created a weaker and baser creature than you thought him to be! Can he, can he do what you did? In respecting him so greatly, you acted as though you ceased to feel any compassion for him – you who have loved him more than yourself! Had you respected him less, you would have asked less of him, and that would have been more like love, for his burden would have been lighter'. For the Grand Inquisitor, man knows no greater burden than freedom of conscience, no greater trial than the demands of universal brotherhood. By setting standards of conduct beyond the scope of the majority, Christ paradoxically condemned them to a life far from God. The church, by contrast, by setting standards fairly low from the start, preferred a version of love which made anthropological sense, and corrected Christ's work by relieving man of his burdens and allowing him to accomplish 'all that he seeks on earth', namely, 'whom to worship, to whom to entrust his conscience and how at last to unite into an incontestable ant-hill…'[28]

The Grand Inquisitor 'dialogue' and its subsequent discussion by Ivan and Alyosha are pervaded by a dualism to be found throughout Dostoyevsky's novels. It is a dualism between two principles claiming universal validity. On the one hand the validity of an amoral or extramoral authoritarian principle which accepts the sword of caesar and the attendant necessity of the worldly domination of some human beings over all other human beings; on the other, the validity of an acosmic ethic of brotherliness and principle of universal responsibility in which every individual is responsible for the fate of every other individual.[29] On the one hand, authoritarian mystery, obscurity, and lies; on the other, the full presence of openness, clarity and honesty. On the one hand, the strategic nihilism of Nicholas Stavrogin; on the other, the childlike innocence of Prince Myshkin. On the one hand, the institutional conception of responsibility of the Jesuit, on the other the personalist conception of taking responsibility for 'everyone else' invoked by Father Zossima.

This opposition between two accounts of how to live a life fascinated Weber. For him, the theme of how to live a life is inseparable from those of personality formation, development, and maturation, and neither the institutions of constituted secular authority as Dostoyevsky defines it, nor the everyday settings in which an acosmic brotherliness is exhibited, can provide the conditions in which individuals might *form* both the world and themselves, might lead a life rather than allowing it to happen. While the one sets standards of personal conduct which are too low – the member of the Catholic church 'lives ethically from hand to mouth'[30] – the other requires a capacity for Christ-like conduct which 'today' is impossible 'for purely external reasons'. What they share is the sponsoring of an essentially *childish*, immature mode of conduct. 'We shall prove to them that ... they are mere pitiable children, but that the happiness of the child is the sweetest of all' says the Grand Inquisitor; 'we shall permit them to sin ... and they will love us like children for allowing them to sin.'[31] And at the opposite extreme, numerous commentators have noted the destructiveness of Dostoyevsky's most Christ-like creation, Prince Myshkin, who destroys others precisely through a childlike ethic of love, openness and honesty practised without regard for consequences, through a humility which serves only to burden others with a moral responsibility for which they lack the strength.[32]

Weber's robust conception of adult behaviour largely avoids this alternative, which in political thought is that between Hobbesian hierarchy and Rousseauian egalitarianism. Hobbes and Rousseau, too, share an antagonism toward plural, particularistic association, be it sectarian or corporative. Moreover, neither the Hobbesian nor the Rousseauean tradition contains a theory of political education appropriate to a democratic polity as Weber understood it. Weber's idea of maturity, of self-formation and self-development, stands opposed both to the Hobbesian idea of self-preservation, and to the Rousseauean idea of self-perfection, and in this sense is far closer to Hegel than has been acknowledged. Too often Weber's social philosophy has been presented in terms of stark existential alternatives of the sort which pervade Dostoyevsky's novels. Hence, the acceptance of power and violence as a constitutive horizon of our political life is seen in terms of a pact with diabolic forces. Against this view two points need to be made. Firstly, what D. H. Lawrence said in criticism of Ivan Karamazov is true of Weber: 'The man who realises that Jesus asked too much of the mass of men, in asking them to choose between earthly and heavenly bread, and to judge between good and evil, is not therefore satanic.'[33] If Weber endorses the Grand Inquisitor's view of the inescapability of domination, he does so for pragmatic as much as philosophical-anthropological reasons. Secondly, despite the fact that Weber's profoundest statements about politics are about the calling of the political leader, and despite the fact that he seems to endorse democratic institutions only in so far as they are a seedbed for the moral resources which leadership requires, the wartime essay 'Suffrage and Democracy in Germany' explores the idea of political education from a more recognisably democratic, if unconventional, point of view.[34]

The obvious route between Hobbes and Rousseau is one which leads via de Tocqueville and Durkheim, where civil associations or professional bodies educate their members in the idea of shared social duties and thereby act as proving grounds for democratic citizenship. But Weber asks whether there is an extent to which the nation state itself can be treated *as if it were a voluntary association*, just as he describes the Calvinist conception of the church as one shot through with sectarianism. The sect itself renounces universality, rests upon free association, is an *aristocratic* formation of the religiously qualified, rejects institutional grace and office charisma, and is made up of members whose charisma is either given or sought after. There is a Tocquevillean moment when Weber describes the sects as the unwritten but thereby most important component of the American constitution, because they 'exert the strongest influence on the formation of the personality'.[35] It is this which prevents America being 'an incontestable anthill'.

But in *Germany* he is more reticent about the political significance of voluntary associations. The sect 'is a specifically anti-political or even apolitical formation.'[36] It is just this, so it seems, which allows it to expect certain qualities from its members, while large scale political institutions are mechanisms for the selection of *leaders alone*. But Weber disrupts this neat distinction by asking whether in a formally democratic polity there is a set of qualities, an ideal of personality formation, to which *all* citizens can aspire.

Political versus Social Democracy

Weber's most explicit treatment of this theme, which grafts the sectarian problematic onto the state, is contained in the wartime essay 'Suffrage *and* Democracy in Germany' (my emphasis). If political democracy presupposes something common to all – an equal right to participation – do the members of a democratic polity share the same substantive 'qualities'? Weber answers that social democratisation is by no means a consequence of the extension of suffrage. But the distinctive feature of his argument is the description of the process of 'social' democratisation. Here a set of qualities peculiar to an *aristocracy* is diffused 'downwards' by a process of imitation. Hence the question: *are* the characteristics of the German-Prussian ruling class imitable and democratisable? For in a state which is a true community of fate, a 'true aristocracy can stamp an entire nation with its own ideal of distinguished conduct', by means of a process in which 'the plebian imitates the gestures' of the aristocracy.[37]

The German-Prussian aristocracy's qualities were not imitable, and in the worst sense. They were that combination of features summed up by the

German term *Satisfaktionsfähigkeit*, the capacity to give satisfaction, a 'virtue' embodied in the institution of the duel, and pervading the two arenas which had the key formative influence on younger members of the German ruling class, namely the officer corps and the student fraternities. (See Ay, Chapter 5.) *Satisfaktionsfähigkeit*, far from capturing a set of qualities worthy of imitation, signifies a virtually insurmountable *barrier* between the Junkers and the rest of German society. It was considerations of this sort that were to lead Karl Mannheim to develop one of the most powerful analyses of the crisis of Weimar culture: democratisation brought with it a cultural and political crisis because it brought onto the political stage groups whose leading strata exhibited incommensurable 'styles of thinking' and lacked a shared mode of communication.[38] Among them Mannheim discerned a genuinely aristocratic style of thinking. Weber, by contrast, describes the Prussian Junker class as plebian,[39] tied to a process of agricultural embourgeoisement that has brought it irrevocably into the sphere of interest conflict. Mired in the realm of necessity, it lacks genuinely aristocratic social distance.[40]

> Anyone who knows the much (and often unjustly) maligned and (equally unjustly) idolised Junker of the eastern provinces is bound to take delight in them on a purely personal level – when out hunting, drinking a drop of something decent, at the card-table, amidst the hospitality of the estate farm – in these areas everything about them is genuine. Everything becomes false only when one stylises as an 'aristocracy' this essentially 'bourgeois', entrepreneurial stratum ... If one tries to put the stamp of an aristocracy, with its feudal gestures and pretensions, onto a social stratum which depends nowadays on plain, bourgeois-capitalist work, the inevitable result will simply be *the physiognomy of the parvenu*.[41]

In a nation which lacks a genuine aristocratic social form, whose officialdom is thoroughly middle-class, all attempts to emulate the manner and bearing of that class on the mistaken assumption that it is aristocratic will produce not emulation, but caricature. Nowhere was this danger greater than in the spread of the student fraternities, which, far from being the proving ground which might nurture the aristocratic qualities required by 'men of the world', had become nothing more than a mechanism for selecting officials.

In support of this view Weber compares German, Anglo-Saxon and 'Latin' political culture and social forms. Just as he wrote on problems of *Lebensführung* with half an eye on Russia, so he wrote on the advent of democracy and parliamentarianism in Germany with an idealised image of English politics to hand. Thus, having lamented the absence of a democratisable German social form, he writes:

> The forms governing the behaviour of people in Latin countries, right down to the lowest strata, are produced by imitating the *'gesture of a cavalier'* as this evolved from the sixteenth century. The conventions of English-speaking countries, which also shape the behaviour of society down to the lowest stratum, derive from the social habits of that section of society which set the tone from the seventeenth century onwards ... 'gentlemen', who were the bearers of 'self-government' ... The Latin code of honour, like the very different English one, was susceptible of being democratised to a great extent. The specifically German concept of 'being qualified to give satisfaction', on the other hand, cannot be democratised.[42]

The methodological doubts about this passage notwithstanding, Weber is making a crucial point about the relationship between democracy as a political form and a democratic social form. The *internal relationships* of the officer corps and of the student fraternity are dominated by caste conventions of command and obedience which, though hierarchical, are not 'aristocratic'. They lack the *aesthetic* dignity of true aristocracy, embodied in an outward grace and bearing, and inner coolness and reserve, in a proper balance between the formal and the informal aspects of behaviour.[43] Such a balance he believes he can discern in the gentleman, and the club which is his milieu, 'built on the principle that all gentlemen are equal'.[44]

In the absence of 'gentlemen', Weber remarks that if democratisation were to do away with the prestige attached to a university degree, no politically valuable social form would have been destroyed. 'It could then perhaps clear the way for the development of formal values which would be appropriate to our middle class social and economic structure and therefore be both genuine and distinguished. Such values...can only be developed on the basis of inner distance and reserve in one's personal bearing.'[45]

Conclusion

The essay on suffrage and democracy, then, like 'Politics as a Vocation', reveals a yearning for a social form which lies between the extremes of detachment (The Grand Inquisitor) and involvement (Prince Myshkin), between submission to an authoritarian state and acosmic brotherliness.

Although far from convinced, Weber believed that the ultimate goal of political education in a centralised democratic polity was to produce citizens capable of exhibiting an inner ethical balance. For all his admiration for the *Gesinnungsethiker* who populated Dostoyevsky's novels and appeared on the streets of Munich in his own day, in his mind Weber associated the virtues of inner distance and reserve, or cool reflection, maturity and judgement, with the Puritan sects, the Western European city, and the Northern European bourgeoisie.

The methodological shortcomings of a diffusion/democratisation approach are obvious: do the barriers to the democratisation of qualities reside in those qualities themselves, or in the communicative relationship between groups? But his remarks retain a twofold significance. Firstly, Weber is recommending an approach to political culture which connects political form with external behavioural codes, an approach which is gaining in popularity today among the followers of Bourdieu and Elias. Secondly, it testifies to the centrality Weber attached to the sectarian associational form, not merely as a proving ground for a particular set of substantive human qualities he admired, but as the paradigm case of such a proving ground. It is this idea, and not an anti-democratic impulse, which led him to express the hope that democracy in a formal sense might give rise to the integration of all citizens into the state, not as its co-rulers, but as politically educated 'master-race'.[46] By this expression he meant nothing more – but nothing less! – than a nation of adults rather than children, who would accept political authority without submitting to it, seek liberty within rather than beyond the world, and pursue equality freed from the illusions of universal brotherliness.

NOTES

1. H. Arendt, *Lectures on Kant's Political Philosophy* (Chicage: Chicago University Press, 1982), p. 23.
2. F. Dostoyevsky, *The Brothers Karamazov* (London: Penguin, 1957), p. 377.
3. See Max Weber in his discussion of Ernst Troeltsch at the first German Sociological Society meeting, 'Das stoisch-christliche Naturrecht und das moderne profane Naturrecht', *Verhandlungen des ersten deutschen Soziolgentages* (Tübingen: Mohr, 1911), p. 199; *PW*, p. 361; Marianne Weber, *Max Weber* (New York: Wiley, 1975), p. 490.
4. P. Honigsheim, 'Max Weber in Heidelberg', in R. König and J. Winckelmann, *Max Weber zum Gedächtnis* (Cologne: Westdeutscher Verlag, 1964), p. 241.

5. Under the influence of younger thinkers such as Lukács, Weber came to take Russian versions of consistency of conduct as seriously he did Calvinist and Puritan versions. See *Georg Lukács: Selected Correspondence 1902–20*, ed. and trans. J. Marcus and Z. Tar (New York: Columbia University Press, 1986).
6. M. Weber, *Economy and Society* (Berkeley: California University Press, 1978), pp. 54–5, 1163–4, 1196–8, 1204–10.
7. This problem was central to Troeltsch's thinking in *The Social Teachings of the Christian Churches* (London: Allen & Unwin, 1936).
8. See G. Poggi, *Calvinism and the Capitalist Spirit. Max Weber's 'Protestant Ethic'* (London: Macmillan, 1983).
9. J. Alexander, 'The Cultural Grounds for Rationalisation', in his *Structure and Meaning* (New York: Columbia University Press, 1988).
10. See W. Hennis, *Max Weber. Essays in Reconstruction* (London: Allen & Unwin, 1989); L. Scaff, *Fleeing the Iron Cage* (Berkeley: University of California Press, 1990).
11. See Hennis, op. cit., chapter 1.
12. This view, it has to be admitted, is not common in the literature which over-whelmingly discusses parliamentary democracy as a proving ground for statesmen. See W. J. Mommsen, *Max Weber and German Politics* (Chicago: Chicago University Press, 1984); R. Eden, *Political Leadership and Nihilism* (Tampa: University Press of Florida, 1983). But see also L. Scaff, 'Max Weber's Politics and Political Education', *American Political Science Review*, 67 (1973), pp. 128–41.
13. This was also an expression of his thoroughgoing objection to any organicist social ethics.
14. *FMW*, p. 450.
15. E. Troeltsch, *The Social Teaching of the Christian Churches* (London: Allen & Unwin, 1936), pp. 91, 94.
16. Ibid., p. 94.
17. Ibid., p. 94.
18. E. Troeltsch, 'Das stoisch-christliche Naturrecht und das moderne profane Naturrecht' *Verhandlungen des ersten deutschen Soziologentages* (Tübingen: Mohr, 1911), pp. 169–73. Translated as 'Stoic-Christian Natural Law and Modern secular Natural Law', in O. Gierke, *Natural Law and the Theory of Society* (Cambridge: Cambridge University Press, 1957). Page references refer to the German original.
19. Ibid., pp. 170–3.
20. Ibid., pp. 173.
21. Ibid., p. 199.
22. Ibid., p. 200.
23. G. Simmel, 'The Conflict of Modern Culture', *On Individuality and Social Forms* (Chicago: Chicago University Press, 1971).
24. See the letter to Harnack of 1906 quoted by Jaspers in his *On Max Weber* (New York: Paragon House, 1989), pp. 168–9.
25. On Weber's Russian sympathies see Marianne's account of the fiftieth anniversary of the Russian library in Heidelberg, op. cit., pp. 466–7. Weber's written references are somewhat oblique: *The Russian Revolutions* (Cambridge: Polity, 1995), pp. 230–3; letter to Ladislaus von Bortkiewicz ,

12 March 1906, 'your "epistemological" politicians in Russian are a unique people. And yes! Would that so much idealism could appear in Germany.', *MWG, II/1*, p. 47.

26. 'The Nation State and Economic Policy', *PW*, p. 27.
27. See Weber's comments on Luxemburg and Liebknecht in Marianne Weber, op. cit., p. 642.
28. F. Dostoyevsky, op. cit., p. 302.
29. Ibid., p. 377.
30. *PESC*, p. 116.
31. Dostoyevsky, op. cit., p. 304.
32. The private destructiveness of Prince Myshkin is the other side of the political destructiveness of figures like Shatov who appears in *The Devils*. In Weberian terms, what unites them is a philosophy of the deed, without regard for consequences, without any institutional mediation, and without any need for self-legitimation. It was Walter Benjamin who remarked that, 'The destructive character has no interest in being understood.' See 'Der destruktive Charakter', *Illuminationen* (Frankfurt: Suhrkamp, 1977) p. 290.
33. D. H. Lawrence, in R. Wellek ed., *Dostoyevsky* (New York: Prentice Hall, 1962), p. 94.
34. *ES*, p. 1207.
35. Ibid., p. 1207.
36. Ibid., p. 1207.
37. *PW*, p. 108.
38. K. Mannheim, 'The Democratisation of Culture', *From Karl Mannheim* (New York: Oxford University Press, 1971); *Ideology and Utopia* (London: Routledge & Kegan Paul, 1936) especially pp. 1–29 and 130–236.
39. Weber is serious enough about this to moot the posssibility of creating a genuine landed aristocracy by means of a forest clearance programme in the East.
40. *PW*, pp. 108–29.
41. Ibid., pp. 114–5.
42. Ibid., p. 120.
43. This theme is brilliantly explored by Norbert Elias in *The Germans* (Cambridge: Polity, 1996). Diffusion through imitation plays a major role in the work of Elias, especially his account of the development of 'warriors into courtiers' and of the aping of courtly gestures by a nascent bourgeoisie. See *The Civilising Process* (Oxford: Blackwell, 1993). Weber himself may have taken it both from Nietzsche and from Tarde, a copy of whose *Laws of Imitation* he possessed. See G. Tarde, *On Communication and Social Influence* (Chicago: Chicago University Press, 1969), pp. 177–91.
44. Weber, op. cit., p. 117.
45. Ibid., p. 122.
46. Ibid., p. 129.

9 The 'Science of Reality' of Music History: on the Historical Background to Max Weber's Study of Music

Christoph Braun

'He has never, we said afterwards, done anything more incredible. We were all completely dazed and dumbfounded.' Bewilderment clouds the admiration with which the Heidelberg theologian Hans von Schubert comments, presumably in late 1912, on a lecture by Max Weber on the 'sociology of music' given in his Heidelberg home on Ziegelhäuser Landstrasse.[1] It shows the difficulty Weber's contemporaries faced in fitting his widely diverse interests within the canon of academic disciplines. How did the trained jurist, economist, historian and cultural analyst come to be directing his enquiries towards fields so foreign to his subject as music? A few motifs taken from the history of Weber's works as a whole and from his biography, described below, should provide an insight into this and demonstrate the nature of the theoretical musical analyses as well as their connection with the general interests of the social and cultural scientist.

First, when the history of the texts is followed, a thread is found to extend from the two foundational works of 1904–5, '"Objectivity" in Social Science and Social Policy',[2] and *The Protestant Ethic and the Spirit of Capitalism*, to the study of music of 1912–13, and reveals that this is the science of reality applied to music history, with a cultural and sociological line of enquiry. Second, a connection will be made that has so far been overlooked, between Weber's sociology of culture and Karl Vossler's sociology of literature.

1. An Economist 'Astray'

Hans von Schubert's comparative, 'more incredible', indicates that Weber's musical interests were not the first or the only things to cause disciplinary confusion. The thirty-year-old Berlin jurist had already caused a stir by being appointed full professor of economics in Freiburg and through a colossal amount of work familiarising himself with the subject matter of economics, which was very closely related to legal, political and cultural history. The loss of his teaching position which accompanied his mental and physical breakdown did not put a stop to his productive powers; just the opposite. Both the 'Objectivity' and the 'Protestantism' essays from the years 1904–5 led to debates which crossed disciplinary boundaries. These were sparked off for one thing by the epistemological concepts of *Verstehen* (of the 'meaning' of social action) and 'ideal type' as the means of a specifically *cultural*-scientific, i.e. value-related, 'objectivity'. With these concepts their author dissociated himself from the intuitive 'experience' (*Erleben*) of the traditional humanities subjects and history, as well as from naturalism and the rebellious natural sciences which were now claiming the monopoly over 'science'.[3] For another thing Weber's contemporaries reacted strongly to his practical test of forming an ideal-type concept in the 'Protestantism' study, which seeks to grasp in the ascetic Protestant way of life the fundamental elements of the psychogenesis of that 'earth-shattering process of reshaping which our economic life and with it our cultural existence in general experienced through the advance of capitalism.'[4]

In the 'Objectivity' – as in the 'Protestantism' – essay Weber largely remained the pupil of the traditional 'historical school' of economics, as which he saw himself and as which he sought, from very different perspectives, to understand the 'cultural significance' of capitalism as the most powerful cultural factor of the present day. The response was indeed enormous[5] to these two works, which were fundamental to the way the modern social sciences understood themselves and the process by which they were set up; but it was not marked by such bewilderment as with the later 'detours' into the sociology of music and culture. These become recognisable from 1908–9 and culminate in the plan for a 'comprehensive sociology of culture'; the study on music of 1912–13 can be regarded as the only part of this that reached a finished form.[6] As should be emphasised from the start, it was, in Weber's terminology, an 'empirical history of music' based on comparative universal history, with a sociocultural, value-related, line of enquiry.

As early as 1909 Weber proclaimed the 'unavoidable' necessity, as a sociologist, of working 'at the edges of the field and in neighbouring fields'.[7] He demonstrates his own activities in other disciplines from time to time in downright sarcastically conducted debates with colleagues who widened their interests into the field of art, especially music, and in the process displayed their 'dilettantism' to a greater or lesser degreee. Thus to the sociologists and 'technologists with a purely scientific training', Wilhelm Ostwald and Ernst Solvay, who applied knowledge of the laws of the natural sciences to the field of art and judge this from the standpoint of thermo-dynamics and the production and conversion of energy, Weber makes the objection: 'Awkward – that "art" *begins* precisely where the "points of view" of the engineer *leave off*! But perhaps it is always and everywhere the same with what we call "culture"?'[8] A year later, at the first conference of the German Society for Sociology, which he had helped to found, in Frankfurt am Main in October 1910, Weber corrects his friend Werner Sombart's lecture on 'Technology and Culture' – a 'piece of journalism' – with empirical facts and concrete questions. Sombart's question about the 'effects of technology on culture' is made concrete and given its place in the discipline.[9] More interesting than Sombart's 'problem [of the] dependence of artistic developments on the general, *extra*-artistic, technical conditions of life', because it is more ambitious than this, appears to Weber to be the 'special, much more specific problem … [of the] dependence of the devel-opments in an art-form on *its* technical means'. It is a case here of 'intrinsic laws' (*immanente Gesetzlichkeit*) in an art's technical means, faced with the 'rule' by which 'the artist's will engenders the technical means of solving a problem'. In disciplinary terms, Weber assigns this 'question of the connec-tion between artistic will and the technical means of music' to the field of 'music *history*'; while '*sociology* poses the other question, about the connec-tion between the 'spirit' of a particular music and the *general* technical bases of our present, and especially our big-city, life, which influence the tempo of life and our feelings towards it.'[10]

In the reply to Sombart it becomes apparent where Weber's own ven-tures into other disciplines have led him: to music-historical and instru-mental details relating to the 'question of the connection between artistic will and the technical means of music'. The development of the wind, stringed and keyboard instruments and of the modern orchestra as a whole, and the consequences of this development for the work of the composers Bach, Haydn, Beethoven, Berlioz, Wagner and Richard Strauss,[11] not only show him that 'rule' but also make him aware of the ideal-typical contrast between subjective artistic will and the objective technical means employed in realising this artistic will. The dual process of showing that socio-economic and technical factors *participate* in artistic phenomena and, where they do not play a role, of also giving the autonomy of artistic creativity its due – this dual process becomes the leitmotif of Weber's sorties into the sociology of art and music over the decade 1909–1919.

Weber devoted the study on music predominantly to the objective, tech-nical, historically developing conditions of music. This at least is what is shown by the provisional version that we have of it. Judging by that, it is not, or only marginally, a 'music sociology' in the sense of the Frankfurt sociology conference as cited above, but rather it is a specific 'history of music'. That is indicated explicitly by the essay on the 'The Meaning of "Value Freedom" in Sociology and Economics' published in 1917, which places the results of the study on music, written four years earlier, within the 'history of music'.[12] 'Its central problem, from the point of view of the interest of the modern European, is ...: why music oriented to harmony was developed only in Europe and in a particular period from the polyphony which had come about in the musical tradition almost everywhere, whereas the rationalization of music took a different and in fact usually diametrically opposite path everywhere else. Elsewhere intervals (usually the fourth) developed towards being divided spatially instead of according to harmony (the fifth).' The answer: 'The central problem is therefore the origin of the third in its harmonic significance: as an integral part of the triad; and then of harmonic chromaticism; and further of modern musical rhythm, ... of rational musical notation, ... of rational polyphonic singing' – 'all those are "advances" in music's *technical* means which have greatly determined its [western] history'.[13]

How did Weber arrive at these insights so foreign to his own subject and scarcely comprehensible to his colleagues? It is known that the close friendship with Mina Tobler, the Swiss pianist living in Heidelberg who was introduced into Weber's Sunday circle in Heidelberg in 1908 by Emil Lask, provided the biographical and musical foundations.[14] Over and above that, however, continuities within the history of Weber's work show that in his remarks of 1912/13 and 1917 Weber did not really pursue new questions or sudden inspirations. The 'detours' into music theory rather expand on the two (new) solutions to (traditional) economic questions already presented in the 'Objectivity' and 'Protestantism' studies.[15] This expanding out follows two lines of argument, one which analyses cultural objectifications in their social, economic and technical dimensions from the point of view of sociology of culture, and one from the point of view of rationality theory which looks at cultural objectifications as cultural spheres becoming more differentiated and independent under their own momentum. The former links the 'Objectivity' essay with the contributions to the debates at the Frankfurt and Berlin sociologists' conferences (1910 and 1912), the section of the music study on instruments, and the essay on 'value freedom'. The analyses of rationality start with the 'Protestantism' study and lead via the 'rational bases' section of the music study to the 'Author's Introduction'('Vorbemerkung' of *Gesammelte Aufsätze zur Religionssoziologie*).[16]

2.   The 'Science of Reality' in Music History

In the 'Objectivity' essay Weber includes aesthetic cultural objects in his analyses, though from the dominant economic viewpoint of their being economically determined. That 'earth-shattering' fact mentioned in the 'Geleitwort', that (modern) capitalism has fundamentally altered life, is as true of them as of all cultural phenomena.[17] Aesthetic objects too are and always were determined partly by economic factors. Now, however, in the age of modern capitalism, the influence of economic realities is a more subtle and sustained one: the 'indirect influence of social relationships, institutions and groupings of people, all under pressure from "material" interests, extends (often unconsciously) to all areas of culture without exception, and into the finest nuances of aesthetic and religious feeling'.[18] The section of the music study dealing with instruments puts this in concrete terms. Weber pays particular attention to economic competition in the manufacture of pianos and its effects on the way people composed. The 'market conditions of the now capitalist production of instruments decided the fate of musical instruments'[19] – in two respects: first, when the early piano appeared, the immediate predecessor of our present-day concert grand and of the 'bourgeois "furniture"', the domestic upright, the 'older types of instrument, the clavichord and harpsichord, which were weaker in tone but more intimate and intended for more sensitive ears' were supplanted; second, however, 'the fierce competition between factories and virtuosos involving the specifically modern means of the press, exhibitions, and finally, by analogy for instance with the sales techniques of the breweries, the instrument manufacturers' creation of their own concert halls ... achieved that technical perfection of the instrument which alone could satisfy the composers' ever-increasing technical demands. The older instruments would not have coped even with Beethoven's later works'.[20] Weber sees similar causal interrelationships between the economy and art in the development of very early medieval stringed instruments (forms standardised to a norm – musical guilds – stable market), in the development of the modern violin (striving for beauty of tone – manageability of form – player's freedom of movement – functionality of the parts of the instrument and qualities of the wood) and in organ building (wealth of the monasteries – ecclesiastical use of the organ – its technical development – its mechanical principle – its significance for the harmonisation of medieval music towards chordal harmony).[21]

It is not only at the concrete level of the interconnection of the economy and aesthetic feeling that the music study points back to the 'Objectivity' essay. Its starting point is also to be found here, in the programmatic definition of 'science of reality': 'We aim to understand the reality of the life around us, into which we are placed, *in its particularity* – on one hand the connection and the cultural *significance* of its individual phenomena in their present shape, on the other the reasons for their historical having-become-so-and-not-otherwise'.[22] The music study carries out this programme with precision for *musical* reality as it presented itself to Weber the music expert and music lover at the turn of the century.[23] With it, as Weber tells his sister Lili in 1912, he wanted simply 'to write something … about music *history*. i.e. just about certain social conditions from which it can be explained that *only we* have a "harmonic" music.'[24] From this modest 'something', however, resulted a tremendously compressed 95-page treatise which made its author the first universal historian of music on an empirical, that is, phonographically checked, basis.[25]

Its central concern is with the comparison of 'tonal systems'. This itself points again to the 'Objectivity' essay and the concept of 'culture' that is used there: ' "Culture" is from the standpoint of the *person* a finite segment, invested with meaning and significance, of the meaningless infinity of events in the world'.[26] Weber discusses tonal systems as cultural forms rationalising the stock of notes found naturally; the systems are finite segments, invested with meaning and significance, of the infinity of the natural range of notes, and have become differentiated according to 'value standpoints' in cultural history, music theory and/or musical practice. The music study enquires as to the peculiarities of the modern European tonal system and discovers them, through universal-historical comparisons, in chordal harmony and the equal tempering of the pitch of the intervals. In the 'Introduction' to 'The Economic Ethics of World Religions', presumably written shortly after the conclusion of the music study was provisionally set down, Weber puts his remarks on music very precisely. The 'Pythagorean "comma"', a small, scarcely audible interval, symbol of the (unrationalised) pure tones of nature, 'resists total rationalisation oriented to acoustic physics'. Weber distinguishes 'the various great systems of music of all peoples and ages' by 'the manner in which they have either covered up or bypassed this inescapable irrationality or, on the other hand, put irrationality into the service of a wealth of tonalities.'[27]

Weber's music study shows – to take up those summarising sentences of the 'Introduction' – with what means, modern European musical culture covered up, or rather bypassed, the acoustic irrationality of the Pythagorean comma: it eliminated this 'trouble-maker' through equally tempered pitch. In contrast, the non-European and pre-modern European (ancient and medieval) musical cultures left the intervals at their natural values and used them for a wealth of 'tonalities' on the basis of a spiral of notes (*Tonspirale*) which is in principle infinite. In non-European cultures can be found – analogously to a highly differentiated world of deities – hundreds of 'keys',[28] in each case with different intervals of the same category varying by minimal amounts (varying sizes of semitones, whole tones, etc.), with individual patterns in the succession of intervals, and individual 'characters' ('*Ethoi*').[29] In contrast, the modern European stock of twelve kinds of key in the closed, tempered 'circle of fifths', which moreover no longer knows anything but *one* semitone, *one* whole tone, *one* fifth, etc. and two types of pattern for the succession of whole-tone and semitone intervals (the 'major' and 'minor' species of octave) seems a relatively meagre though thoroughly calculated product; its components stand in precisely regulated, rational relation to each other.

3.   'Musical Life' and Ideal-Typical Reason

The intention of the first and final thirds of the first, 'rational bases', section of the study is to draw systematic comparisons between tonal systems as the means of 'understanding in its peculiarity the reality of the surrounding [musical] life within which we are placed'.[30] Its middle part – likewise following the 'Objectivity' essay's 'science of reality' – discusses the 'reasons' for European musical culture's 'historical having-become-so-and-not-otherwise': the complex 'interconnection of circumstances' (Verkettung)[31] which led to the emergence of the musical 'peculiarities' specific to the modern West. Weber stresses the modern system of notation, which sets down the polyphonic parts in a musical 'score'. Through setting down the notes' relative time-values and the fixed scheme of organisation in bars 'the progression of the individual parts in relation to each other' becomes 'clear and unambiguous', which makes 'a really polyphonic "composition"' possible.[32] Further central 'circumstances' found only in the West were a special feeling for harmony oriented to harmonic thirds, a polyphony in the form of contrapuntal musical parts regulated by strict theory with rules and prohibitions, together with a chromaticism harmonically linked into this polyphony during the Renaissance, and lastly – as the 'final thing in the development of our music towards chordal harmony' – the equally tempered tuning of the intervals.[33]

As regards method, the music study is a paradigmatic application of the concept of 'ideal type' which Weber first uses in the 'Protestantism' essay, in the concept of the 'spirit' of capitalism which is constructed synthetically from complex historical reality.[34] In the music study Weber works with ideal types of tonal systems and forms of polyphony, which in their intellectual construction and their function as a *means* of knowledge cannot be thought of in the same way as musical practice, but which help to order the complex universal-historical reality of this practice and to enable comparisons to be made. Weber compares the melodic way of producing and ordering intervals with the harmonic. The former follows the principle of juxtaposition, the spatial arrangement of notes within the basic interval of the fourth, and sets up numerous 'tetrachord' sequences of notes which are often subtly distinguished from each other by only the smallest of intervals. These foster and demand a good ear, but do not really offer any means of comparability or systematisation, which are necessary especially for the transposition of melodies. It is just such means which the harmonic way of producing intervals holds; this subscribes to the principle of affinity and consonance between notes, and instead of dividing up (the fourth) by spatial distance, orders the intervals by means of harmonic division – prototypical is the fifth divided by the major or minor harmonic third. Melodic logic (*Ratio*) is manifested in the essentially linear music, in one or (purely quantitatively) several parts, of non-European cultures and of European antiquity and the European Middle Ages, and corresponds to the natural, 'pure' tuning that is oriented to subtle nuances of pitch and a wealth of keys; in contrast, harmonic logic underlies modern European music, major and minor chordal harmony based on a qualitative feeling for harmony, and needs equally tempered tuning for its expressive possibilities to unfold freely. The rational 'operation' of the tonal system, however, is at the high cost to the modern European – this is one of Weber's sociocultural value standpoints – of a 'dulled' ear for intervals.[35] In contrast, 'other cultural circles', according to Weber in the letter to his sister, possess 'a much better *ear* and much more intensive musical *culture*'.[36]

With its characterisation of the different paths taken by musical rationalisation as ideal types, the music study particularly reflects that sentence which Weber wants to put 'at the beginning of every study which essays to deal with rationalism': 'one may ... rationalise life from fundamentally different basic points of view and in very different directions'.[37] And again, there is a connection here with the concept of 'rationalism' first put forward in the 'Protestantism' essay and later expanded in 'The Economic Ethics of World Religions' in terms of universal history. The 'spirit' of capitalism, which shows itself as a 'spirit' that plans in a rational-functional and impersonal way, leads Weber to recognise a specific kind of rationalism which increasingly determines not only human economic activity but the whole of culture from the start of modern times.

Weber looks for and finds this rationalist 'spirit', first understood in terms of the sociology, or more precisely psychology, of religion, in music too, as well as in the various 'contents of culture' (*Kulturinhalte*) examined to a greater or lesser extent from 1910 on, which were intended to form the basis of the planned sociology of 1913. Where the 'Protestantism' essay discussed 'rational conduct on the basis of the idea of the calling ... born ... from the spirit of Christian asceticism' as one of 'the fundamental elements ... of all modern culture',[38] which with its 'tremendous cosmos of the modern economic order' reveals itself as a culture which is particularly rational, the music study takes this up formally by understanding equally tempered chordal harmony based on a self-contained, rationally conceived tonal system as one of the constitutive components of modern European cultural life. Not only the 'rationality' of 'the peculiar modern Western form of capitalism', but also the rationality of the peculiar modern western form of music is, as the 'Author's Introduction' can be taken as implying for the music study, 'essentially dependent on ... calculability'.[39] In contrast, the historical and non-European forms of both economic activity and music-making (and of tonal systematising) are distinguished essentially by incalculability, freedom, improvisation, spontaneity.

The drawing of parallels and the internal linking of cultural spheres (here, of economic and musical behaviour in the widest sense) is explicitly emphasised by Weber in the 'Author's Introduction' – embedded in the negative question: 'Why did not the scientific, the artistic, the political, or the economic development there [e.g. in China or India] enter upon that path of rationalisation which is peculiar to the Occident?'.[40] The music study puts the positive way round – for its own subject: 'why did both polyphonic and harmonic-homophonic music, and the modern tonal system in general, develop from the polyphony which was after all fairly widespread, at just one point on the earth rather than other places with an ... at least equal intensity of musical culture?'[41]

The ever-present eye to the 'rationalisation' of tonal material and of other cultural contents and materials is known to have served Weber 'in recognising the special *peculiarity* of western, and more precisely, of modern western rationalism and in explaining its origins'. And nevertheless, to call Weber exclusively a, or even *the*, theoretician of modern rationalism would be to take too narrow a view of his intentions. Rather, his reflections on musical logic are of a dialectical nature. They are first and foremost of a demonstrative character: they mean to show 'that in music too, and precisely there – in this art which apparently springs most purely from emotion – logic plays such a significant role; and that its peculiar nature in the West, just like that of western science and all western state and social institutions, is conditioned by a specific kind of rationalism'.[42] That music in particular is an especially strong emotional force, Weber knows not only from his own personal experience;[43] it is the cultural theorist and sociologist of religion, too, who knows it, who – following Schopenhauer, Kierkegaard, Nietzsche and Jacob Burckhardt – concerns himself with the aesthetic and erotic spheres in the sense of 'life forces' and calls music and its 'purest form: instrumental music' the '"most inward" of all the arts'; it is music that he counts among those 'this-worldly forces of life whose being is of a fundamentally arational or antirational character' and to which he ascribes the power of 'a this-worldly salvation ... from the routines of everyday life, and especially from the increasing pressures of theoretical and practical rationalism'.[44] So much the starker does the contrast appear between the music study – the analysis of the rationality of music taken as a sphere of material structured according to its own laws – and the 'Zwischenbetrachtung', with its idea of music as an art of the emotions with power over the conduct of life because it is inwardly moving. The two appear to contradict each other – appear to. For Weber's rationalist destruction of illusions, his disenchantment of music as an emotionally oriented bourgeois substitute for religion by means of mathematical formulae and the analysis of the '"inner logic" of tonal relationships', is only antithesis. Where is the synthesis that has been obscured by the label of rationalism?

It lies in Weber's insight into the power of the 'irrational' forces of (music) history. Time and again Weber returns to the need for passionate expression which makes itself felt with increased intensity at particular epochs in almost all developed cultures. This striving for expression has been manifest in 'baroque' scales which deviate from traditional patterns. It has always given the tonal systems handed down from the past a dynamic developmental impetus. Moreover, the forces of musical rationalisation do not operate alone and have never done so, but always in combination or in conflict with their great adversary, 'musical life', the 'actual realities of praxis', what 'exists in practice', the 'musical habits of the milieu', the 'living motion of the musical means of expression'. Such contradictions and tensions between logic and irrational emotion, chordal harmony and melody, theory and practice, and even between single (adjacent) notes make up the basic tenor of the music study. In that, it is a prototype of Weberian ideal-typical thinking, which finds emphatic expression in 'inner tensions' and the 'irreconcileable conflict' of principles. It is not the label of rationalism which does justice to Weber, but reference to a dichotomous thinking about theory and practice, 'musical life' and 'musical logic'.[45]

4.   Weber's Sociology of Culture and Karl Vossler's Sociology of Literature

The question of 'Why just here?' and 'only in our case?' does not only structure the incomplete sociologies of *Economy and Society* and the discussion of the sociology of religion represented by 'Economic Ethics of World Religions', it also governs the investigations of the music study. It can in general be considered *the* characteristic question for Weber. It is this, however, which reminds us of another sociologist of culture, not paid much attention by Weber research until now, Karl Vossler. Weber had an 'unconcealable admiration, in terms of both style and substance', for the 'congenial' writings of his friend the Heidelberg Romance scholar.[46] Vossler's works on the origins of modern French and Italian poetry, especially on 'Troubadour culture', prompted Weber to plans of his own in the field of the sociology of literature. They anticipate and are closely linked to his plans for music.

For his projected history of the emergence of the oldest modern poetry, that is, Provençal lyric poetry, Vossler wanted to investigate the form that 'economic, social and religious conditions, and cultural conditions in general, took in southern France in the course of the 10th and 11th centuries', but also, beyond that, 'to ask of poetry itself the secret of its birth and to illuminate it by its own spirit'.[47] In this, the Romance scholar's interest was directed first and foremost towards the 'inner causal connection between the flowering of chivalric devotion to women and love poetry and the outbreak ... of various heresies'. He shows himself to be 'astonished' at 'how Petrus Waldus's teaching of renunciation ... flourished best precisely in the most civilised places in Europe, in laughing Provence, how in the same language in which the new muse sang of knights, arms and love a more solemn voice preached of fasting and abstinence.'[48] Weber's reactions to the type and direction of Vossler's questions points directly to the type and direction of the questions in the music study. On 11 December 1910 he thanks his colleague for written material which 'prompted the question to arise again, where I might best find out about the *social* conditions and the 'milieu' of troubadour culture.' Weber meets Vossler's astonishment at the spread of ascetic teachings in Provence, and in its language which was so far removed from asceticism, with the question 'whether and how an oriental input ... could perhaps somehow have had a part in the origination of the specifically erotic element (of troubadour poetry). [...] And then again, as ever: why just in France, or rather Provence, rather than elsewhere, this attitude to women so divergent from the east on the one hand and from the position of women in the west on the other?'[49] That two years after Vossler's study of the origin of Provençal poetry Weber himself makes music his subject in the same way, that is, in regarding the development of its material (its tonal system) as something intrinsic to it, and that in doing so he tracks down 'certain social conditions', that he allows himself to be guided by that 'how-and-why-just-here' question (concerning the origin of the earliest western poetry in Provence), shows how closely the concept of the music study is bound up with Vossler's questions about literary and cultural history. What Vossler analyses in relation to Provence and to literature – the conditions, both socio-historical and those intrinsic to the material itself, for the origination and development of the oldest modern lyric poetry – this is both extended by Weber to the West and the contents of its culture, and is also made specific to music. Weber applies it to the conditions for the development of a music based on chordal harmony.

Beyond the matter of theme and type of question, Weber recognises that he agrees with Vossler's 'demarcation' of sociological work in the field of the arts, with his 'critique of the "sociology" of language'.[50] Both reject positivist and naturalist-nomothetic goals of knowledge in favour of cultural and historical ones which take into account the social groups which were the cultural vehicles; yet they do *not* want this understood as a vote for a sociological explanation of cultural content. In 1911 in his *'Entstehungsgeschichte der französischen Schriftsprache'* Vossler returns to 'practical factors, especially social and political ones', although he warns against rash 'dilettante' sociological attributions.[51] As well as geographic and climatic factors he draws attention above all to the 'spheres of meaning', the 'emotional and intellectual branches' of dialects and languages. In the young Dante's Florence there existed simultaneously: Latin for 'elevated, didactically-slanted scholarship; French for medium-level, elegantly-slanted instruction; Provençal for aristocratically nuanced love poetry [and] Italian for democratic, bourgeois intellectual life'. By such nuances is 'e.g. a German professor governed, when he discusses scholarly questions in France in fluent French while being unable to make a pleasant remark in anything approaching correct style to a beautiful Frenchwoman in the *same* language of the country. His linguistic skill has simply grown up along a different emotional and intellectual branch to that of gallantry.'[52] To Weber this 'charming and wonderfully apt example' seems 'such a particularly happy one in that it warns us against believing that the formation of special kinds of language by social groups is ultimately decided by the external social coherence and homogeneity of these groups as such – and not, much rather, by the inner divergence of the various *mental* provinces concerned.' He thought Vossler had thus with precision 'shown from the start the limits of any attempt at a sociological view of the history of language'.[53]

'Mental provinces', 'emotional states', 'kinds of atmosphere', 'emotional branches' are the concepts which Vossler and Weber use to discuss questions of the origin, development, and differentiation of the contents of culture – concepts which the 'modern linguistic history' of 1911 'no longer understands.'[54] 'Experience of different kinds of mental make-up' and 'provinces of possibilities for mental sensation'[55] are seen by both historians of culture as decisive factors for artistic expression, while facts specific to different strata or classes are seen as *contributing* but not primary elements. According to Vossler, the great linguistic masterpieces and works of art with which literary history concerns itself are 'if not exclusively, still predominantly and essentially creations of genius, not explicable by the taste of their time. Studying contemporary linguistic taste prepares the way for an explanation, but does not provide it.'[56] Weber discusses this connection between the 'collectivist' and 'individualist' viewpoints – again in 1910, at the Frankfurt conference of sociologists – in the field of music, or more concretely, of instrumental history: 'Conditions of a sociological, and partly economic, character, made possible the development of the orchestra as used by Haydn. But the idea underlying it is his own most personal property and not, as it were, technologically motivated', and neither – it should be added – is it specific to stratum or class.[57] *That* Weber took sufficient account of those technical, economic, sociological – social – conditions of the specifically western musical development is shown – at least in as far as the 'technical means' are concerned – by the music study's analyses dealing with tonal systems and instruments. They cannot, however, be allowed to disguise the fact that Weber considered these objective factors as only *one* side of artistic development and of the arrival at artistic expression. The other side was for the sociologist, or rather social historian, of music the 'most personal artistic will'.

It is not just with this striving for artistic expression that cultural historians set 'boundaries' to sociology.[58] Sociology has to be modest even with the development of music, or more concretely of archaic stereotyped phrases of notes used in cult and magic, into an 'art' in the sense of an 'area of culture that has become independent and that objectifies itself through its own techniques and principles of order (*Regelhaftigkeit*)',[59] sociology has to be modest. Where language becomes 'literature', 'art', according to Vossler 'sociological interest will not die away, it is true, but must have the sense to restrain itself and be patient, like a woman's escort stops at the door of the room she uses for her toilette and, as a real man of the world, does not wish to see the arts she uses to renew and heighten her charms.'[60] With the sublimation of language to 'literature' and 'art' there begin – to use Weber's terminology drawn from music – the 'internal dynamics' and 'autonomous laws' of the development of its means of expression which are intrinsic to the material, and are not directly accessible to sociology.[61]

Weber's study of music takes up Vossler's limitation of sociology's claims to provide a sociological explanation. Where music develops from the 'use of traditional phrases of notes for a practical purpose' in the cult to 'art', and a *'Melopoiie'* and a 'music theory' in the sense of a rationally regulated and regulating body of rules for the craft of composition arise,[62] there begins a rationalisation of this sphere of culture with its own momentum which sociology can, as it were, only look at from outside. It can at most name social groups who stand in 'relationships of elective affinity' to certain systematic tonal arrangements and developments, such as the Cistercians who, 'according to the rules of their order, maintained a puritanical avoidance of all aesthetic refinement' and therefore embraced the 'ethos' of the pentatonic, or more correctly the diatonic, and were 'antipathetic' to 'chromaticism's striving for passionate expression'.[63] Such attributions of 'elective affinities' – made first by Weber in the field of economics, or rather religion and ethics, in the 'Protestantism' study – such references to 'spiritual complementarity (*Adäquanz*)'[64] between the ethos of the way of life of a social group, stratum, estate or class and the 'ethos' of certain musical materials, sociology is in a position to make; it cannot, however, provide an explanation of why the material of music has developed and become differentiated in this direction and no other, if it wants to stay empirical and true to the historical facts.

Yet it was not with such thoroughly reasonable and comprehensible relationships of 'elective affinity' and 'complementarity' that Weber will have provoked the bewilderment he did among his colleagues, but rather with his efforts to discover the characteristics of the material of music, its 'internal momentum' and intrinsic 'autonomy'. These efforts were directed to the question which interests Weber 'in the last resort the most': 'to what extent have "natural" affinities between notes operated as an element of developmental dynamics?'.[65] Here Weber is on completely alien musicological, or rather acoustic, territory – with the result that Weber criticism has paid no attention to this 'most interesting' of questions. Weber knew the scale of the question. Behind it lay the controversy between traditional European music history of Hugo Riemann's stamp, and the rising universal-historical comparative musicology (the later so-called ethnomusicology) of the Berlin School around Carl Stumpf and Erich Moritz von Hornbostel, a controversy above all about the 'nature' of notes, about the apparently natural ordering of the European tonal system and the apparent imperfection of its non-European, to a greater or lesser degree 'primitive', counterparts. The positions which Weber takes up in this controversy make the music study a paying of critical respects to Hermann von Helmholtz's epoch-making *Lehre von den Tonempfindungen*, which in 1863 tried to provide a 'theory of music' on a 'physiological basis', a scientific 'grounding of the elementary rules for the construction of scales, chords, keys' in the perception of overtones.[66] Weber rejects Helmholtz's naturalistic deductions. In this he continues his criticism – though softened by admiration for the 'extremely perceptive' analyses of the universally-ranging scholar[67] – of the 'credulous mindset of naturalistic monism' and the 'powerful repercussions' of this on economics and cultural history[68] – repercussions which moved him in methodological writings from 1903 on to define the position of the social and cultural sciences against the claim to dominance of the natural sciences, especially of chemistry as the leading science and 'ruler of our culture'; these repercussions also led him in particular in 1909 to denounce Ostwald's and Solvay's 'technological' explanations of art and their attempts to subsume it under technology as *'faux-pas'*.[69]

Weber corrected Helmholtz's physiological and physical explanation for the varying tonal systems, based on theoretical deduction from the naturally-existing harmonic series, by using empirical analyses, backed up by phonographic records, undertaken by the Berlin Phonographische Institut under Carl Stumpf and Erich Moritz von Hornbostel. He was hoping for an answer to that question, approached 'by the experts only with great caution and avoiding all generalizations',[70] not from comprehensive 'theories' but only – if at all – 'for concrete cases'. The scepticism of the social scientist who does not wish to see historical reality pressed into the 'Procrustean bed' of a particular theory[71] here becomes concrete and musical. Thus in his music study Weber paradigmatically puts his central premises about scientific theory to the test. In its defence of its methodological and empirical position and its question from cultural science about the 'quality' of listening and about 'musical culture', this sortie into the alien fields of contemporary music history, music theory and ethnomusicology reveals a breadth and depth of thinking and a synthetic achievement which is as yet unequalled, and which now more than ever can serve as the model for a sociology of culture.

Translated by Mary Shields

NOTES

1. Recorded by Eduard Baumgarten, in Baumgarten, ed., *Max Weber: Werk und Person, Dokumente, ausgewählt und kommentiert* (Tübingen: Mohr, 1964), note 482.

2. *MSS*, pp. 49–112.

3. Cf. Friedrich Tenbruck, 'The problem of thematic unity in the works of Max Weber', trans. S. Whimster, *British Journal of Sociology*, XXXI, 3, (1980), pp. 316–51.

4. Weber together with Werner Sombart and Edgar Jaffé in the new editors' 'Geleitwort' to *Archiv für Sozialwissenschaft und Sozialpolitik* XIX (1904), p. II.

5. Cf. the contemporary critiques of the *Protestant Ethic* and Weber's 'anticritiques', edited by Johannes Winckelmann (Gütersloh; Siebenstern 1978, 3rd impression); and also Helmut Fogt's survey, 'Max Weber und die deutsche Soziologie der Weimarer Republik: Aussenseiter oder Gründervater?', in *Kölner Zeitschrift für Soziologie und Sozialpsychologie*, Sonderheft 23 (1981), pp. 245–72.

6. Cf. Weber's postscript in his letter of 30.12.1913 to his publisher Paul Siebeck: 'Later I hope to manage a sociology of the *contents* of culture (art, literature, *Weltanschauung*) for you sometime, separate from *this* work [the *Grundriss der Sozialökonomik* and the parts of this collected in *Wirtschaft und Gesellschaft* (WuG)], or as an independent further volume of it' (Bayerische Staatsbibliothek, Munich, Collection 446, Weber-Siebeck correspondence). The music study itself (hereafter *MUS*) was published posthumously in 1921 with the title *Die rationalen und soziologischen Grundlagen der Musik* by the then lecturer in music at Munich Theodor Kroyer and Marianne Weber. For its genesis and its publishing history, see Christoph Braun, *Max Webers 'Musiksoziologie'* (Laaber: 1992), pp. 95–140.

7. 'Energetische Kulturtheorien', in: *Gesammelte Aufsätze zur Wissenschaftslehre* [WL], ed. Johannes Winckelmann, (Tübingen: Mohr, 1982), 5th impression, p. 424; and 'Wissenschaft als Beruf', in: ibid., p. 588.

8. *WL*, 416

9. *Verhandlungen des Ersten Deutschen Soziologentages vom 19–22 Oktober 1910. Reden, Vorträge und Debatten*, Tübingen 1911, p. 99ff. For the 'journalism' accusation, see Weber's letter of 28.10.1910 to Franz Eulenberg, *GStA*.

10. *Verhandlungen*, 1911, p. 99ff. [Part of Weber's contribution is translated in S. Whimster and S. Lash, *Max Weber, Rationality and Modernity* (London: Allen & Unwin, 1987), pp. 278–80.]

11. 'It can e.g. *perhaps* – I cannot be judge of this – be claimed that Beethoven did not venture to follow his own musical ideas to their logical conclusion because the wind instruments of his day still did not have the full chromatic scale that valved trumpets have. But, as Berlioz proved even before its invention, this deficiency was not absolutely impossible to overcome technically, and Beethoven himself did not shrink from astonishing experiments in overcoming it ...' (ibid.).

12. *MSS*, pp. 1–47.

13. *MSS*, pp. 30–1. The 'Vorbemerkung', written two years later, to the *Gesammelte Aufsätze zur Religionssoziologie* (GARS) repeats the list in similar form (Tübingen: Mohr, 1978), 7th impression, photographically

reproduced, vol. 1, p. 2). For English translation see 'Author's Introduction', *PESC*, pp. 14–15.

14. Cf. Ingrid Gilcher-Holtey, 'Max Weber und die Frauen', in: Christian Gneuss and Jürgen Kocka, eds, *Max Weber. Ein Symposion* (Munich: Deutscher Taschenbuch 1988), p. 151. It is no exaggeration to say that without Mina Tobler the music study would not have come into being. Weber himself in a letter to Mina of August 1919 talks of the 'direction' of the pianist, under which he wrote the work. He owed much of his knowledge of the musical canon to this friend; in particular she played piano arrangements of operas and orchestral works for him as well as piano compositions. This found direct expression in the music study, cf. MUS, p. 94, and Braun, *Webers 'Musiksoziologie'*, op. cit. pp. 24 ff., 40 (with reference to the relevant until now unpublished letters).

15. That this largely remained unrecognised, not only by Weber's contemporaries but also until now by Weber exegesis, stems from both thematic and editorial bewilderment at the music study, which is hardly accessible to non-musicologists and which one can also, with Eduard Baumgarten (see note 1 above), call stylistically extremely hard-going.

16. The 'Author's Introduction' is to be found at the start of *PESC*, pp. 13–31.

17. See above, note 4.

18. *MSS*, pp. 65–6.

19. *MUS*, p. 90.

20. *MUS*, pp. 90–95.

21. *MUS*, pp. 82–5, 88.

22. *MSS*, pp. 71–2.

23. For the breadth of Weber's musical experience, which goes considerably beyond that usual among the educated bourgeoisie, includes sound standards of judgement, and culminates in a Wagner-worship, or rather Wagner-scepticism, which is astonishingly similar to Nietzsche's, see Braun, *Webers 'Musiksoziologie'*, op. cit., pp. 21–49.

24. *GStA*, Max Weber Nachlass, Rep. 92, no. 26, sheets 45–6 and MWGII/7 (in press) p. 754. Critical reception of the study has not taken much notice of this statement of intent. Rather, the 'social' was soon – even as a result of the title – disregarded, or reinterpreted as 'sociological'. It was given attention not by sociologists, with the exception of Hermann Matzke, *Musikökonomik und Musikpolitik. Grundzüge einer Musikwirtschaftslehre*, (Breslau, 1927), p. 8, but by music theorists: Tibor Kneif, 'Gegenwartsfragen der Musiksoziologie', in: *Acta musicologica* XXXVIII (1966), p. 77; Heinz-Dieter Sommer, 'Max Webers musiksoziologische Studie', in: *Archiv für Musikwissenschaft* 39 (1982), p. 81, note 8. For more on its reception, see Braun, *Weber's 'Musiksoziologie'*, op. cit., pp. 11f., 97f., 137f., and Braun, 'Grenzen der Ratio, Grenzen der Soziologie. Anmerkungen zum "Musiksoziologen" Max Weber', in *Archiv für Musikwissenschaft* 51 (1994), p. 18ff. The title of volume I/14 of the Max-Weber-Gesamtausgabe (MWG) will take Weber's intentions into account and be: *Rationale und soziale Grundlagen der Musik* [rational and social bases of music].

25. This distinction remains to the Heidelberg sociologist of culture even when one bears in mind that he obtained his knowledge at second hand, from the fieldwork especially of the Berlin Phonographische Institut. More on this later.

26. *MSS*, pp. 80–1. Cf. also Lawrence A. Scaff, 'Max Webers Begriff der Kultur', in Gerhard Wagner and Heinz Zipprian, eds, *Max Webers Wissenschaftslehre. Interpretation und Kritik* (Frankfurt am Main: Suhrkamp 1994), pp. 678–700.
27. *FMW*, pp. 281–2.
28. Understood here as a section extracted from the tonal system which orders the notes of an actual melody according to pitch within an octave.
29. *MUS*, pp. 17ff., 30–2.
30. *MSS*, p. 71. (Addition by C.B.)
31. *PESC*, p. 13.
32. *MUS*, p. 67.
33. *MUS*, pp. 64–76.
34. *PESC*, pp. 47, 172–3.
35. *MUS*, pp. 79, 94.
36. Cf. also Christoph Braun, 'Vom Clavichord zum Clavinova. Kulturanthropologische Anmerkungen zu Max Webers Musik-Studie', in *Historische Anthropologie* 3 (1995), pp. 242–66.
37. *PESC*, pp. 77–80.
38. *PESC*, p. 180.
39. *PESC* . p. 24
40. *PESC*,. p. 25.
41. *MUS*, p. 64. This puts in concrete terms those 'certain *social* conditions' mentioned in the letter to Lili of August 1912, 'from which it can be explained that *only we* have a "harmonic" music […] Strange! – that is the work of monasticism, as will be seen'. Monasticism was the most important vehicle of the above-mentioned medieval 'circumstances' of rational notation, rationally regulated polyphony, etc., the interconnection of which put European musical development on the path of modern chordal harmony.
42. Marianne Weber, in her preface to the second edition, of 1925, to *Wirtschaft und Gesellschaft*, reprinted 5th edition (1972), p. XXXIII.
43. Weber's admiration for Wagner's *Tristan* and *Mastersingers* is the musical equivalent of that 'genuine pathos' of 'self-abandon' which belongs to what is 'most inwardly genuine and real in life'; cf. the 'value-freedom' essay, *MSS*, pp. 2–3, 16. Those two works, as also the second act of the *Valkyrie* mentioned in his 'Protestantism' essay (*PESC*, pp. 107–8), Weber counts among the 'truly "eternal" works that Wagner has created'. *Tristan* in particular is to Weber 'the kind of great experience that one very seldom has, a work of great human truthfulness and unparalleled musical beauty. The extrahuman and superhuman additions are simply not there' [in contrast to *Parsifal*, which Weber, like Nietzsche, finds a game, 'empty sweetness'; C.B.]. The companions were 'completely carried away by its ecstasy and experienced this work of art as the highest transfiguration of the earthly': Marianne Weber, *Max Weber. A Biography* (New Brunswick, N.J.: Transactions, 1988), pp. 501–3; and Braun, *Webers 'Musiksoziologie'*, pp. 26ff., 47ff., with reference to the impressions of operas in Weber's letters).
44. *MWG, I/19*, p. 499ff.
45. This is also made more than clear by the passage in the 'Categories' essay, presumably written shortly after the music study: from music history, Weber would like 'to clarify some time how the relationship between the

model of correctness of a behaviour and the empirical behaviour 'works', and how this developmental factor relates to sociological influences, e.g. in a concrete development in art'. 'Particularly in cultural history', it is 'those connections, i.e. the seams where tensions between the empirical and the model of correctness can burst out,' that are 'of extremely great significance in the dynamics of development'. The final sentence of the rational-bases part of the music study puts this concisely: "The relationship between musical logic and musical life is one of the most historically important of the various creative tensions in music' (WL, p. 438, note 1).

46.   Weber in a letter of 5.5.1908 to Vossler, *MWG, II/5*, p. 557) and also of 11.12.1910, *GStA*.

47.   'Die Kunst des ältesten Trobadors', in *Miscellanea di studi in onore di Attilio Hortis*, Trieste 1910, p. 419.

48.   *Die philosophischen Grundlagen zum 'süssen neuen Stil' des Guido Guinicelli, Guido Cavalcanti und Dante Alighiere* (Heidelberg: Carl Winter, 1904), p. 2ff.

49.   Letter to Vossler of 11.12.1910.

50.   Ibid.

51.   In: *Germanisch-Romanische Monatshefte* 3 (1911), p. 52. Vossler is thinking of De La Grasserie's *Des parlers des differentes classes sociales*, Paris 1909. For Vossler's and Weber's harsh criticism of naturalist-nomothetic 'nonsense' in Karl Lamprecht's *'Entwicklungslinie' der deutschen Kulturgeschichte*, see *WL* pp. 7ff., 24ff., 414; *PESC*, p. 244, n.114, and *MWG II/5*, p. 25; Vossler, *Die philosophischen Grundlagen*, op. cit., pp. 1, 5, 8.

52.   *Entstehungsgeschichte der franzosischen Shriftssprache* (1911), p. 160. Another example: 'Alfonso el Sabio wrote his prose work in Castilian, his love poetry in Galician and a particularly courtly style of minnesong in Provençal' (Ibid., p. 159ff).

53.   Weber, in a letter to Vossler of 15.11.1911, *GStA*.

54.   Vossler, *Entstehungsgeschichte*, op. cit., p. 159.

55.   Weber, in a letter to Dora Jellinek of 9.5.1910, in which he talks in detail about the poetry of Stefan George and Rainer Maria Rilke (*GStA*); see also Marianne Weber, op. cit., pp. 455–464.

56.   'Grammatik und Sprachgeschichte oder das Verhältnis von 'richtig' und 'wahr' in der Sprachwissenschaft', in: *Logos* 1 (1910/11), p. 92.

57.   *Verhandlungen*, p. 100. That Weber considers monocausal 'explanations' and economic-materialist deductions of a vulgarly Marxist kind as refuted not only, but above all, in the realm of the aesthetic and artistic, does not need to be especially emphasised here; cf. e.g. *MSS*, p. 64f.; *PESC*, p. 277, n. 84.

58.   Cf. Vossler's 'Grenzen der Sprachsoziologie', in: *Hauptprobleme der Soziologie. Erinnerungsgabe für Max Weber*, ed. M. Palyi (Munich and Leipzig: 1923), p. 361 ff.

59.   Cf. A. Zingerle, *Max Webers historische Soziologie. Aspekte und Materialien zur Wirkungsgeschichte* (Darmstadt 1982), p. 152; for the development of music into 'art', see also G. Simmel, 'Psychologische und ethnologische Studien über Musik', in: *Zeitschrift für Völkerpsychologie und Sprachwissenschaft* 13 (1882), p. 268.

60. Vossler, 'Grenzen der Sprachsoziologie', p. 389.

61. The two concepts run like a leitmotif not only through Weber's music study but also the part-sociologies from the outline of social economics; see, for example, the '"autonomous laws" of the "bureaucratic organisation" which lie in its technical structure itself' (*WuG*, p. 578), the 'autononous laws of party mechanics' (*WuG*, p. 669); in the case of 'religious affairs' too he speaks of 'highly independently-minded autonomy' (*WuG*, pp. 704, 264, 356, 700; *PESC*, p. 277, n.84); and of the 'intrinsic rational autonomy' of the judicial system (*WuG*, pp. 361, 392, 506), of the market (*WuG*, p. 383) and of the 'form of political administration' (*WuG*, p. 780).

62. *MUS*, p. 31ff.

63. *MUS*, p. 12. Examples of other analyses of elective affinities in music: 'Chromaticism is antipathetic to the early church just as to e.g. the ancient Hellenic tragedians and the bourgeois Confucian musical teaching' (*MUS*, p. 12). For the concepts of 'ethos', 'conduct of life' and 'elective affinity', cf. Klaus Lichtblau and Johannes Weiss, 'Einleitung', in: Lichtblau and Weiss, eds, *Max Weber: Die Protestantische Ethik und der 'Geist' des Kapitalismus*. Textausgabe auf der Grundlage der ersten Fassung von 1904/5 mit einem Verzeichnis der wichtigsten Zusätze und Veränderungen aus der zweiten Fassung von 1920, (Bodenheim: Hainstein 1993), p. vii and note 2.

64. Cf. *PESC*, pp. 91–2, 166–7 and *GARS* vol. 1, 'Antikritiken', pp. 55, 303. 'We will have to continue to discuss such relationships of adequacy (*Adäquanz*)': WuG pp. 201, 293, 704ff., 724.

65. *MUS*, p. 25.

66. See above pp. 202–3.

67. *MUS*, p. 25. Among these, as can be seen from the fundamental historical question of the music study, Weber counted Helmholtz's explicit and in his time still extremely unusual appreciation of the (melodically conceived) 'music without harmony refined over thousands of years' in Europe and 'even now among non-European peoples' (*Lehre von den Tonempfindungen*, Braunschweig: 1863, p. x).

68. *MSS*, p. 86

69. Cf. also Wolfgang Schluchter, *Religion und Lebensführung* (Frankfurt am Main: Suhrkamp, 1988), vol. I, p. 53ff. and Hubert Treiber, 'Zur Genealogie einer "science positive de la morale en Allemagne". Die Geburt der "r(e)ealistischen Moralwissenschaft" aus der Idee einer monistischen Naturkonzeption', in: *Nietzsche-Studien* 22 (1993), p. 192.

70. *MUS*, p. 25. From the wealth of ethnomusicological monographs evaluated by Weber, see: Hornbostel, 'Studien über das Tonsystem und die Musik der Japaner', in *Sammelbände der Internationalen Musikgesellschaft* 4 (1902/3), p. 302ff.; Hornbostel, 'Melodie und Skala', in *Jahrbuch Peters* 19, p. 1ff.; Carl Stumpf, 'Tonsystem und Musik der Siamesen', in Stumpf, ed., *Beiträge zur Akustik und Musikwissenschaft*, Heft 3, (Leipzig: 1901), pp. 69ff.; and Carl Stumpf, *Die Anfänge der Musik*, (Leipzig: 1911). For information on the reception of the work by ethnomusicology and music history, see Braun, *Webers 'Musiksoziologie'*, op. cit., pp. 235ff.

71. *MSS*, pp. 93–4

10 Love and Death. Weber, Wagner and Max Klinger[1]

David Chalcraft

In his eulogy for Weber of 1920 Troeltsch attempts to answer 'what was at the core of this man, whose virtually magic influence radiated far and wide?' One of the things he tells us is that 'He was an admirer of Max Klinger.'[2] This statement is confirmed by visitors to the Weber household in Freiburg who were provoked into comment by the conspicuous display of a large collection of Klinger's etchings and drawings. As Marianne recorded,

> And on their walls there were Klinger etchings, some of them showing nudes. Was it really possible to sit down on the sofa under a little Eve meditating by a dusky forest pond? Or could one take an unembarrassed look at the nude figure of a male stretching toward the light from a dark ground, which the artist had called 'Und dennoch'?[3]

When Weber's mother came to stay she was obviously shocked by the display of nudity so evident and asked them 'at least remove the Klingers from their walls'. This became a matter of some comment within the family and when Helene's sister Ida Baumgarten visited, she wrote to her daughter that the Klingers 'decorate all the rooms'. And when a young Else von Richthofen visited the house the impact of the Klingers was sufficiently strong for her to comment on them some decades later to Eduard Baumgarten, who recorded: 'On the wall opposite Max Weber's desk hung an original etching by Max Klinger. On the way home she wondered what kind of person would have hung this picture on the wall opposite him.'[4]

Max Weber presented Marianne with 'the almost complete etchings of Max Klinger' on the first anniversary of their wedding.[5] That was in 1894 during their first year at Freiburg, although Max Weber almost certainly would have been aware of Klinger before in Berlin.[6] By 1894 Klinger had published 12 cycles of etchings, numbering some 184 prints. In 1906, in order to finance a move from Heidelberg's Hauptstrasse to the Fallenstein

Villa on the banks of the Neckar, they sold the 'original Klinger etchings, which they still loved but which they had now absorbed completely.'[7] These were sold to the Kaiser-Friederich Museum in German Posen and the museum's records show that 118 etchings were bought for 6790 Marks (or about £50 000 in today's values).[8]

On at least two occasions the Webers made gifts of Klinger's work to close friends and relatives. When they left Freiburg for Heidelberg they gave the sculptress Sophie Rickert the extensive cycle of *Amor and Psyche* (Opus 5).[9] And in October 1918 Max Weber wrote to Wina Müller that the Klinger print he was giving her for her birthday previously 'hung here (in Heidelberg) in my room and because of that could be seen as rather "personal"'.[10] In addition Weber's cousin, Fritz Baumgarten, gave Marianne the Klinger print 'Glück' for Christmas in 1894.[11]

It does seem possible to gain some access to Weber's private family life and personal development through studying the contexts in which Klinger's art was displayed and discussed by Weber and members of his immediate family and closest circle of friends. An analysis of these discussions shows that in various degrees the older generation had not yet come to terms with the role of carnality within the convention of marriage. Klinger, alongside Tolstoy, represented the new realism. It also shows that Marianne and Max did not have a naturalistic attitude towards sex. Max Weber was interested in the strongly expressive eroticism of Wagner and Klinger without actually pursuing that life-style himself. It was through their interest and study of Klinger that the couple came to an aesthetic sublimation of their relationship. Actual sex, as explored in Sudermann's naturalistic dramas, in Wagner's *Tristan and Isolde* and in Klinger's graphic art (all subjects of discussion in the family), leads to dishonour, loss of self control and death. This provides an insight into Weber's intimate life and his attitudes towards chastity, eroticism and death. It was the contemporary artistic treatment of these themes that reinforced Weber's own renunciatory outlook on life.

This chapter will also show that Klinger's graphic work carried a heavy dose of the psycho-sexual, a taint of decadence, and symbolism (both textual and intellectual) that was wrapped in a dream-like, pre-Freudian evocation. We need, however, to distinguish between the private and public consumption of Klinger's art. In his day Klinger was best known for his polychrome Beethoven statue that was selected, in an act of homage, as the centre-piece of the 14th Exhibition of the Vienna Secession in 1902.[12] Weber seems to have been drawn neither to Klinger's monumental sculptures nor to such mammoth paintings as, for example, 'The Judgement of Paris' or 'Christ on Olympus'.[13] Of the graphic work his favoured genre was the allegorical and 'Phantasiekunst' works of Klinger rather than those works dealing with social awareness and realism, as for example the cycle 'A Life'. Varnedoe and Streicher capture this balance when they argue that Klinger's modernity is based on 'subjectivity and fantasy on the one hand, and social awareness and realism on the other'.[14]

What was attractive to bourgeois consumers of Klinger were the possibilities of prolonged private viewing, the communication of the subjective, the symbolic representation of desire and its destructive tendencies, the expression of the inexpressible, and the invitation to internalise and extend their fantasies. On the cycle entitled 'Brahms Fantasies' the composer himself commented to Clara Schumann, 'They are not really illustrations in the ordinary sense, but magnificent and wonderful fantasias inspired by my [music] texts. Without assistance ... you would certainly miss the sense and connection with the text. How much I should like to look at them with you and show you how profoundly he has grasped the subject and to what heights his imagination and understanding soar.[15] Reisenfeld captures the situation well when he writes: 'The subjectivity of Klinger's prints and the format of the folio lent themselves to presentation in an intimate space, suitable for sustained viewing and intellectual reflection, after the fashion of the traditional print connoisseur and his albums, in the drawing room, study, club, bookstore, or small gallery, either laid out for study on a table or framed on a wall.'[16]

Equally important for the view was the sense of narrative in the print cycles in which the prints are viewed alongside each other, each having a proleptic and a recollective function for the whole series.[17] Further, Klinger's imaginative use of borders and frames to contextualise and comment on the central action of the print provided interpretative signposts at the same time as extending the range of meaning. These two latter features of Klinger's graphic art need to be kept in mind throughout if he and his reception are to be interpreted correctly.

As a cosmopolitan bourgeois Weber might well have purchased the Klingers as an investment.[18] But on his departure from Berlin to Freiburg his choice is significant. It was a statement of independence and a display of avant-garde taste alongside the other young Freiburg intellectuals. However this statement raises a number of questions as to how Weber did confront the themes of the unconscious and sexuality. Equally the shock encounter of the Klingers within the privacy of the Webers' household triggered a discussion by the older generation, to which I now turn.

Reading Klinger

The cycle of six prints 'Eve and the Future' recurs in family discussion. Marianne explicitly describes Eve, the first print in the cycle. In her recollections, Marianne stresses more the reaction to the pictures and what they symbolised socially rather than the content of the prints and the artist's treatment of themes. She writes, recalling the period in Freiburg around 1895, 'Outwardly the life of the couple was typical of their circle. Yet they attracted attention as being different. Among other things, they had social views of the relationship between the sexes that were unfamiliar to those around them. And on their walls there were Klinger etchings, some of them showing nudes.' As already quoted above, how could one sit down in the living room and not be embarrassed by such uncompromising nudes?[19]

Marianne takes the Klinger pictures as an index of her forward looking attitudes, but it is interesting that 'outwardly' their life seemed to conform to the norm. Outward respectability also appears to be the issue for Helene Weber when she visited in 1894. Marianne, in her account, almost revels in recording the manner in which she was unconventional, drawing attention to her involvement (as a woman) in social work and her attending the philosophy seminars of Heinrich Rickert; she is proud of holding 'unusual views'. But this display of the Klinger etchings, especially given their content, in the private sphere of their home, alarmed Helene. In such a setting how could one avoid intimate contact with depictions that one could choose not to engage with in a public gallery? She tried to persuade them to change their life-style and 'at least remove the Klingers from their walls'.[20] Helene considers public decorum and the opinions of others, whilst Marianne, equally conscious of this semi-public gaze, revels in the 'scandal'.

Helene did not object to the content *per se* it seems, although someone with religious sensibilities like Helene might well have objected to nudity in renderings of biblical and religious themes. Certainly Klinger's 'Crucifixion' of 1887 caused a storm of protest precisely because of its depiction of a robeless Christ.[21] Nevertheless, Helene seems to feel that unusual views or possessions can be explored but must be done privately so not to offend others or to appear outwardly as too liberal.

Helene gave exactly the same kind of advice to Marianne, when she learned of her reading Tolstoy's *Kreutzer Sonata*, which Marianne had found among Weber's books and read aloud to Helene in early November 1893. Tolstoy's short story, while ostensively about the murder by a jealous husband of his wife, whom he suspects of infidelity, actually manages to expose the whole range of social ethics and practices surrounding men's sexual education, courtship between couples, marriage and the raising of children. These arrangements Tolstoy portrayed as being rooted in nothing but an animality, geared to sensual gratification to the moral detriment of all persons involved. Married life is nothing but 'a pigsty existence'.[22] The story's purport is to raise the ideal of chastity before society's eyes: 'The sex instinct', Tolstoy opines, 'no matter how it's dressed up, is an evil, a horrible evil that must be fought, not encouraged as it is among us'. And again Tolstoy comments, 'Of all passions, it is sexual carnal love that is the strongest, the most malignant and the most unyielding. It follows that if the passions are eliminated, and together with them this ultimate, strongest passion, carnal love, the goal of mankind will be attained and there will be no reason for it to live any longer'.[23]

Helene wrote to her sister, Emilie Benecke on 4 November, 1893, 'Do you know Tolstoy's Kreutzer Sonata? A dreadful book really, and only to be read in the privacy of one's own room, but a dreadfully serious sermon'. The story had undoubtedly touched a raw nerve. Helene continued to her sister, 'it made many things clear to me' and 'was bitter medicine' and yet 'helped me in several ways'. She concluded, 'But keep that to yourself'.[24] With regard to Marianne, Helene mentioned to her sister that she seemed particularly mature 'in understanding things like that'. Yet she cautioned Marianne to steer away not only from books and ideas of this kind but also not to discuss them with Max, so as 'not to get a distorted view'. It is not clear whether Max was trying to persuade Marianne that such celibate ideas were a nonsense or whether he endorsed the ascetic sentiment with even more force than Tolstoy, and with totally damning attitudes to 'normal' married life and the raising of children to boot. The latter would seem more likely.

Following the latter interpretation of asceticism the matter of the Klingers requires further explanation. Gilcher-Holtey has speculated that Weber was seeking to communicate a degree of sensuousness to Marianne through the purchase of Klinger's etchings (an unsuccessful attempt in her opinion).[25] This, of course, is to take the depiction of eroticism in Klinger as an invitation to enjoy such pleasures and eroticism as the main theme of the etchings. Whilst 'Eve and the Future' certainly implies eroticism, it is in cycles such as 'A Love' that the narrative is most explicitly erotic. For Helene and for Marianne the issue was nudity.

It was the same for Ida Baumgarten, who recalled for her daughters how difficult it was to avoid seeing the Klinger prints. But Ida is altogether more interested in the art for its own sake and more liberal than her sister, Helene, with regard to the nudity question. She wrote, 'I have to admit that a powerful creative force asserts itself here and new, interesting points of view. I can also see that the Adams and Eves with which he is mainly concerned should not run around clothed among the high masses of rock which close Paradise off to them, and even less on the fragrant meadows and in the cool groves of paradise'. Ida is even handed enough to appreciate the possible historical/textual accuracy of Klinger's depictions of Adam and Eve. And yet, like her sister Helene, she objects to having these prints and their content thrust upon her attention. As she goes on in her letter, 'But I still cannot admire the fact that these completely naked figures come out at you from every wall, all the less as they are not even beautiful, but expressive'.[26]

Marianne's response to Helene was somewhat truant and truculent but with Ida she appears to have spoken more honestly. Ida informed her daughters that Marianne justified the nudity in the prints precisely because of their expressiveness, and that apparently she 'admires the spirit expressed in the naked figures …' Perhaps this is the spirit of unconventionality once again, but what Ida appreciated in the outward life of the young couple is the tasteful luxury of their 'magnificent flat', the furnishings of which clearly convey to her that they are 'both children of wealth'. Her uneasiness with the Webers' conspicuous consumption registers on the issue of the Klingers, as the only 'point of contention'.

There are other features of Ida's letter worth recording. First, that Klinger seems to be generally well known within Weber's wider family, for she recalled that Dora Benecke (a niece of Ida and Helene) 'had already been talking about the new prophet of art, Max Klinger'. Also, in writing to her daughters who were staying at a clinic, she asked them to inquire whether the doctor knew anything about Klinger – reflecting either that the doctor (Wildermuth) was interested in art, or that Ida had spotted something psychological or pathological in Klinger. Ida seems to have given the subject some thought: 'He always strikes me as like Sudermann, transposed to the field of the visual arts'.[27]

Sudermann (1857–1928) through his writings challenged conventional complacency, exposed *Kulturlüge*, portrayed the seedy side of life, donned a social conscience, enjoyed the open discussion of sexual and erotic issues, and explored the emergence of the 'new woman'. Yet his naturalism comes down on the side of conventional sexual ethics and the need for birthcontrol, advising restraint rather than the ecstasy of experience and the decadent embrace of death.[28] In drawing this comparison, Ida Baumgarten may have been recalling aspects of Klinger's cycle 'A Life, 'a moralising tale of sin and suffering',[29] which the Weber's owned since it is listed in the Posen inventory.

Eve and the Future: Reading the Cycle

Whatever the essence of Helene's and Ida's and Marianne's assessment of the meaning and significance of Klinger it is beyond question that none of them draws attention to the complete cycle. They treat the depictions of the nude figures of Adam and Eve as the central aspect of the cycle, or at least those aspects of the cycle they were willing to talk about in their letters, perhaps taking the nudity as a generalisation of their more deep-seated discomfort. A closer assessment of the cycle allows us to question their understanding and perhaps to move closer to Weber's own appreciation and the reasons for Klinger's ability to disturb.

Scaff reflects on the Helene episode by saying that 'Culturally, the depiction of androgynous figures and of an unconventional 'freer' woman surely drew the Webers in the 1890s'.[30] He may well be right in a general sense, but it can be argued that he has taken Marianne's own interpretation at face value without studying those examples of Klinger's work the Webers owned. Marianne is perhaps more impressed with the example of Sophie Rickert – an artist and one-time pupil of Klinger – than the depiction of women in the art of Klinger. Even if Klinger's work as a whole was studied, a single clear view of the treatment of women would not appear, since his work runs the gamut of personifications. As such, 'Eve and the Future' needs to be looked at from more than one perspective. In many ways, 'Eve and the Future' is quite a traditional depiction of the sin of Eve and its consequences. What is unusual in Klinger's treatment, and typical of his exploitation of the potential of the cycle format, are the three 'fast-forwards' which disrupt the unfolding of the traditional narrative to highlight the future. The future is treated in a heavily symbolic and mythical fashion, barbaric and shocking in its depictions of the horror, death and destruction brought into the world through Eve's deed.

Taking the cycle as whole, and beginning with the first print [Plate 1], we first encounter a depiction of Eve pensively, if also coyly, twirling her flowing yet matted hair, surrounded by a lush and fertile lakeside, perhaps a little bored by her sleeping husband Adam. The lake, with its possibility of reflection, has perhaps awakened in her a consciousness of her own beauty and latent unfilled and previously unexperienced sensuality. In the third print in the cycle [Plate 3] she stands before the Tree of Knowledge, sideways on to the viewer, on tip-toes to make full use of the mirror held before her by the uncoiled serpent smiling beguilingly. The mirror, like the lake, offers reflection and the gaining of self knowledge. What Eve sees and learns about herself relates to her looks, her body; the serpent appeals to her awakening vanity and sensual desires. Klinger does not strictly follow the account in Genesis, but emphasises the sexual dimensions of the growth of self knowledge. Their self knowledge does not extend to their nakedness. Unlike the biblical story there is no shame attached to the body; Eve remains naked throughout.

In the fifth print of the cycle [Plate 5], Klinger portrays the expulsion of Adam and Eve from Paradise. They do not walk separately, neither does the man cower in shame. Rather a resolute and strong Adam carries Eve, her face hidden from our gaze, as well as from the sword bearing angel standing guard at the natural stone pillared entrance to the garden of Eden. The landscape is barren and rocky. As Varnedoe and Streicher observe, 'here, as in the whole cycle, Klinger seems to assert that woman is weaker, and is primarily to be blamed for the Fall, while man the stronger and less guilty must literally bear the burden'.[31] It is female vanity and sensuality that leads to expulsion and death in the all too near future. If Marianne is attracted to the bold expressiveness of the naked figures, in the latter print at least, it is Adam who stands tall and defiant, and there is no confident striding woman.[32]

The future is depicted particularly bleakly in three 'flash forwards' in prints number two, four and six in the cycle. Each future represents a commentary on the biblical story in Genesis. In the 'Second Future' [Plate 4] Klinger depicts a demon of his own creation, carried by a leech on a river of blood, greedily seeking out the next victims – a phallically situated harpoon jutting forwards. In the 'Third Future' [Plate 6], 'one of Klinger's most chilling images' say Varnedoe and Streicher,[33] a skeleton 'relentlessly and gleefully' crushes human beings with a pounder. This is Death as the Leveller. The cross in the left hand corner of the print suggests an ineffectual role since the pounding continues regardless and there appears to be no salvation. In this print, as against certain sentiments in the cycle 'On Death Part 1', death does not appear to be a highest wish providing release from this mortal coil but a destructive force from which there is no protection. And, moreover, it is woman, symbolised in the figure of Eve, that is the root cause of such a calamitous future.

If this is a defensible reading of the cycle it renders the comments of Marianne, Helene and Ida somewhat anodyne in contrast. It even suggests a degree of misunderstanding, whether wilful or not, on the part of the young Marianne. The interpretation equally challenges Scaff's comments. The reading put forward here tends to agree more with that aspect of the work of Klinger recently pointed out by Dijkstra. In discussion of the portrayals of the sexual encounters between Zeus, taking on the form of a swan, and Leda, Dijkstra describes Klinger as 'one of the period's most relentless reporters of woman's bestial proclivities'.[34]

I have left discussion of the second plate [Plate 2], the 'First Future', in the cycle until this juncture, since the viewing of it in the Weber household in Freiburg provides a further example to place alongside the reactions of Ida Baumgarten and Helene Weber. In this instance, Eduard Baumgarten records for us the young Else von Richthofen's memory of seeing the print. Baumgarten bases his anecdote apparently on a written note of Else's which recalled her visiting the Weber's in 1894 or 1895. He writes, drawing on her note: 'On the wall opposite Max Weber's desk hung an original etching by Max Klinger. On the way home she wondered what kind of person would have hung this picture on the wall opposite him. The picture, entitled, 'The First Future' ... shows a colossal tiger sitting up straight at the end of a ravine which in the writer's memory was 'paved with skulls'.[35]

Baumgarten does not go on to tell us what opinion, if any, Else eventually reached regarding the meaning of the print and what it said about Weber. Baumgarten, though, does go on to speculate on what the print may have conveyed to Weber, although he is sceptical of the attempt. He takes up Schmidt's reading:

> An interpretation of the etchings which had the agreement of the artist is given in Max Schmid's monograph (1st ed., 1899): 'What we think of is how Dante, lost in the forest, beneath the image of the spotted panther found the path through life barred by the passions of the flesh.' It is a futile question whether Max Weber was aware of this interpretation, and if yes, whether he accepted it. Presumably he will have known the story of every single print in the collection of these original etchings which he owned and loved, and what lay behind them. But it does not need to have been Klinger's conception of endangered man that caused him not just to tolerate but to love the picture; it can just as well have been the imperious figure of the defiant, bolt-upright animal in the perfected form of its own mightiness'.[36]

While Baumgarten may well be right, since the animal is indeed majestic and powerful, this interpretation is somewhat pedestrian and fails to place the print in the context of the cycle as a whole. The leopard in the first Canto of *The Inferno*, does indeed bar the way; it waits to devour the entrant who has descended into hell on account of the sin of sexual promiscuity. The Leopard metes out the punishment earnted through sexual misdeeds on earth. This would tend to confirm that the sin of Eve depicted in the cycle is of a sexual nature and that it is sexual activity that she is contemplating at the opening of the cycle. Weber may well have had it above his desk as a reminder of the view that the wages of sin (and for 'sin' read unrestrained sexual intercourse) is death, or as an example of this view of sensuality.

'Eve and the Future' represents a much more unconventional view of woman than Marianne suggests, and the issue of nudity is really rather innocuous in the face of the depictions of sexual longing and the grotesque portrayals of its consequences. Perhaps the unconventionality of the Webers lay in their acceptance of chastity as a noble virtue,[37] a virtue that was becoming more fashionable perhaps in the light of the *Kreutzer Sonata* and infractions of this code led to decay and death as Klinger (and Tolstoy) so clearly portrayed. What made the women of the older generation uneasy, particularly Helene, was perhaps seeing the illustration, directly and indirectly, of a carnality they themselves may have unwilling experienced in their own relationships. It is in this context that Fritz Baumgarten's gift to Marianne of a Klinger print is significant. In Ida Baumgarten's letter to her daughters at Christmas 1894 she also recorded that 'For Max, Fritz had the Dürer etching which Max so admired once, which my father left, and then for Marianne "Das Glück" ...' There is probably little doubt that this print was number 5 from the cycle 'A Love'(first edition 1887). The content of the print is quite remarkable [Plate 7] (especially as a present from Weber's married cousin to boot) in as much as it depicts an act of sexual consummation of a 'brief encounter' and presents it as 'Happiness'.

This would seem to contradict all the readings of Klinger we have been putting forward. If put in context, however, Klinger's point is a clear one and negative: after this encounter the woman becomes pregnant, is shamed and ostracised by society and dies alone in childbirth or during an abortion. The prints in the cycle prior to 'Happiness' depict the pursuit of a female by a man in secret groves of luscious parkland and it seems that Klinger is more critical of the motivations of the man in the partnership rather than the woman as in 'Eve and the Future'. In some editions of the print a motto from Schopenhauer was appended to this print that reads: 'After Coitus the cackle of the devil is heard.'[38] It remains to be seen whether a similar theme of love and death pervades the second cycle to be discussed, to which we now turn.

On Death Part I

We have already seen that Max had presented Marianne with 'the almost complete etchings of Max Klinger' as an anniversary present in 1894.

Marianne goes on to record that one print in particular carried Weber's anniversary message.

> On one of the prints from the cycle *Vom Tode* which depicted Death as Saviour, he wrote the following verses: 'Once I hoped I would be vouchsafed an early death in the full vigour of my youth. I no longer desire such a death, for I have found here below what gives human hearts eternal youth. When one day the end of our life approaches, my child, we shall lay down our work and cheerfully walk together on the dark paths of death into an unknown land'.[39]

The print [Plate 8] needs to be placed in the context of the cycle. It opens with 'Night' which depicts a man in deep reflection. The subject of reflection is death. The moth attracted to the lily in the picture suggests a dilemma between the veracity of the Easter message and the inevitability of death. The next two prints have a sea-theme – 'Sailors' and 'Sea'. The imminence of death is indicated by the scene of sailors fighting on rocks over responsibility for a wrecked ship with a sea still threatening to devour them. In the lower part of the picture hell is depicted. A demon with open mouth awaits the arrival of still more dead, ushered in by death with his scythe. The sailors soon will follow. The next prints in the cycle, 'Road', 'Child', 'Herod', 'Farmer', 'On the Tracks', 'Poor Family', all depict various scenes where death has arrived unexpectedly: a lightening bolt in 'Road', a train crash in 'On the Tracks'; death has taken his victims whether they be young or old, poor or noble. It is perhaps only in the print, 'Poor Family', that death has come at an expected hour, and the light around the dead man's head has a halo effect. Yet the stillness of the scene seems to represent resignation and exhaustion rather than peace and release for the family. The bereaved woman and child are at the garret window, perhaps looking to the future. But the skeletal figure of death appears on the left of the composition and there is also a view of a man digging a grave which suggests that they too will soon meet a similar end, hurried along by poverty.

Klinger disputes the traditional Christian view of death and resurrection. There is no salvation. Rather it seems that all bodies, reaped by death's harvest, are feasted upon by creatures, demons, other mythical figures and even by corpses. Klinger shares the Baudelarian fascination with the cadaver, the corrupting corpse, rejecting the view of death as release, just reward, and a transcendent firmament.

The print singled out for mention by Marianne Weber 'Death as Saviour' strikes a somewhat different note. The print depicts [Plate 8], on the right hand side, a terrified group of people in classical garb fleeing from the figure of death, whilst one figure, apparently in modern western dress, remains in a position of worship. The print concludes the cycle in so far as, unlike the previous images, here the hour of death appears to be known if not actually positively sought after by the obeisant figure. The print also appears to comment on the entire cycle through the inscription which reads: 'Wir fliehen die Form des Todes, nicht den Tod; denn unsrer hoechsten Wuensche Ziel ist: Tod' (We flee from the manner of death, not from death itself; for the goal of our highest desires is death).

The message for the desire for death would appear to be a singularly inappropriate gift for a first wedding anniversary present. The poem that Weber inscribed on its reverse does temper its import somewhat. The border to the picture also appears to present quite inappropriate details since it contains some quite graphic and bestial depictions as a comment on the scene. For example, in the lower margin 'a woman resists the grasp of a giant beast, part human, part toad, while on the left, a woman is raped by a giant lobster'.[40] A range of morbid fantasies are intimated: is this what happens to women after death, is it a comment on woman's supposed bestial sensibilities – a not uncommon motif in Klinger – that lead to death, or is the fear of death to be ranked with the fear of sex on the part of women? The point remains, however, that without Weber's gloss in the poem he composed the 'gift' of this print would appear rather odd.

Apart from the differences in dress the central action containing women and children echoes the image in *The Protestant Ethic and the Spirit of Capitalism* of Christian in Pilgrim's Progress, leaving his wife and children behind to seek salvation from fear of death.[41] Only when he reaches the celestial city does it occur to him that it would be good to have his family with him. It is in this context, in the revised version of the *Protestant Ethic* of 1920,[42] that Weber adds Siegmund's reply to the herald of death from Wagner's *Die Walküre*.[43] Siegmund refuses to die and be awarded a hero's place in Valhalla since that would entail abandoning his beloved. In the poem, Weber gives expression to the importance of companionship in giving life meaning and how this renders death an unwelcome and tragic interruption when it occurs before the appropriate hour.

The final line of the poem is an allusion to *Tristan und Isolde*, hence, the linkage between Klinger and Wagner is made by Weber himself. In the opera, Tristan beckons Isolde to follow him into death (Act 2, Scene 3), 'Where Tristan is now bound for, will you Isolde follow? The land Tristan means where sunlight sheds no beams; it is the sacred realm of night from which my mother sent me forth'. Isolde accepts the invitation – it is only in death/night that their love can find its fulfilment. She replies, 'Where Tristan's home may be there goes Isolde with thee'. Marianne and Max saw the opera in Berlin in 1893 in their first year of marriage. They also attended a performance in Munich in 1912. Of all the Wagner operas, with the exception of *Die Meistersinger von Nürnberg*, Tristan, captured for them the greatness of Wagner and the German spirit.[44] Performances of *Tristan and Isolde* were heard as so passionate and evocative that bourgeois ladies, especially in Russia, otherwise repressed, were said to swoon during performances; like the effect of the presto of Beethoven's *Kreutzer* Sonata on Podznyshev's wife and her musical partner in Tolstoy's story. The music was so explicit to Minna Wagner that, enraged with jealously at her husband's relationship with Mathilde Wesendonck, she said, 'the text is appalling: the passion in it is almost indecent'.[45] Likewise Marianne Weber could write 'they were completely carried away by its ecstasy and experienced this work of art as the highest transfiguration of the earthly'.[46] While the crescendoes and surging music in the second act according to some commentators leaves nothing to the imagination,[47] the opera can be linked to a chaster more abstemious theme.[48] The Schopenhauer theme of abnegation in the face of carnality and death can be given equal weight in interpretation to the biographical context of Wagner's ecstasy with Mathilde Wesendonck.

For Tristan and for Isolde, the link between fulfilled love and death is inextricable. Their union, mental and physical, can only be fully consummated in death, which they long for and welcome. Their tragic situation means that fulfilment in this world, in the world of politics, of the day and the light, would only lead to destruction, as indeed it does. Or rather, the very fact that their love is incapable of satisfaction, with each experience only serving to heighten the desire for more, death intervenes as the final release from the desires of the body. This means that the opera can work to advise that such passion is not for the realm of the day but only for the realm of the night.[49] Weber, unlike Tristan, is not devoted to death; he does not seek death at this moment or any moment in the near future. Weber is still alive and wishes to remain alive, in companionship to be sure, but most certainly in the bright light of day where renunciation is an everyday achievement. One feels that Weber's passion was strong, perhaps similar to Tristan's, yet controlled.

The erotic, the satisfaction of elemental passions, in the two cycles of Klinger we have discussed, in Sudermann, in Tolstoy, and in Wagner disrupts the everyday world and leads to destruction of honour, independence and even life. This is supportive of a version of the chaste option as championed by Tolstoy in the later stages of his life.[50]

Postscript: Ascona, 1913

While he was at Ascona in 1913, Marianne sent Weber a letter on his birthday. We only have Weber's reply of 21.4.1913. (See p. 51, above.) 'Your dear beautiful letter has just arrived and 'Tristan' as symbol...I cannot look at myself with such great and beautiful eyes as you do so all that is 'given up' rather than 'given.' She had evidently alluded to Tristan. Weber thanks her for the 'poem' she has sent him. The whole episode is difficult to decipher, but one feels Weber's discomfort with Marianne using the symbol of Tristan to apply to him. Indeed, Weber expresses surprise at her memory of some twenty years (back to the time of the gift of 'Death as a Saviour') and suggests that her view of him needs correction. Nonetheless, he is grateful for her fine and elevated view of him. He concludes, before passing onto other matters, with: 'keep your love for me, most trusting Mädele – since you are still so young that one cannot call you otherwise – then in the coming year and the years that are allotted to us we will be happy and always going forward together'.

These statements are reminiscent of Weber's original poem of 1894, but there is a feeling that things have changed, that Weber must ask that trust from the young Marianne should continue. Although he wishes and plans to remain with Marianne, perhaps another side of his nature has been opened up by 1913 and the private and intimate meaning of the Klingers and of Wagner's operas had been broken. Weber would not continue to remain silent, but shared his nature and his passion with others.[51]

Klinger and Wagner had been consumed in private, although not in a private enough context for the more reserved and guarded older generation. Tolstoy, Sudermann and Klinger were obviously known and discussed amongst Weber's closest circle of family and friends, especially during the Freiburg years, but even here generational and ethical differences would mean that not everyone was comfortable. Helene may well have approved of Weber's reading of the prints, but he rarely confided in her what his own views on these matters were. Weber, given his upbringing and his knowledge of his mother's experience of married life and child-bearing, would not have been unresponsive to the ascetic message found in Tolstoy. The mastery of the passions became a central feature of a mature personality.[52]

In this context, the Klinger etchings on his walls in the two decades either side of the turn of the century reveal different aspects of Max Weber. They show his leaning towards the avant-garde and the unconventional, his modernity, and his attempts to make a statement of independence through an indulgence in conspicuous consumption made possible through the new privatisation of seeing. Equally they served to remind him, perhaps in an entertaining fashion, of the consequences of unbridled passion, a view which he shared with Marianne. His own attitude to Marianne perhaps meant that he regretted, for example, the patriarchal treatment of Eve in Klinger and he toned down the force of the meaning of Klinger on occasions. Weber's mind was of the cast that he could entertain the opinions of others whom he did not necessarily follow in their entirety and yet find them interesting and worthy of analysis. Weber, then, controlled the anarchy of his passions through the culture of renunciation.

NOTES

1. I would like to acknowledge the support of the School of Social Sciences, Oxford Brookes University for funding research at the Max Weber Archive at the Bavarian Academy of Sciences in Munich, and the *Museum für bildenden Künste* in Leipzig; to Dr Mary Shields for many useful conversations and for invaluable assistance with the German language; to Professor Guenther Roth for drawing my attention to, and providing transcripts of, two unpublished letters; and to Sam Whimster for sharing his knowledge of references to Klinger in Weber's correspondence.
2. E. Troeltsch, *Religion in History* (Edinburgh: Clark, 1991), pp. 362–3.
3. Marianne Weber, *Max Weber. A Biography* (New Brunswick, N.J.: Transactions, 1988), p. 203. Marianne slightly misrecalls the title of the print, which is almost certainly 'Und doch'.
4. E. Baumgarten, *Max Weber. Werk und Person* (Tübingen: Mohr, 1964), p. 474.
5. Marianne Weber, op. cit., p. 201.
6. The poets Richard Dehmel and Stefan George, the academic Wilhelm Wundt, and the musicians Richard Strauss, Max Reger and Brahms all revered Klinger (D. Gleisberg and H. Arikawa, *Max Klinger. Werke aus dem Besitz des Museums der bildenden Künste Leipzig und des Nationalmuseums für Westliche Kunst* (Tokyo: 1988), p. 26. Max Weber visited Leipzig in October, 1909. According to the Gesamtausgabe editors he met Max Klinger, who lived in Leipzig, and his woman friend, Elsa Asenijeff (*MWG, II/6* 287, 289). Or he may have viewed some Klingers. His two letters (to Marianne) are unclear, referring to going 'zu den Klinger's' (letter 12 October) and a Herr Bruck going with him 'zu den Klingers' (letter 13 October). [Klinger had just finished a 3 year commission to paint a gargantuan mural in the main lecture hall of Leipzig University. This was destroyed by Allied bombing in 1944.]
7. Marianne Weber, op. cit., p. 359.
8. As researched in *MWG, II/5*, 52. The Webers had given 46 prints (Opus V) to Sophie Rickert in 1879.

9.   See W. Hennis, *Max Webers Wissenschaft vom Menschen* (Tübingen: Mohr, 1996), p. 205. The cycle is now owned by Hennis.

10. *GStA*, 10.10.1918. Wina Müller was Marianne Weber's mother's sister who helped in her upbringing on the death of her mother. Wina was the centre of the family at Oerlinghausen where the Webers often visited for family anniversaries and festivals including their own wedding and silver wedding anniversary. It is difficult to determine which print he sent her. Weber mentions that the print was somewhat mildewed but that 'it has always given us pleasure because it is a good print '*avant la lettre*'; a suggestion of the progressiveness of Weber's taste.

11. Fritz Baumgarten was Weber's cousin who had befriended the teenage Max in Berlin whilst he was training to be a teacher and who now worked in Freiburg. Marianne Weber, op. cit., pp. 489, 204.

12. C. E. Schorske, *Fin de siècle Vienna. Politics and Culture* (Cambridge: Cambridge University Press, 1981), pp. 254–63; P. Vergo, *Art in Vienna. 1898–1918* (London: Phaidon, 1975), pp. 65–77.

13. Weber appears to have been against monumental art stating that the Hamburg monument to Bismarck was 'the only truly valuable example of monumental art in Germany' as opposed to the 'monstrous monument to Bismarck' and the 'wretched cathedral' in Berlin ('Wahlrecht und Demokratie in Deutschland' *Zur Politik in Weltkrieg*, Studienausgabe, (Tübingen: Mohr, 1988), pp. 174; *PW*, pp. 108–9).

14. J. K. Varnedoe and E. Streicher, *Graphic Works of Max Klinger* (New York: Dover, 1977), p. xvii.

15. M. Musgrave, 'The Cultural World of Brahms', in R. Pascal ed. *Brahms: Biographical, Documentary and Analytical Studies* (Cambridge: Cambridge University Press, 1983), p. 11.

16. R. Reisenfeld, 'The revival, transformation and dissemination of the print portfolio in Germany and Austria, 1890 to 1930', in R. A. Born and S. d'Allesandro, eds, *The German Print Portfolio 1890–1930. Serials for a Private Sphere* (London: Wilson, 1977), p. 21.

17. C. Hertel, 'Irony, dream and kitsch. Max Klinger's paraphrase of the finding of a glove and German modernism', *Art Bulletin*, 74, (1992), pp. 91–114; Max Klinger, *Malerei und Zeichnung: Tagebuchaufzeichnungen und Briefe*, ed. A. Hübscher (Leipzig: Philip Reclam, 1985), pp. 19–20.

18. G. Roth, 'Max Weber as a Scion of the Cosmopolitan Bourgeoisie', un-published paper, Max Weber Study Group Conference, 1995.

19. Marianne Weber, op. cit., p. 203.

20. Ibid., p. 204.

21. R. Lenman, 'Painters, Patronage and the Art Market in Germany 1850–1914, *Past and Present*, 123, (1989), p. 112.

22. L. Tolstoy, *The Kreutzer Sonata and other Stories* (London: Penguin, 1985), p. 77.

23. Ibid., pp. 54–6; cf., 65.

24. Helene Weber to Emilie Benecke, 3.11.1893, Deponat Max Weber-Schäfer, Bavarian State Library. Helene would have been particularly sensitive to Tolstoy's late views on childbirth and child rearing. Helene was over-whelmed with grief at the loss of her 4 year old daughter, little Helene. (Marianne Weber, op. cit., pp. 37–9.) Undoubtedly Helene did not receive

the support she required from Max Weber Sr and it would not have been uncommon for him to have expected conjugal realtions to continue during this period. Helene contined to have children at regular intervals, with Klara born in 1875, Arthur in 1877, and Lili in 1880. The protagonist in Tolstoy's *Kreutzer Sonata* Pozdnyshev says, 'a woman has to go against her nature and be expectant mother, wet-nurse and mistress all at the same time' (p. 61). This would have been particularly poignant, especially with her anxiety regarding the health of the children after Helenchen's death; something that is echoed by Tolstoy (pp. 69–71). Helene's own mother took the view there was no spiritual bond either in her own marriage or Helene's. This again echoes with Pozdnyshev's view that men are only interested in the woman's body (p. 45) and that 'shared ideals' and 'spiritual affinities' are a nonsense. 'There's not much point in going to bed together if that is what you're after.' (p. 34)

25. I. Gilcher-Holtey, 'Max Weber und die Frauen', *Max Weber. Ein Symposion*, ed C. Gneuss and J. Kocka, (Munich: Deutscher Taschenbuch, 1988), pp. 146–7.

26. Ida Baumgarten to Anna and Emmy Baumgarten, 24.12.1894, Deponat Max Weber-Schäfer, Bavarian State Library.

27. Ibid.

28. Sudermann rose to fame on account of his drama *Die Ehre* in 1890 and this was followed by two further plays *Sodoms Ende* (1891) and *Heimat* (1893). At first these plays were considered risqué and performances were prohibited. See J. Osborne, *The Naturalist Drama in Germany* (Manchester: Manchester University Press, 1971), pp. 174–6, and H. F. Garten, *Modern German Drama* (London: Methuen, 1964).

29. J. K. Varnedoe and E. Streicher, *The Graphic Works of Max Klinger* (New York: Dover, 1977), p. 81.

30. L. Scaff, *Fleeing the Iron Cage* (Los Angeles and Berkeley: University of California Press, 1989), pp. 145–6.

31. Varnedoe and Streicher, op. cit., p. 77.

32. One is reminded of Weber's contrast between the Catholic's and the Puritan's attitudes to the world as represented by Dante and Milton. In Milton the couple look forward to the challenges of life outside paradise, 'They hand in hand with wand'ring steps and slow/Through Eden took their solitary way' (*PESC*, p. 80, although these lines from *Paradise Lost* are actually omitted in the English translation – my thanks to the editor for pointing out this discrepancy.) This 'walking together' echoes the walking together of Weber's poem of 1894 to Marianne, Wagner's *Tristan and Isolde* and countless other examples in which 'Liebestod' is central.

33. Ibid., p. 77.

34. B. Dijkstra, *The Idols of Perversity: Fantasies of Feminine Evil in Fin-de-Siècle Culture* (Oxford: Oxford University Press, 1986), p. 315.

35. Baumgarten, op. cit., p. 474. Baumgarten adds in parentheses, 'It was quite possible to take the menacing unevenness, the creviced nature of the path through the ravine, for skulls'. That Else remembered 'skulls' is significant since it suggests that Else has conflated the Third Future (in which the skulls are crushed by the skeletal figure of death) with the First. This in turn would suggest that the Webers did have the whole cycle on display.

36. Ibid., p. 474.
37. In the absence of clear evidence to document whether Marianne and Max consummated their marriage, it is a hostage to fortune to build up a strong argument in favour of Weber's 'chaste option'. However, even if we must finally talk of restraint rather than chastity, Weber's asceticism remains as does his readings of Klinger and of Wagner.
38. Varnedoe and Streicher, op. cit., p. 85.
39. Marianne Weber, op. cit., p. 201.
40. Varnedoe and Streicher, op. cit., p. 88.
41. *PESC*, p. 107.
42. D. J. Chalcraft, 'Bringing the text back in: on ways of reading the iron cage metaphor in the two editions of *The Protestant Ethic*', in Larry Ray and Michael Reed, (eds), *Organising Modernity* (London: Routledge, 1994), pp. 16–45.
43. D. J. Chalcraft, 'Weber, Wagner and Thoughts of Death', *Sociology*, 27, 3 (1993) pp. 433–49.
44. Marianne Weber, op. cit., pp. 502–3.
45. P. Wapnewski, 'The Operas as Literary Works', in U. Mueller and P. Wapnewski, *Wagner Handbook* (Cambridge, Mass.: Harvard University Press, 1992), p. 70.
46. Marianne Weber, op. cit., p. 502.
47. B. Millington, *The Wagner Compendium. A Guide to Wagner's Life and Music* (London: Thames and Hudson, 1992), pp. 299–300.
48. E. Newman, *The Wagner Operas* (Princeton, N.J.: Princeton University Press, 1949), p. 186.
49. J. L. Rose, 'A Landmark in Musical History', in *Tristan and Isolde*, (London: English National Opera, 1981), pp. 12, 16.
50. J. S. Carroll, 'Tolstoy', in J. Hastings (ed.), *Encyclopaedia of Religion and Ethics*, vol. 12, (Edinburgh: Clark, 1921); W. L. Shirer, *Love and Hatred. The Stormy Marriage of Leo and Sonya Tolstoy* (London: Aurem Press, 1994).
51. Chalcraft, op. cit., 1993.
52. *PESC*, p. 119.

11 Max Weber and German Expressionism
Mary Shields

Recent writings have extended our understanding of Weber as a personality torn apart by the dichotomies, evident throughout his writings, of irrational experience and rational knowledge, empathy and understanding, subjective and objective, private and public, content (seen as amorphous, dynamic and anarchic) and form (seen as static and rigid). It is recognised that Weber's sense of disintegration gives him a great deal in common with the creative writers of his time; all were in some way aware that the social and intellectual framework which formed their heritage was no longer sustainable. This resulted in an overwhelming sense of cultural crisis – *Kulturkrise*.

One writer who has analysed Weber's work in these terms particularly clearly is Edith Weiller in her book *Max Weber und die literarische Moderne*,[1] which draws largely on Scaff's analysis.[2] Weiller concentrates on Weber's heroic attempt to endure the dichotomies for the sake of preventing total disintegration, in contrast to some creative writers who she sees as prepared to let disintegration take its course and to face up to chaos. She draws illuminating parallels between Weber's thinking and Stefan George's use of form as a bastion of the private against chaos, or the dogged effort of Thomas Mann's characters to 'hold out' against the decadent forces assailing them. In general she considers Weber, in his attempt to build barriers around the private self to protect it from the external, public world, to be closest in spirit to the writers of the Decadent movement.

Weiller does not, however, consider the development of Weber's work over time. But when a more developmental approach is taken, one finds that the balance between subjective psychic energy and objective form shifts in Weber's work. Thus, right at the end of his life, he is able to contemplate the possibility of an eruption of subjective energy from the private into the public sphere, thereby effecting a transformation of the public and a transcendence of the dichotomies. In looking at this process, the work of the German Expressionists provides some interesting comparisons.

The Expressionists on the whole represent a younger generation to Weber himself and those of his contemporaries that Weiller talks about. The 'Expressionist decade' when most of their work was produced was 1910–1920. Given that the writers and artists involved were still little known then, at least initially, it is unlikely that he would have come across their literature and paintings; if he had, he would almost certainly have been perplexed and probably horrified by them. Yet Weber and the Expressionists (as also the writers who Weiller considers) were reacting to the same cultural crisis. Not only did Weber share some important concerns (such as cultural criticism) with these artists and writers, but some of the themes he wrote about later in life and even his language show parallels with those of the Expressionists. Thus looking at Expressionism can throw light on some aspects of Weber's thought which have until now received relatively little attention. The early twentieth century in Germany was, after all, a period of enormous social, intellectual and aesthetic ferment, and the same questions were voiced in many different areas of life. Artists, for instance, were greatly impressed by particle physics, or writers by Freudian psychology. As Vietta and Kemper write in their book on Expressionism, Expressionist writing can help us to understand the epoch as a whole, not just its literature.[3] Before we think about Expressionism and Weber's later thinking, however, we need to examine Weber's attitude to the individual and the relationship between individual and external world prior to this period.

Weber pre-1909 and the Diversion of Psychic Energy

Psychic energy is an important theme of Weber's work. *The Protestant Ethic* can be seen *inter alia* as a tale about what happens to the personality when psychic energy is denied its normal outlets, and what happens to rationalised social forms when the psychic energy which created them has been spent. Thus the original Puritans were denied the outlets of mysticism, eroticism, intoxication, aesthetic enjoyment, normal sociability and even deep affection within the family: 'Every purely emotional, that is not rationally motivated, personal relation of man to man easily fell in the Puritan, as in every ascetic ethic, under the suspicion of idolatry of the flesh'; even friendship was seen as fundamentally irrational.[4] This, according to Weber, had two important consequences for western culture: psychic energy on one hand turned inward instead of being outwardly expressed and resulted in the introspective anxiety, 'that disillusioned and pessimistically inclined individualism',[5] of the Puritan mentality; and on the other hand was expressed externally in devotion to work, which

resulted in modern capitalism. Weber was also interested in the pathological conditions connected with this forced channelling of psychic energy:
he mentions 'the often definitely pathological character of Methodist emotionalism' as being possibly connected with asceticism[6] and is interested
in the hysterical states that devotees of religious sects were prone to. He
also, however, seems to see the 'normal' Puritan mentality as in a sense
pathological: its representatives are plainly inhumane towards their fellow
humans.[7] Most important, the Puritan experienced an 'unprecedented inner
loneliness of the single individual'[8] – and the emotional intensity of this
statement suggests that Weber feels the Puritan was not alone.

Western capitalism arose because ascetic Protestantism diverted psychic
energy into an unusual path. As the power of ascetic Protestantism was
relaxed, however, capitalism was gradually drained of its 'spirit' and
became an empty, rigid shell (*stahlhartes Gehäuse*[9]), with its overtones of
impersonality, over-intellectuality and repressive mechanisation, so characteristic of much social critique of Weber's period; and not only is the shell
empty, but also the people who inhabit it: 'specialists without spirit, sensualists without heart'.[10] The only way to exist in the modern world is to
become a 'Persönlichkeit' equal to dealing with it, and this is only achieved
through the rational ordering of one's own life, the conscious mastery over
one's inner impulses. Goldman talks of the Puritan 'subjugation of the
natural self and its unification from within through devotion'[11] and of
Weber wanting to go back to this self-shaping as the only means of achieving the creation of personality under conditions of modernity, when 'the
ideals of *Bildung* and broad self-development were no longer adequate for
equipping the self to meet the demands of a world dominated by rationalization and disenchantment.'[12] Thus the rational ordering of the self is the
only way by which the individual can accommodate to a rationalised
society comparable in its 'inhumanity' to Puritan repression; while the nonrational psychic energies that are thereby repressed can only surface as
something alien to this order, and therefore threatening to it. This idea of
the rational ordering of the personality is one that Weber shared with others
(Goldman focuses on Thomas Mann) and has been commented on often
enough. But whereas in Weber's early work it seems to reign supreme, in
the later work a tension arises between this view and a more dynamic one
which allows greater expression to irrational aspects of the personality.

In the methodological essays on Roscher and Knies written concur-
rently with the *Protestant Ethic* (in 1903–6), Weber does talk a little about
the irrational, or nonrational. One form is benign, as the inspiration or
intuition which benefits the scientist although it comes from outside
the realm of science and cannot have any part in its methods, and it is

therefore treated with great circumspection. The other form is more ominous, as the incalculability of both the madman and natural cataclysms (Weber here equates the calculable with the rational[13]). Both forms appear to be rather mysterious and alien; and the mad and the natural of course represent a threat to rational human civilisation. Although Weber talks about them in the most neutral tones, a sense of this threat becomes apparent when one considers his examples, which include a boulder crashing from a cliff in a storm, the spread of syphilis, and so on. That these natural cataclysms might also be functioning unconsciously as symbols of the psychic irrational for Weber is suggested particularly by the image of the flooding of the Dollart, which is used on at least three occasions. This medieval invasion of the sea into vast areas of farmland and habitation can be seen as a powerful image of the threat of some nonrational, elemental power to rational civilisation.[14] And when one considers Weber's own 'volcanic' temperament and his efforts to keep his rebellious 'animality' in check,[15] it seems as though Weber himself saw that part of his own nature which was not rationally ordered was some kind of threat to his ordered existence. This all suggests a model of the developed personality as keeping vital psychic forces at a distance, carefully monitoring the benign ones, and repressing the disruptive ones.

The repression or loss of psychic energy was of course a common motif of the period. The writers of late-nineteenth-century Decadence provide ample examples of the disappearance of vital energies, not only in the bourgeois decline of Thomas Mann's *Buddenbrooks* (1901), but in an obsession with death generally, seen most quintessentially perhaps in Wagner's linking of that most vital energy, the erotic, with death in the *Liebestod*. The similarity of Weber's imagery to the imagery of petrifaction often found in the literature of the period has also been noted.[16] At the same time, however, there was an increasing sense at the time that what was repressed did not just disappear but must resurface, either in pathology (Freud) or in a socially inappropriate form, as with Thomas Mann's composer Aschenbach in *Death in Venice* (1912), or Heinrich Mann's *Professor Unrat* (1905). These last two examples are both of intellectuals who exist on a purely cerebral plane and have lost touch with their emotions until they are overwhelmed and destroyed by them.

Finally, among Naturalist writers the raw clash between natural impulses and social convention can be a common theme, as in Frank Wedekind's play *Spring Awakening* (1891), in which the conflict beween the adolescent awakening of sexuality and conventional bourgeois life leads to tragedy. Although during this period the existing social order was often felt to be so strong that finding a new emotional vitality could in the end have only destructive consequences for the individual, the threat of socially disruptive forces is implicit and the beginnings of the vitalist emphasis on individual experience are apparent in such works. There was in general the complaint that modern capitalist society was rigid, impersonal and over-intellectual. And Weber certainly shared the view of society as impersonal; as early as 1894, he complained of the impersonality of industrial domination, as opposed to the 'personal relationships of domination' that had previously existed (in an essay in *Die christliche Welt*[17]). His Methodological Introduction of 1908 to the survey of industrial workers that he engaged in for the Society for Social Policy also shows a deep concern about the effects of modern industrial operations on personality and culture. It finishes by saying that 'the "system" as it is today ... has changed, and will go on changing, the spiritual face of mankind almost to the point of unrecognisability.'[18]

Contemporary Views of Cultural Form versus Psychic Energy

The sense of disjuncture between individual and culture was clearly articulated by Georg Simmel, who distinguished between on the one hand the 'objective culture' of material things and 'forms of culture', and on the other hand the 'subjective culture' of personal development, and attributed 'the disharmony of modern life, in particular the intensification of technology in every sphere combined with deep dissatisfaction with it' to a mismatch between the two.[19] He has an image of human culture as a stream of life ('constant flow'), throwing up cultural forms which harden and evolve towards ever-increasing differentiation but increasingly lose their inner vitality and reason for existence.[20] This is helpful for understanding the period, in which the dichotomy between form and content, objective external world and subjective person, is central (while his statement of this theme is evocative of the 19th-century German intellectual tradition of Hegel, Schopenhauer and Nietzsche). This way of thinking about form and content, objective and subjective, is also apparent in Weber's work. His concept of the rationalisation of cultural phenomena leading to their increasing specialisation and divergence is in some ways similar to Simmel's idea of cultural forms – with the important difference that Weber does not have Simmel's vitalist idea of the flow of life as the source of all forms. This kind of thinking does, however, show the significance of Weber's 'empty shell' of capitalism.

The question of the relationship between form and psychic content was a common one in the period, although not always approached in the same way. The art historian Wilhelm Worringer's *Abstraction and Empathy* (published in 1908 and extremely influential: by 1910 it was in its third edition) was inspired by Simmel.[21] His starting point was that 'at all times art proper has satisfied a deep psychic need';[22] and his theory was that primitive people and people in other historical periods marked by insecurity 'in relation to the cosmos, in relation to the phenomena of the external world'[23] produced abstract (originally geometrical) art, from 'the urge – in the face of the bewildering and disquieting mutations of the phenomena of the outer world – to create resting-points, opportunities for repose, necessities in the contemplation of which the spirit exhausted by the caprice of perception could halt awhile'.[24] To paint an object abstractly is 'to tear it out of the flux of happening, ... to eternalise it', whereas naturalistic art was produced in those periods of confident 'empathy' 'between man and the phenomena of the external world'.[25]

Simmel's and Worringer's ideas represent two sides of the same coin: form for both represents an arresting of the flux that is the unformed continuum of life: but whereas Simmel stresses the organicity of this process, which happens as a matter of course, Worringer introduces a new note of anxiety, in the human psychic need to impose form as a refuge from chaos and insecurity. Both kinds of thinking are echoed throughout the period.[26]

Different again, but also extremely influential, were the painter Wassily Kandinsky's ideas on abstract art in *Concerning the Spiritual in Art* and 'On the Question of Form' (both 1912). Whereas for Worringer, abstract art represents a refuge from the chaos of contingency, for Kandinsky (a Russian living in Germany, credited with producing the first non-representational painting, around 1911) it is a language in which spiritual reality can be communicated. His idea of art as expressing the artist's own interpretation of reality rather than the way reality conventionally appears is typical of Expressionist thinking, as is also his idea that if the artist ignores artistic form as such and simply paints his inner vision, form will take care of itself as a direct expression of content. Kandinsky's transcendental view that in expressing his subjective vision the artist was also tapping into a spiritual reality that would give the world new content and form was one strand of Expressionism.

As Kandinsky illustrates, in Expressionism a new relationship between dead form and vital irrational content is postulated. Whereas in earlier work psychic energy often seems to have disappeared or to be unable to make any impact on existing forms, it returns in full force in Expressionism. Expressionism was not a unified movement in the sense of being a definite group of people with a definite programme, but instead comprised numerous small groups and individuals. Moreover, many different views and ways of thinking are represented in Expressionism, so that generalisation about Expressionist ideas is always dangerous. But in very general terms, whereas the Naturalists showed the existing order as maintained despite the conflict with individual energies, the Expressionists often showed the existing bourgeois order as crumbling under attack from new energies or disintegrating of its own accord, as in Jakob van Hoddis's ironic poem 'End of the World' of 1911:

> From pointed pates hats fly into the blue,
> All winds resound as though with muffled cries.
> Steeplejacks fall from roofs and break in two,
> And on the coasts – we read – flood waters rise.
>
> The storm has come, the seas run wild and skip
> Landwards, to squash big jetties there.
> Most people have a cold, their noses drip.
> Trains tumble from the bridges everywhere.[27]

The theme of apocalyptic destruction is common in Expressionism, and is also found, for instance, in Ludwig Meidner's series of apocalyptic paintings, showing the human civilised world being swept away by colossal natural and/or metaphysical forces (and we remember Weber's image of the Dollart here too); Meidner's other favourite theme, the figure of the prophet, is also common, representing the hope for a new order. Looking at both Kandinsky's and Meidner's paintings, it is clear that they are painting not in a naturalistic but a visionary way – even though Kandinsky is concerned more with the spiritual and creative, and Meidner with the destructive.

Simultaneously there is also an eruption of irrational and often violent and destructive forces from within the human psyche. In the Austrian Oskar Kokoschka's play *Murderer, Hope of Women* (1910), for instance, or in Georg Heym's story 'The Madman', this destructive urge is horrifyingly irrational and gratuitous; but in other cases it is directed against the authoritarian existing order, of which the father is the symbol, as in Reinhard Sorge's play *The Beggar* (1912), or Walter Hasenclever's *The Son* (1914). In these two plays, and also others, the murder of father by son is an important theme. That violence is, at least in part, the result of a repressive, authoritarian society in general, and of the war in particular, is shown by Fritz von Unruh's play *Ein Geschlecht* ('One Race', written 1916), whose protagonist's 'vitalism, perverted, turns to self-destruction' as a result of the uncontrollable aggressive violence which the war has fostered in him.[28] Another erupting psychic force is the erotic, which also breaks down existing conventions – in August Stramm's play *Sancta*

Susanna (1914), for instance, it fuses with the spiritual in a mystical experience which can no longer be contained within traditional religious bounds and is therefore considered blasphemous.

It is not simply the fact that these repressed psychic energies come to the fore that is characteristic of Expressionism; indeed, although they are particularly frequently and strongly expressed here, they were also found to an extent in Naturalism, as we have seen. It is also that they are presented in a way which strips them of their social contingency, and through the form of their presentation makes them into universal forces. Thus the characters in Expressionist plays are types rather than individuals; they often do not have individual names at all but are called simply 'the father', 'the girl', 'the bank clerk', etc., and they have no individual character of their own but behave as cyphers for particular roles. They represent life principles in a pure, universal form, not crystallised into individual people as in traditional drama. So we can say that the clash between psychic energy and established social forms is presented in a way which itself sweeps away dramatic conventions.

This rejection of traditional aesthetic forms in order to present the universal, dynamic essentials of experience is characteristic of Expressionism, which shows the search for new forms more appropriate to their psychic content. This was not always apparent. Early Expressionist poetry, particularly, still often used traditional forms and frequently then a tension arose between strict form and dynamic content, as though the form were still just managing to contain the explosive energy. This is the case with the van Hoddis poem quoted above. And in Stadler's 'Form is Joy', form, characterised as peace and satisfaction but also as restriction, is explicitly contrasted with the dynamic urge for life and experience – all expressed through antithesis in traditional rhyming couplets. In the poetry of August Stramm, however, not only traditional form, but also normal syntax, is dispensed with in order to reach the universal essence of experience, as in 'Melancholy' of 1914:

Striding striving
living longs
shuddering standing
glances look for
dying grows
the coming screams!
Deeply
we
dumb.[29]

The dynamism of Expressionism is apparent here in the predominance of verbs in the poem.

The search for new forms resulted in the development of twelve-tone music (by Arnold Schoenberg) and of abstract art (both representational and non-representational). Again, it is important to remember that for Kandinsky and his followers, non-representational art was not simply a matter of finding pleasing combinations of forms and colours, but was a new *language* for spiritual meaning; non-representational did not mean dispensing with communicable content. It is clear in this case that traditional form was seen to represent an obstacle to the communication of the spiritual universals common to all humanity. These spiritual universals are summed up in the emphasis on *Seele*, soul, which for some Expressionists became programmatic. They saw the soul as the part of the personality linking individuals to each other and to the cosmos. It was of course a subjective and nonrational part of the personality, as opposed to the rational intellect.

It was not only in artistic and literary forms that the Expressionists looked for the new, but in new social forms too. Drawing on Ferdinand Tönnies's ideas in *Community and Society* (1887), they tried to find ways of making *Gemeinschaft* the basis for a new society. From the turn of the century there had been attempts to put it into practice by forming close-knit groups of like-minded people; these were predominantly artistic groups, but some were also anarchist or syndicalist, like the Neue Gemeinschaft in Berlin, whose members included the anarcho-syndicalist thinker Gustav Landauer and the poet Erich Mühsam. Later experiments included the hermetic theatre group (1918–21) attached to the journal *Der Sturm*. This attempted to create a *Gemeinschaft* of actors and audience through its productions.

The isolation of the individual in an impersonal society was often felt to be a problem, and much Expressionist poetry expresses the wish to reach out beyond the isolated self to other people, such as Franz Werfel's poem 'To the Reader' which begins: 'My only wish is to be related to you, Oh man.' Some Expressionists, like the group around Franz Pfemfert's journal *Die Aktion* in Berlin, became politically active and championed democratic reform. One cause of individual isolation was felt to be the self-conscious intellect, and some Expressionists tried to transcend its limitations through eroticism, mysticism or primitivism. In a 'Song', Gottfried Benn wishes he were a lump of primeval mud, in order to get back to the totality which predates individuation and the split between self-conscious subject and external world.

Incidentally, there is a sense in which the *Protestant Ethic* also displays primitivism. By going back to the time of the Reformation, Weber traces modern introspective anxiety to its origin – the moment of the Fall when public and private became split.[30] There is also a possible link here with one of the cycles of Klinger prints which Weber owned, 'Eve and the Future'. For Klinger's Eve is tempted not by an apple but by a mirror.[31]

The sense that the relationship between the experiencing subject and the external, 'modern' world has become fractured is fundamental to Expressionism and underlies many of its themes. Vietta and Kemper talk about this 'ego-dissociation' (*Ichdissoziation*) as the result of the confrontation between a pre-modern epoch, schooled on the assumption of a harmonious reality, and a modern, unharmonious world.[32] They see it as manifested in the two antithetical (but frequently coexistent) tendencies, fundamental to Expressionism, of measured social and cultural criticism and of the messianic pathos of proclaiming 'Seele' and the New Man who will transform society.

The Expressionists, then, were characterised by an awareness that the psychic energy that had been lost from traditional social and aesthetic forms could still be tapped at source; tapping it was fraught with danger, because these forms could no longer contain it and would be destroyed by it, and also because this energy had so long been repressed that it could erupt in pathological ways. But alongside violence and pathology this energy also represented spiritual truth, and needed only new forms 'adequate' to it. The influence of vitalist thinking is of course very clear here, and vitalism is an important aspect of Expressionism.[33] Thus repressive, static, 'civilised', conventional life was often linked with over-cerebral rationality, and contrasted with a nonrational and dynamic vitality achievable through ever more experience (*Erlebnis*).

Energy versus Form in Weber post-1909: the Transformative Power of Charisma

This search for energy and new forms to express it brings us to Weber's 'Religious Rejections of the World and Their Directions' ('Intermediate Reflections'), published in 1915 but written some time after 1909,[34] in which Weber put forward his idea of conflicting 'life orders'. Here he explored nonrational and creative aspects of the personality in a way he had not done earlier. He starts by contrasting 'rationally active asceticism', which 'in mastering the world, seeks to tame what is creatural and wicked through work in a worldly "vocation"', with mysticism, in which 'the individual is not a tool but a "vessel" of the divine'. Here again we see the form – content contrast: rational asceticism represses and denies its vital content; mysticism is 'possession' by unbounded spiritual (nonrational) content.[35]

Weber goes on in the essay to describe the various 'spheres' into which the rationalised world is divided: the economic, the political, the aesthetic, the erotic, the intellectual – all of which conflict with religion and in many cases with each other. For Weber, it is no longer possible to live life as a consistent, holistic totality: acting in one sphere will inevitably produce conflict with another. And the most tension between the spheres seems to be between the rational spheres (ascetic, economic, political and intellectual) and the nonrational (mystic, aesthetic and erotic). These spheres of the irrational, as Weiller points out, constitute enclaves of 'salvation' from rational, impersonal life, from 'the cold skeleton hands of rational orders';[36] and the language which Weber uses to describe them is remarkably vitalist. Thus the aesthetic and erotic are 'this-worldly life-forces';[37] art provides 'a *salvation* from the routines of everyday life, and especially from the increasing pressures of theoretical and practical rationalism'[38] (and conflicts with the ethical because of its irresponsibility), while extramarital sexual life has been in intellectualist cultures the only thing linking ascetic vocational man 'with the natural fountain of all life'.[39] 'Salvation' thus appears to involve loss of the self through surrender to some vital energy which forms the antithesis of rational intellectual knowledge and its 'disenchantment of the world and its transformation into a causal mechanism'.[40]

Weber's model of salvation is thus one of tension between psychic energies which now indubitably exist and are no longer completely repressed but are allowed a limited role, and rational life which keeps them in check for most of the time; between occasional private spiritual fulfilment and public aridity. In the case of mysticism, however, there is a glimpse of the potentially explosive nature of this inner energy: 'The most irrational form of religious behavior, the mystic experience, is in its innermost being not only alien but hostile to all form', and the mystic 'believes precisely in the experience of exploding all forms'.[41] By virtue of this inner, nonrational, potentially explosive force, the mystic can become a prophet – and this force is, of course, charisma.[42] The explosive power of charisma in relation to rationalisation is stressed by Brubaker.[43]

At this point Weber seems to have reached an accommodation with the nonrational by integrating it into the personality as a positive force. Its threatening element of incalculability seems now to threaten only the external order rather than the integrity of the individual, while the external order itself remains rigid enough to withstand the threat to its security.

Charisma is seen mainly as a private matter, the means to individual self-fulfilment, while any revolutionary consequences for society that it might have are mentioned very little and at a historical distance. In this way, Weber at this point contains any major threat to present society (as the Expressionists do not); and a precarious balance between individual and society is reached. It might perhaps be no coincidence that this was a time at which Weber himself was most socially active in his capacity as military hospital administrator; while Mitzman suggests that the appearance of Weber's concept of charisma in around 1910 was connected with personal sexual fulfilment putting him in touch with 'all those underground regions of the self which Victorian culture had kept in chains and which were now, in a true return of the repressed, rising painfully to the surface of consciousness'.[44]

Weber's view of charisma in 'Religious Rejections' can now be compared with his view in 'Politics as a Vocation' (which originated as a lecture in January 1919), in which Weber considers the possibility of a political leader arising who could provide real leadership, and the qualities that such a person would need. These are seen to be the rational ability to weigh up a situation and decide on the best course of action, but also that creative force of personality with its roots in the nonrational – charisma, 'the exceptional, personal, *"gift of grace"* which inspires trust and devotion to the person of a leader'.[45] It is 'the "charismatic" element in all leadership' which gives the satisfaction of working for an individual 'rather than for the abstract programme of a party composed of mediocrities',[46] and which is the root of the idea of vocation: 'Devotion to the charisma of the prophet or the war-lord or the exceptional demagogue in the *ekklesia* or in parliament means that the leader is personally regarded as someone who is inwardly "called" to the task of leading men, and that the led submit to him, not because of custom or statute, but because they believe in him'.[47] Thus, even though he is not optimistic about the chances of its actually happening, Weber does now consider it possible that charisma might operate in the present as a political force.

Mommsen has pointed out the increased immediacy of Weber's later view of charisma,[48] but not the two other major differences in the development of Weber's thinking about it: First, that it is no longer confined to the private, irrational spheres of art and mysticism with a certain potential for affecting the course of history through religious prophecy, but that it has entered the public, rational world of politics. Second, that, through its association here with what Weber says about leadership in general, it seems to have become more forceful, to an almost mythic extent.

The reason for these changes, I suggest, lie in the nature of the political situation Weber is facing. The lecture was given in Munich during the revolutionary turmoil of 1918–19, and at this point power there was briefly in the hands of idealistic revolutionaries, before the chaotic and bloody denouement of spring 1919. Mommsen sees Weber's lifelong view of the existing political order as stultifyingly bureaucratic;[49] but the text itself suggests that at this point Weber no longer sees the greatest danger for a vital but stable political order as bureaucratic ossification, but as irrational demonic energy (both aspects are present in the text, but the former is outweighed by the latter). And the source of this demonic energy lies in what Weber calls the 'masses', who although he does not mention this, are now theoretically no longer contained within traditional political structures.

The demonic irrational is present in the essay when Weber talks about not only the destructive emotions that politics unleashes, but also actual violence, which is implicit in any political action.[50] Therefore whoever engages in politics 'is becoming involved ... with the diabolic powers that lurk in all violence.'[51] The leader (who, as we have seen, is by definition charismatic) has to engage with these diabolical, irrational forces, for instance by harnessing the base motives of his following, such as class hatred and the craving for revenge; he cannot change these emotions, but merely hold them in check through people's devotion to him personally.[52] This task of harnessing the masses is one that only the exceptionally strong personality can achieve. Thus it is not surprising that the politician by vocation must be a hero as well as a leader.[53]

Here we find a sense of dynamic, irrational forces threatening human order on a far greater scale than before, one almost reminiscent of the apocalyptic Expressionists. The balance has finally tipped – this challenge of violent emotionalism and of the 'ethical irrationality of the world'[54] is one that, we must infer, rationality itself cannot deal with. The leader, Weber stresses, does of course need outstanding rational abilities in weighing up and deciding on courses of action; but in this situation, we conclude, the power of the irrational can only be overcome by another power transcending rationality – the creative, life-giving power of charisma. This power enables the hero-leader not only to overcome violence by force of personality, but its essential creativity also gives him new value-orientations, which his force of personality, again, enables him to impose on public life. Thus to meet the extreme situation of social disintegration, the charisma that Weber had formerly seen as effective only in seclusion from public life or at a historical distance he can envisage now as providing a psychic energy capable of transforming the contemporary extraordinary political situation.

'Charismatic' Leaders in Expressionism

As mentioned earlier, social criticism is an important element of some Expressionist writing; and the desire for new social forms reflects the general desire for new forms to match rediscovered vitality. The aridity of the capitalist system, and especially the dehumanising effect of its rigid specialisation of work, is a common complaint, and is seen especially clearly in the plays of Georg Kaiser. In *From Morning to Midnight* (written 1912) the revolt of the bank clerk against his dreary everyday existence is a purely personal, vitalist one, with no hint that the social order itself might be changed; but in *Gas I* (published 1918) the messianic hope of a New Man who will bring about a new humanity is held out – only to be dashed in *Gas II* (published 1920) because man's own irrationality and stupidity bring about a final apocalyptic cataclysm. It is interesting to note the similarity between Kaiser's complaint here that people have been reduced by their industrial labour to nothing more than a hand, a foot or a pair of eyes, and Weber's comment in *Economy and Society* about American 'scientific management', by which: 'The final consequences are drawn from the mechanization and discipline of the plant, and the psycho-physical apparatus of man is completely adjusted to the demands of the outer world, the tools, the machines – in short, to an individual "function".'[55] (This process of rationalisation, Weber explicitly makes clear here, widens 'the grasp of discipline' and 'restricts the importance of charisma and of individually differentiated conduct'[56]).

Another Expressionist playwright concerned with the transformation of society and with the idea of the leader who can achieve this was Ernst Toller, Weber's former student and admirer, who took part in the revolutionary events in Munich in 1918–19 and was later defended by Weber when charged with treason. As a proponent of the 'ethic of conviction', he must have been one of the people against whom 'Politics as a Vocation' was directed. Yet despite the fundamental divergence identified by Weber between their views, their thinking about political leaders bears several noteworthy similarities. Toller's view is expressed in his play *Transfiguration* (written 1917–18), which embodies his idealistic view of how a social order in which people are completely degraded by war and poverty might be transformed. It certainly lacks any notion of political reality, as Weber might have objected; but this is not the point for Toller. The important thing is that social change comes primarily not from political action, but from a complete change of hearts and minds in the people – Weber's 'masses'.

This inner transformation occurs first in the sculptor Friedrich. Already artistic and therefore, by Expressionist thinking, receptive to spiritual truth, he undergoes a spiritual regeneration, after which he attains an all-embracing love of humanity. He also finds the persuasive power to communicate this to others and bring about the same transformation in them; in fact, he is closer to being a religious prophet than a politician. This enables the masses to take power not by violent means, demanding revenge, but peacefully as dignified human beings and in a spirit of forgiveness. In this way, the cycle of suffering is broken. Thus, first, Toller and Weber both agree that the situation is such that only a leader with exceptional personal qualities is capable of taking control; and second, that one of these qualities is a form of creative inspiration coming from outside normal rational life. There is also, however, an important difference between Weber's leader and Toller's.

It is significant that Toller's messianic leader is an artist, as this idea of the artist as leader is common in Expressionism. It is seen in Walter Hasenclever's poem 'The Political Poet' (1917), or Max Pechstein's cover for the revolutionary pamphlet 'To All Artists' of 1919, where we see the artist literally with his heart aflame and setting the world alight. The religious leader and the artist are both, in the view of many Expressionists, exceptionally gifted with the power to perceive spiritual truth. And for the Expressionists, spiritual truth is universal; even if the masses are dehumanised by the existing order, they still have the potential to respond to it. Herein lies the great difference between Weber and many of the Expressionists. The Expressionists tended to see the human order as part of the cosmic order, or at least to believe that the very fact of common humanity entailed some universal value. Therefore they often had a positive view of fundamental human nature, as opposed to Weber's profoundly negative one.[57] For Toller and those who thought like him, destroying the old order enabled the spirit of humanity to rise again with renewed vigour in a form that would be more appropriate to it. Weber agreed with them about the need for new vigour and new social forms – but could not agree that humanity itself might provide them, with shared values arising from shared experience. Thus whereas the Expressionist leader, as Weiller points out, did not need to be an impressive personality but merely a conduit for spiritual truth, Weber's leader operated at a purely individual level, as the fundamentally aristocratic hero devoting his exceptional energy and talents to holding the base and irrational population in check.

Whereas many Expressionists thought that by expressing their subjective inner selves they were also expressing the universally human, or even a transcendent spirituality, Weber's profoundly rational world view was unable to accept this. This does not mean that they thought that social regeneration was actually any more likely than Weber did; Kaiser's plays, and Toller's later ones, are pessimistic. But they did sense that if it was to come at all, it could only come through a shared humanity.

This difference does not, however, obscure the fact that Weber appears to have shared much of the thinking and experience characteristic of Expressionism – in particular the antithetical thinking and 'ego-dissociation' of many individuals sensitive to the tensions of the time, who often suffered profoundly under them (actual mental breakdown was common, for instance van Hoddis's schizophrenia, Gross's mental illness, and Georg Trakl's suicide on war service) and who engaged in the social criticism/transformational pathos dialectic. Weber in later life shared the general desire to explore new (political) forms to find a more fitting vessel for the elemental energy of the masses (plebiscitary democracy); the idea that only a new leader could actually produce such a new political form (even if this leader in his eyes epitomises the personal power of the heroic individual rather than symbolises a new emphasis on humanity as such); and the urge to set a vitalist force coming from within the individual personality against the inhuman bourgeois order. In charisma, Weber too, like the Expressionists, postulates a subjective, nonrational force that is able to transcend political conflict and achieve an organic unity of public order and private values – originally at a historical distance but later as a contemporary possibility.

For Weber, charisma has the force to disrupt the modern rationalised order and meld its isolated individuals into a whole again – one almost thinks of a new *Gemeinschaft*. In 'Politics as a Vocation', Weber finally envisages a new form of those 'personal relationships of domination' which he complained in 1894 had been lost from modern industrial society. In producing this personal vision of social regeneration, Weber shows that he shares many of the Expressionists' deepest concerns.

NOTES

1. E. Weiller, *Max Weber und die literarische Moderne: ambivalente Begegnungen zweier Kulturen* (Stuttgart and Weimar: J. B. Metzler, 1994).
2. L. A. Scaff, *Fleeing the Iron Cage: Culture, Politics and Modernity in the Thought of Max Weber* (Berkeley, Los Angeles and London: University of California Press, 1989).
3. S. Vietta and H.-G. Kemper, *Expressionismus*, 2nd edn, Deutsche Literatur im 20. Jahrhundert vol. 3 (Munich: Wilhelm Fink, 1985), p. 19.

4.   PESC p. 224.
5.   Ibid., p. 105.
6.   Ibid., p. 252, note 165.
7.   Ibid., p. 104; pp. 225–6, note 34.
8.   Ibid., p. 104.
9.   The translation of 'Gehäuse' as 'shell' is suggested by D. Chalcraft in
     'Bringing the text back in: On ways of reading the iron cage metaphor in
     the two editions of *The Protestant Ethic*', in: L. J. Ray and M. Reed, eds,
     *Organizing Modernity: New Weberian Perspectives on Work, Organiz-
     ation and Society* (London and New York: Routledge, 1994, pp. 16–45),
     p. 30. I am in general much indebted to David Chalcraft for the many dis-
     cussions in which the ideas in this chapter were developed, and especially for
     his promptings about Weber's fascination with the Dollart, mentioned later.
     Weber's 'Gehäuse' of modern life has come to be seen not only as a key
     image in his own thinking, but as a striking encapsulation of how Modernist
     writers and artists in general felt. Richard Sheppard, for example, refers to it
     frequently in *Modernism/Dada/Postmodernism* (Evanston Il.: North Western
     University Press, 1998).
10. Weber, op. cit., p. 182.
11. H. Goldman, *Max Weber and Thomas Mann: Calling and the Shaping of the
     Self* (Berkeley, Los Angeles and London: University of California Press,
     1988), p. 116.
12. Ibid., p. 118.
13. M. Weber, *Roscher and Knies: The Logical Problems of Historical
     Economics*, trans. and ed. G. Oakes (New York: The Free Press, 1975), p. 125.
14. The link between the elemental power of both the psyche and nature
     becomes clearer when one considers the mythological and possibly also
     linguistic connection in Germany between the concepts of *Seele* (soul) and
     See (lake) (as explained in the Duden *Herkunftswörterbuch*).
15. See A. Mitzman, *The Iron Cage: An Historical Interpretation of Max
     Weber*, 2nd edn (New Brunswick and Oxford: Transaction Books, 1985),
     pp. 293 and 285. Mitzman also repeats Baumgarten's claim that Weber's
     chronic sleeplessness was due to a fear of nocturnal ejaculations (p. 285).
16. Weiller, op. cit., p. 309.
17. Quoted by W. Hennis in 'Personality and Life Orders', in S. Whimster and
     S. Lash, eds, *Max Weber, Rationality and Modernity* (London: Allen and
     Unwin, 1987), pp. 52–74, pp. 64–5.
18. In J. E. T. Eldridge, ed., *Max Weber: The Interpretation of Social Reality*
     (London: Michael Joseph, 1971), p. 155.
19. In P. A. Lawrence, *Georg Simmel: Sociologist and European* (London:
     Thomas Nelson, 1976), p. 249.
20. Ibid., pp. 223–4.
21. W. Worringer, *Abstraction and Empathy: A Contribution to the Psychology
     of Style*, trans. M. Bullock (London, Routledge and Kegan Paul, 1967),
     p. viii.
22. Ibid., p. 12.
23. Ibid., p. 13.
24. Ibid., p. 34.
25. Ibid., p. 13.

26. One might also see a similarity with Weber's idea of the historian as arresting the continuum of events by selecting what seems significant; or with neo-Kantian epistemology in general, as perception itself being a matter of selection from the flood of sense-impressions.

27. In M. Hamburger, trans. and ed., *German Poetry 1910–1975: An Anthology in German and English* (Manchester: Carcanet Press, 1977), p. 83.

28. R. Furness, *The Twentieth Century 1890–1945*, The Literary History of Germany 8 (London: Croom Helm; New York: Barnes & Noble, 1978), p. 195.

29. In Hamburger, op. cit., p. 9.

30. A note in the Roscher essay makes clear that Weber sees the division of the domain of human action into public and private as a consequence of ideas peculiar to Puritanism, ideas of very great importance for the 'genesis of the spirit of capitalism' (Weber, *Roscher and Knies*, pp. 83 and 229, note 77).

31. See D. Chalcraft's article in this volume on Weber and Klinger.

32. Vietta and Kemper, op. cit., p. 22.

33. See Furness, op. cit., pp. 161–208.

34. See Scaff, op. cit., p. 93.

35. H. H. Gerth and C. W. Mills, trans. and ed., *From Max Weber: Essays in Sociology*, new edn (London, Routledge, 1991), p. 325.

36. Ibid., p. 347.

37. Ibid., p. 341; Weber's own phrase is "innerweltlichen Mächten des Lebens", in *Gesammelte Aufsätze zur Religionssoziologie I*, 9th reprint (Tübingen, J. C. B. Mohr, 1988), p. 554.

38. Ibid., p. 342.

39. Ibid., p. 346.

40. Ibid., p. 350.

41. Ibid., p. 342.

42. Ibid., p. 340.

43. R. Brubaker, *The Limits of Rationality: An Essay on the Social and Moral Thought of Max Weber* (London, Allen and Unwin, 1984), p. 64.

44. Mitzman, op. cit., p. 251.

45. P. Lassman and R. Speirs, eds, *Weber: Political Writings* (Cambridge, Cambridge University Press, 1994), p. 311.

46. Ibid., p. 339.

47. Ibid., p. 312.

48. W. J. Mommsen, *Max Weber and German Politics 1890–1920*, 2nd edn, trans. M. S. Steinberg (Chicago and London, University of Chicago Press, 1984), p. 422.

49. W. J. Mommsen, 'Personal Conduct and Societal Change', in Whimster and Lash, op. cit., pp. 35–51, p. 37.

50. Lassman and Speirs, op. cit., p. 364.

51. Ibid., p. 365.

52. Ibid., p. 365.

53. Ibid., p. 369.

54. Ibid., p. 361.

55. Gerth and Mills, op. cit., p. 261.

56. Ibid., p. 262.

57. Cf. Weiller, op. cit., p. 229.

Index